MILK TO MOTORWAYS

An autobiography

Fred Smith

2QT Limited (Publishing)

DEDICATION

THIS BOOK IS a tribute to my wonderful family; my wife Margaret and our four children Richard, Carmen, Jonathan and Ben, not forgetting their wonderful partners, whom I would have handpicked for them. I am not going to go on about them as they have forbidden me to do so, however, I am determined to say how heart-warming it is for me to witness the total love and affection that they each have for their mother, no mother could be loved more. I must also pay tribute to my own parents, now long gone, for instilling in me a work ethic, by example rather than by lecture, that no matter how hard things can be with no apparent light at the end of the tunnel, to have confidence in yourself and keep going and eventually that light will appear.

FOREWORD

Firstly I would like to say how honoured I am to have been asked to write this foreword for such a genuine and unassuming man who goes by the name of Charles Frederick Smith.

I was first introduced to Fred almost 20 years ago at Shaw Hill Leisure Club which, as you will read, is a big part of his life and accomplishments. We have spent many hours together in the gym; lifting weights and having competitions against each other. At this point I think I ought to let you know that I am half Fred's age (as we say, I'm his youngest best mate and he's my oldest best mate) so, to compete with someone half his age just shows the pedigree and mind set of the man.

We have travelled to many places together – London, New York, Berlin, to name but a few and all in aid of fitness challenges and marathons. What makes Fred stand out from the crowd is what Fred has achieved in both weight lifting and marathons. To those of you who don't know a lot about training, you rarely see a high level strong man/big man go into marathon endurance training – they really are opposite ends of the spectrum.

Although he has been a very successful businessman, everyone who meets him loves his down to earth personality and the fact that he takes the time to speak to everyone. He's a true gentleman and loved by all.

We've been through a lot together and have lots of great memories but in the same vein we've been there for each other in the bad times too. We talk on a level together and you wouldn't realise there was an age gap at all. I class him as a true friend and I appreciate everything he has done for me over the years and all the predicaments he has helped me out with (and there have been a few!). There are so many great memories and I hope many more to come.

Kieran O'Donnell

ACKNOWLEDGEMENTS

I WOULD LIKE to say a big thank you to the people who have been instrumental in helping me, not only to finish the book but actually to get it started in the first place.

The first person that I told of my idea to write my autobiography was Tom Ungless, a writer himself, who I have only met in recent years as we both go to the same gym and swimming pool at Shaw Hill. Tom has been very supportive and helpful for which I am grateful. When I first mentioned it to him it was January 2016. "When do you think it will be completed?" he asked "March next year" I replied, "Well, good luck with that" he said with a wry smile. As I write this it is the first of October 2017 and still much to do. I now understand the wry smile. Tom also put me in touch with Lesley Atherton who I must thank for her help, advice but most of all her encouragement and confidence in what I was trying to do. I would also like to thank Jenny Hardman for providing her typing skills in the very beginning which helped to speed up the whole process.

A big thank you to Mel Jefferies, Eric Derbyshire and Les Simpson for their patience and support, listening to my ramblings about the book over many a liquid lunch. Also to Cath and Jemma from Shaw Hill for their genuine interest and enthusiasm. To Steve Gill, photographer, for doing an excellent job on enhancing some of the old photographs which otherwise could not have been reproduced. Thank you also to Kerry Gilligan for putting me in touch with Steve and for always being happy to help in whatever way she can. I would also like to thank my niece Charlotte for her friendly advice.

Thanks also to Colin Nelson, a friend and neighbour of mine many years ago who, one evening, knocked on my door and gave me the names of four motorway maintenance depots, contact names and numbers, which I gratefully accepted.

A big thank you must also go to John Cowley for introducing me to my publishers, 2QT Publishing, of Settle, North Yorkshire

I would like to thank everyone mentioned in the book, without whom there would be no book. And last, but not least, a massive thank you to my wonderful (soon to be) daughter-in-law Suzanne, who, in spite of being snowed under at work, always managed to find time to help me with the book. A special thanks to Suzanne's mother, Madge, who unbeknown to me was actually my first reader when Suzanne would take home chapters of the book, freshly typed, for her to read. Madge's enthusiastic feedback on my work in progress was very encouraging for me as it gave me confidence that I was doing something right and kept me on the track.

I hope that any reader will be sympathetic to any mistakes or errors that I might have made and accept that at the age of 74 I've never done anything like this before or thought I ever would and hopefully my amateurism could almost be seen as endearing?

Disclaimer

Although the stories I have told are all true, I have changed many of the details and identifying features so to preserve privacy and confidentiality where necessary.

CONTENTS

THE EARLY YEARS,
AN ELF IN WELLINGTONS

I n Dave Spikey's autobiography *Under the Microscope*, he was advised to start at the beginning because that's a very good place to start. He went on to ask, 'But how do you define the very beginning?' Well, in my case that is very easy because I actually remember being born. Yes, that's a fact – I remember being born. It isn't a memory whereby I sat there thinking 'How long is this going to take?' or 'I wonder what the weather's like out there?' or even 'If she gets on with this I could be born on New Year's Day' (which I was)…

No, it was a memory of indescribable pain and stress and then an equally indescribable feeling of relief when I eventually entered the world. A lot of people rubbish that story but I will never back down – I remember being born! I believe that this has also happened to other people.

At that time my parents and my older brother, Roy, lived at Cowling Farm at the top of Cowling Brow in Chorley. Both my parents were Chorley born and bred, my father being one of four boys. Uncle George was the oldest by one year, then came my dad Jack, then Uncle Fred (who I never knew as he died aged nineteen), and finally the youngest, Uncle Ellis. Although we lived at Cowling Farm it did not belong to us; it belonged to my dad's boss, Mr Pantall. My dad was farm manager.

All my dad's family were miners and there was no farming history in the family. When my granddad, also called Fred, was a young man and was working around the Chorley area, the pit that he worked at closed down. This led to him travelling to Durham, then a large mining area, to find work and that is where he met my grandma, Hannah. I understand she was very active in the Salvation Army, although I only found this out after she died so I have no information on what she did.

I remember my mother telling a story that was in all the local papers at that time. Someone had committed suicide by jumping off a bridge called The Eight Arches and a fifteen-year-old farm worker found the body at five o'clock in the morning as he was on his way to work. My mother never realised that years later she would marry that young farm worker!

All my mother's family worked in the cotton mills around Chorley. Most worked at Talbot Mill, which was always referred to as 'Bagganley', probably because it was situated at the bottom of Bagganley Lane.

My mother was one of six children: Eddie; Nellie; Charlie; Joe; Jenny and, of course, Mary, my mother. My granddad's name was Charlie and I also had an Uncle Charlie. Charlie was a prominent name in my mother's family as Fred was in my dad's family, which explained my being christened Charles Frederick – or so I assume. It's funny really, as all my dad's family always referred to me as Fred whereas my mother's side of the family always referred to me as 'Freddylove' as if that were my name. They would say, 'Would you like a toffee, Freddylove?' or 'Are you enjoying school, Freddylove?' Strange, but nice.

My parents lived at Cowling Farm until I was about two years old, at which time my dad went on to rent a 28-acre farm at the top of Birkacre Brow, Coppull. He also rented a small semi-detached house a few hundred yards away, as the farmland did not include accommodation. Our new house was 4 Longworth Avenue, an address I remember well. I also remember walking down to the farm one day, gathering an armful of straw, taking it back to the house and spreading it all over the small front lawn. My mum and dad saw me and asked what I was doing, to which I replied, 'Planting strawberries.' They loved that – well, it made sense to me!

When we were old enough, my brother Roy and I attended St Oswald's Catholic School and travelled there by bus. In those days buses were manned by a driver and conductor, and there were always quite a few schoolchildren on board. As the bus approached the bus stop at the end of Clancutt Lane, the kids would stand up and start making their way to the door. The conductor always shouted at the kids who were standing up and made them go back, saying we had not to get up until the bus had stopped.

One day, on the way home from school, I was the only schoolchild on the bus (I can't quite remember why) and was determined not to get into trouble with the conductor. I decided I was going to stay in my seat till the bus stopped but, because there weren't a lot of kids on the bus and no one was getting up (and nobody was getting on either), the driver assumed that no one was getting off. He didn't stop! I was a petrified five year old on a bus on my own for the first time in my life, and I didn't know where I was going. Eventually I could tell that the bus was slowing down and people were standing up to get off, so I also stood up and got off.

I started to run as fast as I could in the direction from which we had come. It seemed to take forever and I was crying all the way until eventually I got back to Clancutt Lane – the stop where I should have got off. It was only a short walk home from there but the trouble was not over yet! My mum had been out of her mind and when I walked in she went mad at me for all the worry I had caused her. I didn't argue; I just assumed that I must be to blame, as five year olds do.

When I was young, almost every event or talking point was defined by adults as 'just before the war' or 'during the war' or 'just after the war'. The Second World War was still fresh in everyone's mind and almost every event in everybody's life fell into one of those three categories. You never hear it now.

Money was not plentiful in the 1940s but, because we kept hens and grew vegetables, we ate better than most. We had a field up Chapel Lane (now all houses) in which my dad grew potatoes. The potatoes were grown in what we called 'drills', with the green tops growing through the tops of the drills. Then, at potato-picking time, my dad would go with the tractor and the potato-picking machine threw the potatoes out. After that, my mum and dad and maybe a couple of school lads picked them up and put them into sacks. One year, my dad took the potato picker up an entire row and never discovered a single potato. Someone had sneaked there at night and dug up every one. They'd put all the green tops back and formed the drill back to perfection so it did not look any different to all the other drills. But it was different – there wasn't one potato below the surface!

Another problem we had was people going out at night and breaking into the hen cabins to steal hens. There were no high-tech security systems in those days. I remember my dad loading up his twelve-bore double-barrelled shotgun one night and sitting in the hen cabin all night. I did not question it then but, looking back, what on earth did he intend to do if someone broke in? Murder them?! Luckily for him (and them) no one broke in.

My only other memory of life at Coppull was when we went to Aunty Jenny and Uncle Bernard's wedding in an upstairs room of The Seven Stars on Eaves Lane, Chorley. I was told to stand still until someone came and told me where to sit but I seemed to be standing for ages and no one came. I decided to take matters into my own hands and sat down, knowing that I wouldn't have chosen the right place but also knowing that a grown-up would come and make me move to where I should be sitting. And that's exactly what happened.

Pretty shrewd for a five year old!

All my mother's family lived in the Eaves Lane area of Chorley. Even as they grew up and got married, they always lived 'on't lane'. My cousin Stella still lives on't lane; in fact, she lives in a house attached to The Seven Stars where her parents got married.

In 1948, my father made what I now realise was a very brave decision and we moved from Coppull and the 28-acre rented farm to 100-acre Blindhurst Farm at Heath Charnock. It was a massive step; nevertheless, buying Blindhurst Farm was my dad's dream come true. He now owned his own farm. Blindhurst had no water toilet, no electricity or even gas, just oil lamps in the house and my mother had to cook on a coal fire. But to my dad these were mere details that would be put right in time – and they were.

I remember the first day that the electricity was switched on. It was winter, with dark mornings and dark nights, and my brother Roy and I went to bed early just so that we could read in bed. The following morning, he woke me up at 5.00am, so we could continue to read – a novelty that didn't last very long. By that time I had another brother, Barry, who was four years younger than me.

My dad paid £7,750 for Blindhurst. He borrowed £2,500 from his brother, my Uncle George, and was allowed to pay off the remainder in instalments to the owner, a lady called Mary Brindle from Adlington who, I believe, had inherited the farm. The money that Dad borrowed from Uncle George was just marked on a piece of notepaper and that was the official agreement. There was no such thing as a solicitor, even though £2,500 was a massive amount in 1948. It was all paid back in full (with interest) and I understand that Dad also borrowed £320 from his other brother, my Uncle Ellis. Even as children, my dad was always willing to discuss the business with us, all the ups and the downs, the highs and the lows.

During the early years at Blindhurst, there were times when money was tight. In fact that is an understatement; there were times when it was non-existent and nothing could be paid until the next cheque arrived. I remember sitting in class at school at a very young age and, while the other kids listened intently to the teacher, I was working out how we could get the bank overdraft down and get the bank manager off my dad's back. Never mind the lesson – I would just copy from the kid next to me at the end of the class and if he got it wrong, so what? I wasn't daft enough to copy it exactly; I would make one or two changes so my answers were different.

When we moved to Blindhurst, Roy, Barry and I attended St Joseph's Catholic School in Anderton. The first Christmas we were there, I got a part in the Christmas play as an elf. The school provided the elf outfits but asked if the parents would provide the elf shoes. For whatever reason my mum never got round to getting me any possibly because, apart from running the house, she also helped with the collecting and packing of the eggs. Anyway, whatever the reason, come the day of the play, I had no elf shoes. As it was pouring down, I went to school in wellingtons. I'll never forget my embarrassment when five other elves and I had to hold hands and dance round in a circle while the teacher, Mrs Southworth, played the piano. All the other elves were resplendent in their little shiny shoes and there I was in dirty wellingtons! My mother and Aunty Jenny were in the audience and thought it was hilarious, giving me no sympathy and just having a good laugh! I wanted the ground to open up and swallow me. Why have I never had a complex? AN ELF IN WELLINGTONS?!

Although money was in short supply, my mother always managed to provide a wonderful Christmas. She would fill one table with sweets and chocolates and that would be the first thing that we saw when we came downstairs. I remember one year she bought me a real football (or tube and case, as they were often called in those days). As she was about to go to bed, she realised that it was going soft so she got the pump and pumped it up again. When she was in bed she started to worry that it would keep going down, so she got up at every hour during the night to pump it up so that it would be hard for me when I got up on Christmas morning. The fact that it was down again in half an hour didn't matter to me.

As we got a bit older, my dad started to take us to the pictures at Chorley. We had no car so we had to go on the bus, which meant that we were tied by their running times. In those days the cinema showed two films every night, a short 'B' film and the main feature film, and showed them in what they called the 'first house' (early) then the 'second house' (late). In other words, there were two showings of each film but, because of the times of the buses, for years we watched the end of the first house then the beginning of the second house before leaving to catch the bus home. So, we watched the end first and the beginning last, and so did everyone else that was on our bus – and no one thought anything about it. How stupid was that?

About that time, I had a school friend called Joe Laithwaite. He was a great lad who was very funny and genuine. One day we were in the school plantation, an area that was in fact out of bounds, when for some reason we started to fight. It was nothing serious as we were just fooling around, but suddenly I felt a sharp pain in my left leg near the calf.

'Joe,' I shouted. 'My leg!' I looked down to see it was covered in blood. Lying next to me was a broken, jagged, milk bottle. The cut was quite bad and the scar is still there today. There was nothing else for it: Joe and I had to go and tell the teacher. The damage was too bad to ignore.

When the teacher, Miss Maher, saw my leg she immediately called the doctor to come and stitch it. Within a few minutes Dr Lawrenson arrived. I had to go in the staff room and sit down on a chair with my leg on a stool while he sat at the side of my leg and inserted several stitches into the cut. He didn't freeze or numb it in any way, just kept shoving the needle into the flesh and bringing it out through the other side. Then he pulled the wound together and fastened it. The pain was excruciating and seemed to go on forever. I was almost fainting during the procedure.

Miss Maher stood at my side, holding my hand and trying to comfort me, but she was called out and replaced by Mrs Southworth, who was not as sympathetic. All she could say – and constantly repeat – was, 'I don't like to hit a man when he's down, but you shouldn't have been there.' She asked me if I would like a cup of tea. 'Yes, please,' I replied, so she went and put the kettle on and made me one, but instead of putting sugar in the tea she put two spoonfuls of salt. She did this on purpose, not apparently to punish me but (as she put it) 'Salt is good for cuts.' Really? After the ordeal she ordered a taxi for me and sent me home.

Tragically Joe died while still a handsome young lad in his twenties. I never heard what caused his death but it was a sad loss.

About 1955, when I was twelve years old, my mum and dad took me and my eight-year-old brother Barry to The Royal Lancashire Show, a day out that farmers in Lancashire never missed. Before we set off, Dad rang his friend Norris Riley, a neighbouring farmer, to arrange to meet him and his wife Anne at the show venue, Stanley Park, Blackpool.

We all met as planned at 11am and set off round the showground. After about an hour of walking, we came across some toilets and Barry expressed a desire to go.

'Alright,' said my mother. 'You go to the toilet and we'll walk on ahead.' She said to me, 'You wait here for him to come out to make sure he doesn't get lost. Don't move till he comes out and then catch us up.'

With that, they walked on. I waited and waited but no Barry

appeared. I kept remembering that my mum had said, 'Don't move till he comes out,' so I continued waiting, but eventually I decided that I must go in and look for him. I went into the toilets (which were temporary ones for the show) only to find that there was another exit and he had left by that one.

By then quite a lot of time had elapsed and the grown ups had travelled a long way. I ran as fast as I could, as I was starting to get frightened. Although I was running fast, and in my own mind thinking I should now have caught them up, there were many side avenues off the main one and I was panicking in case they had taken one of those routes. That was it then: I was twelve years old and was lost among tens of thousands of strangers. I was distraught and spent the rest of the day looking for them.

Then, after hours of looking, I heard Dad's voice. 'Fred,' he shouted, and there they all were, including Barry and the Rileys. But, as with the Clancutt Lane saga, the worst was yet to come: the telling off. How could I do it to them? How could I be so disobedient? After a severe telling off I will never forget Mum's last words: 'You've not only spoiled our day, you have spoiled Mr and Mrs Riley's day as well. Come on, we are going home. You've ruined our day.'

The words, 'Don't move till he comes out,' kept going through my mind, but to no avail. It was a long and quiet journey home and then I went to bed, upset at what I had done.

In the late fifties and early sixties my mother was the president of Chorley Lady Farmers' Group, a thriving movement of farmers' wives, daughters and employees. In fact, it was for anyone with an interest in farming even if they were not farmers. Every year they held two social events: a black tie ball and dinner, where tickets cost £2, and a buffet dance (casual dress) where tickets cost 10/6d.

One farmer's wife in the Chorley area decided that she was missing out on any kind of social life, so she joined the Lady Farmers Group.

Her joining coincided with the dinner dance being held so she and her husband, Bill, decided to go. Unfortunately nobody told them that it was formal dress and they both turned up in casual clothes. They were the only two in the room, which quite embarrassed them both.

Eventually the day came for the 10/6d buffet dance and this time there was no danger of them being caught out again. Come the night, they proudly turned up in smart formal attire – and were again the only two in the room dressed that way.

I remember once, around 1952 when I was about nine years old, we went to see *Phantom of the Opera* starring Claude Rains. I have never been so scared in my life. I was petrified but the worse was still to come. When we got home, my dad made me go round the field and shut all the doors on the hen cabins to keep the foxes out. I had to run around our field at eleven o'clock at night in the pitch black and all I could think about was the *Phantom of the Opera*. I have never run so fast in my life. In the film, the phantom played the violin and for years afterwards I was terrified of the sound of violins.

AGE 10-20, THE SPECIAL YEARS

have called this chapter *The Special Years* because, although we don't realise it at the time, they certainly were. This is the decade when more changes and developments occur than at any other time in your life.

This is the decade when you make the transition from being a young boy of ten to a young man of twenty. This is the decade when you leave school; when you get your first job; when you learn to drive when you get your first car and, if you're a girl, then possibly your first pony (the one you will always remember most fondly). You start to take an interest in your appearance, you have your first date, you have your first crush and it's a time when the music of the day that you loved will always have the most memories for you. Many, many years later you will occasionally hear a song or music from that period and it will immediately bring the moment back vividly – maybe a girlfriend, maybe a dance, maybe a distant holiday. Yes, these are the special years!

It's a strange thing but in the fifties most young men went about their daily work whistling or singing – it was just the done thing. The postman would whistle as he delivered the mail, as would the milkman while delivering milk, the wagon driver, the farm worker – in fact, everyone used to whistle the tunes of the day. We had a young lad work for us at Blindhurst named Les Birchall. Les worked for us for about five years in the mid fifties and his wages were £6 per week.

This money was accrued by people coming to the door to buy eggs and my mother putting the money to one side in the hope that by Friday there would be enough to pay Les his wages.

Les also whistled or sang continually – Nat King Cole's 'Unforgettable', Jonny Ray's 'Cry' and Frankie Laine's 'High Noon'. I didn't notice this trend gradually dying out but I certainly never hear anyone doing it today. On the very few occasions I do, it is always someone of my generation.

I remember one week when for some reason hardly anyone came for eggs; by Wednesday my mother was panicking as there was nowhere near enough money to pay Les. So there was only one thing for it – to put the eggs in boxes and send me to local houses in the hope that, although the residents obviously didn't need any eggs, they would have them anyway seeing as I had walked all that way with them. This worked and, after covering miles, as we lived out in the country, enough money accrued to pay Les's wages.

Another trend that seems to have died out was that most young lads carried a comb and would tidy their hair several times a day, with some lads doing it almost continually. Again, it was just what young lads did.

A few months ago, whilst having a conversation with my brother Roy, we were discussing life on the farm when we were young and we counted up all the farms within a five-mile radius of Blindhurst. There were forty-four; today there are only four. All the others have either been taken over by the remaining four or are private dwellings. In the days when there were forty-four, we knew them all and they all knew us. Everyone knew everyone else. I'm not trying to be sentimental or nostalgic here – it's a fact. My dad was very well known in the area, mainly because of the very long hours he used to work. As far as he was concerned work was not a chore, it was something he loved to do. He loved his farm; it was his life, his job, his hobby and almost his sole topic of conversation. Among the other farmers he was always known as Jack Smith from Blindhurst, as if 'from Blindhurst' was part of his name.

To say that the farm was all-consuming to my dad was an understatement and here are a couple of incidents that typify that.

When my younger brother Barry was born, Dad went to visit Mum in the hospital. In those days the babies were taken from the mothers between feeding times and put in a side ward. As my dad was leaving at the end of visiting time, the nurse said to him 'Would you like to see your new baby, Mr Smith?' He replied 'No, it's alright, I'll see it when it comes home,' and went straight back to the farm!

On another occasion when my maternal grandma was very ill, my dad used to take Mum to visit her on Eaves Lane. Mum would stay for a few hours then Dad would go back later in the afternoon to pick her up. One morning, I think it was a Saturday, Dad came back from dropping Mum off just as Roy and I had finished mucking out. We all went in and cooked our breakfast, ate it and read the farming newspapers. The three of us were just about to go out again when my dad said, 'Oh, your grandma's dead.' He'd forgotten to tell us.

You might think from all this that he was hard and cruel but in reality he was extremely kind and humble – just totally consumed by his beloved farm.

Because of his total commitment to the farm, Dad was a hard taskmaster and as we grew older (even though we were still at school) he expected us to work like men. If we didn't perform as he thought we should, he would let us know about it. Though I don't want to sound self-pitying, I usually came off the worst and his tirades against me usually included the expression, 'You're neither use nor ornament.' That insult did not bother me too much as it was a common expression at the time; it was only when I reached adulthood many years later that I realised I never heard him use that expression to Roy or Barry.

It hurt me more then than it had done at the time.

My dad was very critical of me and never paid me a compliment. One day, when I was about thirteen or fourteen, I said, 'Am I a disappointment to you?' I was thinking that I might melt him a little bit and he might say something kind to comfort me but, without hesitation, he said, 'I don't know. I'll have to wait till you are a bit older before I can tell.' Well, that was a great comfort!

I remember the first car we got. We bought it from another farmer who had been keeping hens in it, so you can imagine what the inside was like! The car was a big grey Ford V8 and every night after work we would all go out and sandpaper it down. We then painted it with brushes. Can you imagine three or four people all painting the same car with different brushes? Anyway, we were very proud of the end result and kept the car for about five years.

Uncle George was the relative that we had most contact with. He never drove and used to come up to the farm on his bike; he always took a great interest in the farm. That was good for my dad as it gave him someone to discuss things with and bounce ideas off, and Uncle George was always there at harvest or hay time to give us a lift. I'm not sure that he ever took any money for this.

Uncle George lived at home with his mother, my Grandma Smith, which was normal in those days. I have very fond memories of Uncle George at Christmas; every year, a couple of days before Christmas Day, he would come up to the farm on his bike with three big plastic bags and each one was full of presents for each of us. We all had an idea what day he would be bringing them and we were always excited. Every year it was like we had two Christmas Days: Uncle George's mini-Christmas Day and the big one.

As Uncle George rode home on his bike he had to go up Nickleton Brow, a steep hill near the farm that stretched for about half a mile. There were five trees evenly spaced along the hill and George would always, without exception, cycle to the second tree, get off and walk to the top. He would then get back on again. His routine never varied.

In my early life, Uncle George lived in a lovely house on Rawlinson Lane, Heath Charnock. They called it 'Evergreen'. It was a semi-detached house that my grandparents had bought new for £320 many years before. Uncle George loved gardening and his garden was a credit to him. People would stop to admire it.

Directly across the road were two huge chestnut trees, or conker trees as we called them. Every year when the kids at school used to see who could collect the most conkers, we always had the most as Uncle George gathered up hundreds that had fallen off the two trees. Only this week I drove past those two trees and noticed that they are still full of conkers. They reminded me of Uncle George and how much pleasure he got from bringing us bulging bags of conkers. I also glanced at his house and it's still called 'Evergreen'.

If a farmer had a son or sons, it was expected that they would work on the farm when they left school. As the sons approached leaving age, with perhaps a year or eighteen months to go, the parents would start to get frustrated as they needed the lads on the farm. I can't count how many times I heard parents and friends say, 'He's too big to be going to school,' as though leaving school depended on their size as opposed to their age.

In all my young life on the farm, my dad only took one day off with us that I can remember – and I suspect that was because my mother was giving him some grief. He got dressed up, we all got in the Ford V8 and off we went to Southport Pleasure Beach. We got there at about eleven o'clock and all went well until about one o'clock, when my dad complained that he had a splitting headache. For the next two hours that's all he said – just repeated that he had a splitting headache – so at three o'clock we agreed that we should go home. Days off did not suit my dad. I've no doubt that when he got back home he got changed and started work again, headache gone.

In the early to late 1950s, apart from going to the pictures, most of our entertainment came from the wireless – the Light Programme, the Home Service and Luxembourg. The latter was an independent station. I would argue with anyone that the simple entertainment we got from the wireless was as gripping and as funny as anything we get from today's hi-tech entertainment. Comedy was provided by the likes of Ken Platt, Al Read and *Life with the Lyons*, and excitement came from things like *Dick Tracy, Special Agent*, a kind of 1950s' radio James Bond. Music came from programmes like *Music While You Work* and *Workers' Playtime*.

Then there were the adverts on Radio Luxembourg – how did they get away with them? I'll give you an example. In those days your only hope of getting rich was to win the Pools, the equivalent of today's lottery. You were issued with a football coupon with all the fixtures on it, and you were given ten chances to pick eight matches that would end in a draw. If you picked all eight and nobody else did, you would win £75,000, riches beyond your wildest dreams, worth millions today. There was one radio advertiser, Horace Batchelor (of Keynsham, Bristol) who promised that if you sent him some money (I can't remember how much), he would tell you how to beat the system and win the Pools. He called his system 'The Infra-Draw Method' and he advertised for years. Why would a person who knew how to win the Pools every week tell everybody else? But it was advertised on radio, so obviously people were sending in money.

The mid fifties saw the introduction of television and it was always a great talking point at school. Television was, without a doubt, a status symbol, especially if yours had a seventeen-inch screen. They were the deluxe models, the cheaper ones being nine inch and twelve inch. Almost everyone watched TV in the front room with the lights out and curtains drawn, as this gave a clearer picture. More often than not, the families with the seventeen-inch screens would leave the curtains open so that passers-by could glance in and see the large screen!

At the end of the Blindhurst's drive was a beautiful lake and on the side of the lake was a massive stone house, the home of the Walker family, a very wealthy family who were the owners of Walkers Tannery in Bolton. I understand that Roger Walker, the father, was heavily into spiritualism. They had two children: the eldest one a boy known as Carton (although his full name was Carton De Whyatt Walker) and his sister, Sonia. Carton went to boarding school and all his clothes had his name stitched on, presumably so that they wouldn't get mixed up with other pupils' clothes. As Carton got older and outgrew his clothes, his mother used to wrap them up and give them to my mother for me to wear. It was great; I could wear upmarket, top-quality, expensive clothes instead of the cheap, bought in the sale clothes that my mother used to get for me. The embarrassing part was making excuses to all my mates as to why all my clothes had 'Carton De Whyatt Walker' stitched onto them.

Carton did not go into the family's tannery business; to his father's disgust, he went into the leisure industry and was responsible for developing two sites almost from nothing, The Last Drop Village at Bromley Cross and The Tickled Trout at Samlesbury. Over the years we lost touch but I believe that Carton died very young. He was a character and a bit of a rebel in his day. I remember when his sister Sonia got married it was the wedding of the year. While the church service and reception were limited to family members and the Great and the Good, they invited all the locals to an evening 'do' in a large marquee. Everyone was excited and it was a big talking point but, for some reason, no invitation came to Blindhurst. Although we pretended not to be bothered, we were very disappointed.

One day we saw Mr Walker's big car pulling up in the farmyard. He got out (he was a very commanding figure) and he walked over to my dad. 'Hello Mr Smith,' he said.

'Oh, hello!' replied Dad, faking surprise.

'I suppose you know that Sonia is getting married on Saturday?' Mr Walker said.

'Oh yes,' said my dad. 'I had heard.'

'Well,' Mr Walker said, 'The Street Drive (our shared road) will be very busy with traffic so I wondered if you could keep your tractors and machinery off for the day.'

My dad was taken aback; he thought Mr Walker was bringing the invitation.

Another revelation in the fifties was the introduction of frozen food. I remember my mum coming home from shopping in Chorley one Tuesday (she always went to Chorley on Tuesdays) and bringing some frozen fish, something we had never had before. She put the fish in the oven, cooked the vegetables then proudly served up the meal. Roy tried to stick his fork in the fish but it wouldn't go in. 'This fish is still frozen,' he said to Mum.

She replied, 'Well, it's been in the oven long enough.'

Roy hit back with, 'It can't have been in the oven long enough or it wouldn't still be frozen.'

My mum just burst out laughing, as did Roy, and the fish went back in the oven. My mum had a great sense of humour and no one appreciated it more than our Roy, especially when she was having a sly go at my dad and he didn't realise it.

As I said earlier, everyone in the area knew everyone else. Only a few of the locals had a car but, if you were walking somewhere and a local with a car saw you, they would always stop and give you a lift. Just across the field from Blindhurst were the Yew Tree Inn and three cottages. One day, one of the residents of the cottages, Bert Corless, was walking to the bus stop when Lester, the manager of the Yew Tree Inn, pulled up in his car and asked Bert if he would like a lift. Bert

1960. My younger brother, Barry, coming down the drive at Blindhurst.

1955. My mum getting into our beloved Ford V8 to
go to Chorley to do her weekly shopping.

1948. My mum and Grandma Smith at the door of 'Evergreen' which my grandparents bought new for £320.

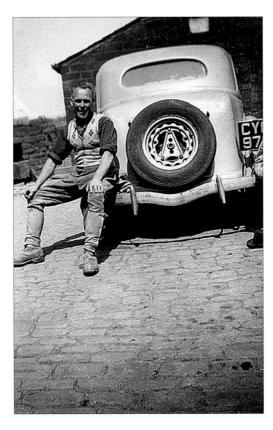

1955. My dad taking a minute's rest sitting on the bumper of our other family member, the Ford V8.

1954. Blindhurst Farm – front view of the house. Donald Holt's bike is in the background. My bedroom was the top right hand window and Roy's was the left.

1964. Margaret with three of her nursing friends, Preston Royal Infirmary.

1957. Mum with me on the right, Barry on the left and camera shy Shep.

1938. Mum and Dad on their wedding day, Sacred Heart Church, Chorley.

Above, **Late 50s.** Nickleton Brow – the road leading to Blindhurst. The Yew Tree Inn, Heath Charnock is in the distance. I love the snow but you never see it now. I feel cheated.

Left, **1964.** Ambition achieved! I won a Health & Strength photographic competition.

STAR GALLERY

FRED SMITH, of Heath Charnock, Lancashire, is a farmer. He is 5ft. 8in. tall; weight 12st. 4lb.; chest 47in.; upper arm 15½in.; neck 16¼in.; waist 31in.; thigh 24in. He is 20. Best lifts are: Squat 410lb.; Bench Press 280lb.; Curl 145lb. He has been training for three and a half years.

1963. In front of the shippon door, *from left to right*, me, my brother Roy, my mother Mary, my dad Jack and my other brother, Barry.

1966. One of many farm walks held at Blindhurst. Blindhurst was *the* farm. That's me dragging the bag of silage.

1962. Me at 18 years old, flexing up at Adlington Barbell Club.

1965. Our wedding day on 2nd May at St Bedes Church, Clayton Green, Chorley. Margaret with her sisters (*left to right*) Jennifer, Carol, Kathleen and Ruth.

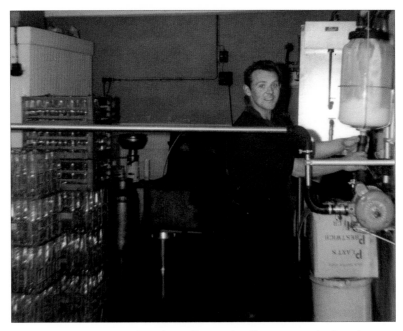

1967. Preparing to bottle milk at Blindhurst, ready for the next day's deliveries.

Circa 1967. Me proudly standing in front of my new electric milk float. Daily fuel cost 9 shillings (45 pence).

got in. While they were travelling, Lester asked if Bert was going to Chorley to which Bert replied yes, so it was agreed that Lester would drop him off there. A few days later Lester received a very severe letter from a solicitor about some minor violation that he had committed, and threatening legal action if it was not put right. The letter was sent on behalf of the solicitor's client, Bert Corless. That had been where Bert was going when Lester dropped him off in Chorley!

As I mentioned earlier, whistling as you went about your day's work was what almost everyone did. Another common practice that seems to have died out was visiting. 'Having visitors' was a regular occurrence for most families. It certainly was for us and, unlike today when we dread visitors, we used to enjoy them. My mother would make sandwiches and brew a pot of tea (she never served alcohol) and everyone would settle down for the night and swap stories. The television never went on then, around ten o'clock, my dad would run the visitors home in the hand-painted car that never let us down.

One of our regular visitors was Donald Holt, the son of a neighbouring farmer. I don't know how he did it but Donald could manage to talk all night without once telling the truth. He basically lived on his imagination. Donald loved to shock and he also loved to be the first one to tell you the local gossip. If there was no gossip or nothing to shock, that was no obstacle to Donald – he just made things up. The odd part about it was that everyone in the room knew when he was lying but nobody ever pulled him up about it. We just went along with it. Maybe we were as stupid as him.

In all the years that he came to visit us, always in the evening, Donald never once sat down. He always, without exception, stood up near the door. My dad never drove him back as Donald always went home on his bike, which never had any lights on. But that was Heath Charnock over fifty years ago – a time when no one bothered about such things. There were no street lights either; Donald pedalled home in the pitch black through the country lanes.

The lack of light made no difference at hay time because, if the hay had been baled, the bales had to be brought in that day. My dad would not allow one bale to be left out overnight. The reason was that if it rained during the night, the bales would have to be reopened to allow them to dry out and then be re-baled. It was too big a risk to take so, no matter what time of the night it was, we didn't finish work until the field was clear. That meant there were tractors and trailers loaded with hay travelling round the country lanes at midnight with neither lights nor indicators and, to make matters worse, between 10.30pm and 11.30pm there were numerous cars leaving the Yew Tree car park (no breathalysers in those days) and the lanes were quite busy. But again, not a complaint from anyone.

Two regular visitors to Blindhurst were Steve and Miriam Finch. Steve had been the agent acting for the lady from whom we had bought the farm and we had remained good friends. He was now elderly and retired but in days gone by he had been a butcher in the village of Adlington, as well as having other business interests. He was quite a wealthy man.

Steve and Miriam lived about two miles from the farm and always walked up to us, with my dad taking them back home again in the trusty Ford V8. They always dressed resplendently, Steve with a three-piece suit and a handkerchief in the top pocket, a walking stick and a bowler hat. Miriam dressed equally well.

Because Steve was well known in the village, and because of his regular visits to Blindhurst, a lot of people thought he was backing my dad financially. Although Steve said that he strenuously denied this, we got the impression that he secretly loved it.

On their visits over many, many years to our house, they were always referred to by everyone, Mum and Dad included, as Mr and Mrs Finch. They were never referred to as Steve and Miriam, except after they had gone home; nevertheless, they were a very entertaining couple and we all enjoyed their visits.

One of the many visitors that came to Blindhurst was an elderly lady called Bessie Strange, who lived in a remote farmhouse on the Nab Moors. Bessie was never referred to as Bessie; she was always known as Black Bess and described as 'strange by name and strange by nature'. She was a harmless and very kind person but a little eccentric.

It was a time before supermarkets and not every shop sold eggs, so she used to make the long walk from her house to the bus route. She would catch the bus to Heath Charnock and make another long walk to Blindhurst, carrying three empty baskets.

She would arrive at Blindhurst at about 7pm and stay till about 10pm, all the time regaling us with stories of her life and experiences. How much of it was true we will never know – but did it matter? My mother would make tea and sandwiches, then fill up her three large baskets with eggs for her to sell to people in Chorley. After that, my dad drove her home in our trusty and rusty Ford V8.

She was not a person to worry about personal hygiene too much and she also wheezed a lot as she spoke but no one ever complained or criticised her, and we enjoyed her visits.

I often compare those days to the situation at our house today. Margaret would have gone into meltdown at the presence of Bessie, and would have had a team of cleaners and fumigators ready to move in. But, as I have said before, that was then and this is now. Things change.

I have noticed, when I think back, that no matter how many people came to our house and stayed for the evening, the TV never got switched on. There was never any alcohol consumed and no one ever swore. In fact, during my dad's entire life not only did I never once hear him swear but I never heard anyone swear in front of him.

There was a couple, Peter and Sybil Brownlow, who lived across the fields from us. Sybil was always known as Syb, and Peter was always known as Owd P. Owd P was a cattle dealer; they lived in a cottage on Dill Hall Brow just near the Yew Tree Inn. Owd P was a regular figure round the country lanes of Heath Charnock. He always wore old tweed suits, brown boots and a tweed trilby and walked with a walking stick – he never drove. He didn't own a farm or any land, just bought cattle from farmers and sold them at the auction. He appeared to be very successful at what he did and he was rumoured to be quite well off, although their lifestyle didn't give this away. Syb, in particular was very careful with money, bordering on tight.

One day, when my mother was in hospital, I was delivering milk to their door when Syb came out and asked me for three eggs. That was unusual, as she always got half a dozen eggs at the weekend, but it was no problem. I went back to the van and got three eggs, which I gave to her. She handed me a cake and said, 'This cake is for you and your family. I have put three eggs in it and I'll be blowed if I am buying eggs from you then putting them in a cake and giving them back to you. So I'll have these three.' Can't argue with that. It was fair enough, I suppose.

When we moved from Coppull to Blindhurst in 1948, Dad continued to run the farm as an arable and poultry farm, though it was always his intention to one day change over to dairy. The main reason for not doing this from the outset was the capital investment; in comparison to dairy farming, arable farming required far less investment. However, by 1953 Dad decided to make the changeover he'd dreamed of from arable to dairy. My dad had a very open mind on farming policies and didn't stick to just one line of products. In time he used his land for arable crops, milk production, beef, poultry and pig rearing.

I remember when he first ventured into pig rearing he bought about twenty newly weaned pigs. Though most people hate the smell of pigs, I loved it. I was about nine years old at the time they were delivered and, when I got home from school, I went to look at them and just sat with them. I loved it – the smell, the noise, just everything – but I didn't realise that I hadn't told my mother where I was and the night was getting darker. She was starting to panic. Also, she had got my dad and Roy looking for me in the shippon, in the fields and all over. Then, as she was passing the pig sty she happened to look in and there I was, sitting with the pigs, happy as a pig in muck.

It was also about this time that the government realised that a lot of cattle were infected by tuberculosis and encouraged farmers to have their cattle tested. Although at this time it was not compulsory, milk from any herd that was tuberculosis free attracted a better price. The value of each cow was considerably increased: a non-TT cow (as it was called) would be worth £45–£60, whereas a TT cow would be worth £75–£90.

After about a year of converting an old building into a new modern shippon, we were ready to buy the first of our herd of TT cattle. This was a major change in our life and we were all excited. Dad had decided that we were going to invest in a herd of Ayrshire Shorthorn cross. I think the reasoning was that Ayrshires were good milk producers and Shorthorns were good beef cattle, so when a cow came to the end of its milk producing life we would get a decent price for it as a beef animal. At least, that was the idea. The new shippon that we had converted held twenty-one cattle and it's true to say that we were very proud of it. Most of the other farmers in the area had shippons holding six to ten cows, so our new state-of-the-art shippon was much admired.

At that time we had a friend on a neighbouring farm who bought all his cattle from a dealer in Skipton; our friend introduced the dealer to my dad. The dealer bought all his cattle from Stirling in Scotland and, even though the cattle were not yet tested because the industry was still in a transitional period, Stirling was a tuberculosis-free area so we felt sure that there would be no problem. Dad took his friend,

Norris Riley, with him on his first visit to the dealer at Skipton. We were all excited about how many cows he might buy on his first visit; my brother Roy and I guessed at four to six, while Les guessed at eight – and he was spot on.

Eight cows were delivered by cattle wagon the following day and I remember us all, Mother included, standing in the yard watching as each one came out of the wagon. That night, milking them was incredibly special for the Blindhurst household. The next morning we were up bright and early ready to start milking, an experience that we had waited years for. It probably took us about six weeks to fill the shippon, buying a few cows every week. When it was finally full, I went into the shippon several times a day to look at our new shippon full of Ayrshire Shorthorns. Their presence was an ambition achieved.

Now that the shippon was full, it was time for us to have the cows tested for tuberculosis so that we could move up to being an official TT herd. The test was a procedure during which the vet would inject all the cattle in the neck and come back three days later to look at their reaction to the injection. If the injected area was flat then it was a pass, but if the area was swollen it was a fail. The size of the swelling was determined by the vet simply placing callipers on the area. I will remember to my dying day the look on my dad's face after the vet had tested the first cow, turned to my dad and said, 'This is not a good start, John.'

My dad just stood there and said simply, 'Is it not?' He was devastated. By the time the vet had tested them all, thirteen out of twenty-one had failed.

We sat in the house that night and hardly anyone spoke. Milking time the following morning was more like a funeral. All the excitement had gone and it was the quietest milking time ever.

My dad rang Fred Wrathall, the dealer in Skipton, to tell him the results. He could not believe it either – he'd never sold any cows that had failed before. I don't remember what the financial arrangements were but I think secretly they were arrangements to suit the dealer. Well, a dealer is a dealer; if they see a chance to make money they take it. So, in due course, the whole testing procedure began again and this time the thirteen replacement cows all came through clean; but – and it is a big but – the eight that had previously passed all failed. This was even more devastating than the last failures. Now there was nowhere to go; we had no money left, we would get a reduced price for the milk and the entire herd was worth a fraction of what we had paid for it. It was a massive blow that took years to recover from. We couldn't swap all the cattle in again as we did not have any money, so we just had to carry on as we were, being seen in those days as second-class milk producers.

All the other farmers in the area heard what had happened. It was big news that Jack Smith's herd of expensive cattle had failed all the tests. They all expressed their sympathy while we knew very well that some of them were secretly gloating. But I suppose you get that in all walks of life.

We got on with life on the farm and the farm next to Blindhurst (the one that Donald Holt and his dad had farmed) came up for sale. We decided it would be a good acquisition. The 40-acre farm was called Nabs Farm and its land bordered Blindhurst land so was a good size to add to ours. I remember that on the day of the auction I was at school and couldn't concentrate; all I could think about was whether we had got the farm. I ran home from school that night and, to great relief, my dad had bought it. He had paid £4,000 and I remember him telling people that it was worth more to us than anyone else, being next door. It was as though he had to justify paying so much. In a short space of time, we sold the farmhouse for £2,750 to a fellow named Pat Kelly. About a year later, Pat bought the barn for £1,500 which, in effect, meant that we had got the forty acres of land for nothing. It was only the land that we actually wanted so it was, all in all, an excellent result.

About three years after the cows failed the TB test, my dad decided that we should go for it again. Not being a premier-league farmer didn't sit well with him; anything less than first class could not and would not be tolerated. So one week, I can't remember the exact year, we sent our entire herd to the auction and a few days later the cheque dropped through the door. It was for £800, which was a large amount in those days, and I was quite excited about it until my dad pointed out to me, 'Yes, we've got £800 but that's all we've got. We've got nothing else.' He was right. We had £800 in the bank but an empty farm. The trick now was to build up a successful dairy farm, starting with that £800.

Over the coming years that's exactly what we did, building up the herd in a calm and professional way and at the same time acquiring two more farms, both bordering Blindhurst: Shaw Place Farm, for which we paid £16,000, and The Barn Fields. These acquisitions took our overall acreage to around 400 acres.

As the years went on under my dad's guidance and drive, Blindhurst was getting recognised as one of the leading and most efficient farms in the North West, and my dad as one of the most successful and knowledgeable farmers.

My dad was a very enterprising farmer and was always ahead of the rest in his farming methods. For instance, in the 1940s when tractors were just becoming popular, he was the first farmer in the area to have a tractor with headlights, which meant that he could work in the fields till well after dark. He often did this; working till midnight was nothing unusual for him. In those days tractors did not have cabs, so sitting on the tractor for hours on end at night was not pleasant but it had to be done. Dad was also the first to make the transition from milking in shippons to using a modern milking parlour and to having the milk picked up by tanker from a bulk tank rather than sending it in ten-gallon churns. He changed haymaking methods and installed three 60-foot tower silos, which was another revolutionary move that separated him from the neighbouring farmers. The list of his enterprising moves is pretty endless.

In those days, the sixties and seventies, there used to be what was known as 'Farm Walks', where a party of anything up to a hundred people would travel by car, or bus, to a certain farm that had been recommended by an official body to look round the farm and fields and see how a farm should be run.

It was a very great compliment to the farmer to be recommended for a farm walk as it meant the farm was being run efficiently, not to mention cleanly. It was a well-known fact that if a farmer kept his farm clean he was a farmer on top of his job. This was because farms, especially farms with livestock, were difficult to keep clean, so a clean farm told you everything about the farmer.

The official bodies who recommended Blindhurst for farm walks were the National Farmers Union, the Milk Marketing Board, the Grassland Society, the Lancashire Education Committee and others that I can't remember.

I remember my dad receiving a letter from a school in Chorley (I can't remember which one) saying that the headmaster had written to the National Farmers Union to say that the school would like to take a party of children round a farm to enlighten them about farming. They had asked the NFU to recommend a farm.

The headmaster's comments to my dad were (and I quote): 'I was delighted to hear from the gentlemen of the NFU that the best possible farm that we could take the children to was right here on our doorstep at Heath Charnock, Blindhurst Farm.' That was the esteem in which my dad and Blindhurst were held. I don't recall any other farm in the area ever being recommended.

There was no money to be made from farm walks; in fact, they were disruptive and probably cost us money, but they were enjoyable and they rightly recognised my dad's dedication to and pride in his beloved farm. Also, when any visitors asked him a question he had the answer at his fingertips. He was completely in control.

When my mother was about forty, she was diagnosed with a blocked valve in her heart and this required a serious heart operation at Blackpool Victoria Hospital. This was the talking point of the whole area; until then, such an operation was unknown. It required her to be in hospital for about three to four weeks. Everyone sent their best wishes to her and sent cakes, scones and treats to those of us that were left at home. None were more generous than Bert and Nan Brindle, who lived in a cottage on Dill Hall Brow. Nan was an excellent cook and almost every day we were sent what you could only describe as a Sunday lunch. Wonderful people.

It turned out that (unbeknown to us at the time) another woman from Adlington had undergone the same operation. The local doctor put her and Mum in touch and whenever they bumped into each other in the village they would always compare notes on their progress. The other lady always let my mother know that she was making better progress than Mum, and loved to tell her that the doctors referred to her as 'Wonder Woman'. She repeated it so many times that eventually Mum also referred to her as 'Wonder Woman' – although Mum said it in a more sarcastic way. Then one day Mum came home from the doctors where she'd been for a routine check-up. We asked her how she had got on, so she gave her report and then she said, 'Oh, you remember Wonder Woman?'

'Yes...'

'She's dead!' You shouldn't laugh.

It was while Mum was in hospital that Roy passed his driving test. That was a great boost to Dad as it meant that Roy could now drive legally on the road and you can't imagine how much that freed Dad up to get on with his job. Roy was also an excellent tractor driver, as was Barry as he got older. I, on the other hand, was not so good – but horses for courses…

When I was about fourteen, my dad and I brought the bull out to serve a cow. The correct way to bring the bull out is with a proper wooden staff, which you connect to the ring in its nose. This gives you more control over the bull. It's not a fallacy that bulls can be dangerous and the rigid staff helps to keep the bull at a safe distance. If it starts to get frisky, you can twist the staff, which means that you are twisting its nose. This usually means that the bull will think better of it and quieten down. On occasions, if the staff wasn't to hand, we used a rope but a rope didn't give you as much control. However, if you had known the bull a long time and you knew its moods and temperament, you could sometimes take a chance and use the rope, as we did on this occasion. Dad went to get the bull out while I went to get the cow and we took them both out into the yard.

After the cow had been served I walked it back into the shippon, leaving my dad to take the bull back. I noticed that he wasn't following me, so I tied up the cow in its stall. When I went back into the yard, I found my dad lying on his back, kicking his feet and legs in the bull's face as the bull tried to gore him with its horns. I immediately ran over to the bull and just managed to get to its nose and grab the rope, which was flying about wildly. I held the rope close to its nose so that I could exert maximum pain and it settled down.

Dad got up off the floor and said, 'That thing's dangerous.' I led it back to the shippon, and the incident was never ever mentioned again – not even a thanks from Dad. This was not because he was ungrateful or anything like that, and neither was he stressed or traumatised; it was because we lived on a farm and these things happen on farms, so are all part of a day's work.

Humour never played a big part in my dad's life. I never once heard him tell a joke or say anything remotely funny although, in fairness, if anyone else cracked a joke he would laugh along with it. He would never be the instigator. In contrast my mother had a wicked sense of humour, which no one escaped. Dad had no sense of humour but had great business acumen; on the other hand, my mother had no business acumen at all but a wonderful sense of humour. But, as Jonny always loves to tell me, I have inherited from both of them. Unfortunately I have inherited my dad's sense of humour and my mother's business acumen.

In those days we had a lot of reps coming to the farm to sell us various farming necessities. They were always referred to as 'travellers' and my mother could do impressions of all of them to a tee. She gave them all nicknames which, unbeknown to them, is what we referred to them by. There was Horace Park who, whenever he meant to say the word 'easy' pronounced it 'yezzi', so he was always referred to as 'Yezzi'. Another man worked for a firm in Bolton called Hollis and he had a little pointed face like a moggie (a mouse), so he became 'Moggie Hollis'. Then there was a tractor salesman with red hair, so he was always 'Copper Knob'. And so it went on. No one escaped.

In those years about twenty to twenty-five people used to visit the farm for some reason or another. There was Les who worked for us, all my family, part-time workers, travellers, and my cousin Bill – and every one of them smoked. At a very early age I decided that I wouldn't smoke. I don't know why, as smoking was not known to be dangerous at that time, but something made me decide I would never be a smoker.

Most young people have their heroes, maybe a film star or a sportsman or some celebrity. With us though, it was farmers; not just not any farmer, but farmers that we regarded, as we put it, as 'being in a big way'. The bigger their land acreage or the size of their milking herd, the more we were in awe of them and we talked about them constantly.

Two local farmers who fell into this category were Jimmy Ashworth of Anderton Hall Farm, Horwich, and Sam Slinger of Becconsall Hall, Hesketh Bank. A trip to either of these farms was a cause for excitement for us all. Sam Slinger was more of a cattle dealer than a farmer, so trips to Hesketh Bank were a regular occurrence while we were in the process of building up the herd. If ever there was an example of combining business with pleasure, this was it. Days out didn't come better than this.

Evening milking always started at seven o'clock. The reason was that nothing would make my dad miss *The Archers*. While we were still milking in the shippon, before we made the transition to milking parlour and covered yard, every cow was identified by the number of the stall that it stood in.

One cow, Number 10, was in the process of calving. After one day of labour, we decided that no progress was being made so we called the vet. After much discussion with my dad, a decision was made that the cow would need a caesarean. She was anaesthetised and arranged in a good position to enable the vet to carry out the operation. The people in attendance besides the vet were me, Roy, Dad and Donald Holt. Incidentally, although Donald still lived at Nabs Farm at that time, he used to work for us on a casual basis. It is also worth mentioning that this was the first caesarean operation that our vet had ever carried out.

It wasn't long after the vet started to cut through the cow's stomach that Dad decided it was not something he could watch as he felt himself going faint, so he beat a hasty retreat. The operation was a success insomuch as the calf was removed. However, the calf was born dead and, although the cow recovered, it didn't thrive and was never a good milk producer. The enormous cost of the vet's bill rendered the operation a bad move and we sold the cow the following year. It transpired that only one other caesarean operation had been

31

carried out on a cow in the North West and that turned out to be for my future father-in-law.

Until about 1957, farmers that sold their milk retail used to transport the milk by horse and float with the milk in ten-gallon churns. The customer would leave a jug on the doorstep, usually with a saucer over it to protect the milk, and the farmer would ladle the milk out of the churn and pour it into the jug then move onto the next customer. If the horse was familiar with the milk round, it would move on by itself while the farmer went up the various house paths and then the horse would stop and wait at the appropriate place – something that years later a van couldn't do. However, the government brought in a law that all milk had to be delivered in bottles as the jug and saucer method was deemed to be unhygienic. This law worked in our favour, as my dad was eager to start selling our milk retail because of the big price differential. Also, most of the farmers delivering by horse were old men who were ready for retirement and they didn't want the hassle of buying bottles and bottle-washing and bottle-filling machines. This meant they put their milk rounds up for sale. The value of the milk round was determined by two things: the obvious one was how much milk you sold each day and, secondly, how compact was the milk round – in other words, how many miles did you have to travel to sell your milk? Terraced houses were popular with milkmen, as you could drop the milk door to door with no long garden paths or drives to walk up.

There were two farmers in our district selling their milk rounds: one was Nathan Smith, and the other was Trevor Edwards. Both had small milk rounds but they were in the same district so, if you combined the two in the same area, it became quite a compact round. At that time, which was over sixty years ago, milk rounds were selling at about £8 to £10 per gallon, so if your milk round sold, say, ten gallons per day you could expect to sell it for around £80 to £100.

Peanuts, I know, for the price of a business but as I said, it was more than sixty years ago. The purchase of Nathan Smith's business went through with no problem although I can't remember what we paid him. However the purchase of Trevor Edwards's milk round was not as straightforward for the most hilarious of reasons…

Trevor walked up to our farm (he never drove) to do the deal. After a bit of a chat, he and my dad got down to how much we were going to pay him for the round. He asked my dad to make him an offer so, as you do when making an offer, he started off at the lowest price.

My dad said, 'I was thinking of £8' meaning £8 per gallon. Trevor was not impressed and said it was worth more – he wanted £10.

Close to where they were standing was a hen cabin in which we kept some point-of-lay pullets. Trevor asked if we would be prepared to sell him some pullets in exchange for the milk round. Dad agreed.

'How much each do you want for them?' asked Trevor.

'Ten shillings,' my dad replied.

'OK, I'll take twenty pullets,' said Trevor.

My dad couldn't work this out and suddenly realised that Trevor had done the deal without having a clue what to ask for; he thought that my dad was offering him £8 for the whole business and Trevor was trying to get him up to £10.

When Dad realised what he was asking for, he couldn't take advantage of him and said, 'Well, go on, I'll give you forty pullets.'

Now it was Trevor's turn to be puzzled and he said, 'A few minutes ago you were trying to knock me down, now you're offering me double what I asked.'

This required some quick thinking and my dad said, 'Well, I always like to barter a bit.'

The Sixties

1960 WAS A very memorable year for me. To start with, January 1st was my seventeenth birthday so out came the L-plates to put on our Bedford milk van. The old Ford V8 car had long gone and by this time we had had the milk round for about three years. Although my dad was happy with the returns he was getting from it, he was desperate for me to pass my driving test and take over from him because it took him away from his farm work for half a day every day (including Sunday) and this was not good. I suppose there was an argument to say that our Roy could have taken over deliveries as he had passed his test two years earlier, but remember what I said about horses for courses? There are some jobs that some people are just not cut out for, so we'll leave it at that.

To speed things up and get me through my test, Dad booked me some driving lessons with the Chorley and Leyland School of Motoring. It was a very expensive and an unusual thing to do in those days. I think the lessons were about £1/10s per hour, which is £1.50 in today's money. My driving instructor was a fellow named Barnes, who was a massive chap and an ex-police officer. He was very smart, with suit and tie, and always wore a big duffle coat with log buttons. He also smoked continually.

My test was booked for the last week in February in the afternoon, so my dad and I delivered the milk earlier that day to give me time to have a last lesson before the test. On the test I don't remember putting a foot wrong but at the end the examiner said, 'I'm very sorry, Mr Smith, but you are not quite up to the standard required.' I was devastated and also I knew what my dad's reaction would be when I got back to the farm. I guessed right! He was not happy, especially as our Roy passed first time with less practice than me. All my dad could say was, 'That's another three months I'll have to go on that flaming milk round!' ('Flaming' was the nearest that he ever got to swearing.)

Anyway, he didn't have to wait for three months as there was a test cancellation for 10th March. I got the place and I passed. To be told that you've passed your driving test is a wonderful feeling. Shortly after that, I had reason to go to Chorley (I can't remember why). On the way back, as I came up Chorley Road, I decided to get an ice cream from Frederick's Ice Cream Shop. Today, Frederick's is quite a spacious shop but in those days, when old Mr and Mrs Frederick ran it, it was much smaller.

As I approached the shop door, I noticed something stuck in the window. When I got up to it, I could see it was a piece of cardboard like the top off a cardboard box and written on it in Biro were the words: 'Push hard, door sticks.' I pushed hard but the door didn't move, so I pushed harder. Still it didn't move, so I gave it the shoulder and it opened. As it did, I heard the latch fall onto the floor.

At that moment, Mr Frederick appeared. 'What's going on?' he demanded, so I pointed to the sign 'Push hard, door sticks'. 'The door's locked' he said. 'We're shut!' I didn't get the ice cream.

'You should have taken the sign down,' I mumbled as I walked away empty handed.

It was expected that I would take over the milk round and Dad would spend all of his time on the farm. It was something I had mixed feelings about. On the one hand it meant that we would get the best price for the milk, or at least some of it, because we were producing more than we sold retail so some was still being sold to the Milk Marketing Board at the wholesale price. But being a milkman and a dairy worker was not what I wanted to do for the rest of my life. However, doing what was best for the family business was the most important thing so I was a milkman for the next few years.

One thing that hurt me over that time was the fact that all my time was taken up by washing bottles, filling bottles then delivering bottles, and I was getting further and further removed from actual farming. At meal times and in the evenings, I was never part of the conversation between Dad, Roy and Barry. They used to discuss at length the plans for the land, the plans for the herd and the plans for the poultry side of the farm – and none of these things involved me. When I was not out delivering, I was confined to one room, the dairy. Still, it was essential to the financial welfare of the family business, so I put my head down and kept going.

Although delivering milk was not the most exciting job in the world, it did have its humorous and unexpected moments. I was delivering a pint to an old couple near the bottom of Babylon Lane. Just as I put the pint of green top on the doorstep the customer, Mrs German, appeared at the door and said, 'I wonder if you could just come in and help me for a minute?'

Without giving it a second thought, I went into the house to help with whatever it was she needed. As we got into the living room she casually said, 'My husband has died during the night, so I wonder if you would help me to bring him downstairs before the undertakers get here.'

WHAT?!! Of all the things I thought she might need, that was not one of them. Anyhow, you didn't argue with customers so up the narrow stairs of this terraced house we went and, sure enough, lying on the floor was Mr German. Dead. I was about seventeen at the time and carrying dead bodies (still warm) was not something I relished. All I could think was, 'Please let me carry the feet end,' but it was not to be.

'You're stronger than me,' Mrs German said. 'So will you carry the head and shoulder end?'

OMG, as we say these days! But, without any argument, I put my arms under his armpits and lifted and he gave the most horrible gurgle as we carried him to the stairs, Mrs German leading the way.

The stairs in those terraced houses are narrow and steep and I think that I was carrying most of the weight – in fact, almost all of it. As we descended the stairs, his head bumped on every step from top to bottom but nothing was going to make me lift him higher because my head was already leaning forward and no way was I getting any closer! All the way downstairs he was bumping and gurgling.

Eventually we got him to the bottom and she said, 'I think we'll put him in the front room.' We carried him into the front room, or parlour as they used to call it in those days. 'Right, he'll do here,' she said, in a very matter-of-fact way, and we laid him down.

Mrs German then sat down on an armchair, put her head in her hands and stared at the floor. Up to this point she hadn't shown any emotion at all. I was in a difficult situation. Did I leave, my job done, or did I stay to help her through her ordeal? As it turned out, I had read the situation totally wrongly. She took her head out of her hands, looked up and said, 'I'd better have an extra pint, there'll be people coming.' At that point I thought it was safe to leave as my work was done.

Although Adlington was only a small village it had several milkmen, one being a lad from White Coppice called John Garlick. He was a very keen Preston North End supporter, and we used to stop and have a chat together most mornings. That was until one morning he told me he had sold his milk round and bought a franchise.

'Oh, yes, and what kind of business will you be doing from now on?' I asked.

His reply surprised me. 'Embalming,' he said.

'Embalming?' I echoed in disbelief.

'Yes,' he said. 'They've given me the Horwich area.' Then, continuing again in a very matter-of- fact way, he said, 'I will need twelve bodies per week to make the same money as I do on the milk round. Any more than twelve and I'm quids in.'

'Oh, well, good luck with that,' I said, still trying to take in what he had just said.

He got into his van and, as he was driving away, he shouted back, 'I wouldn't like you to die, Fred, but if it's inevitable, try and die in Horwich.'

'I will, John.'

Where is Mrs German when you need her?

Strangely enough, only a few hundred yards away from Mrs German was another customer who was not in the best of health and not very mobile. Every morning I used to have to take the milk into the kitchen, put it in the fridge then get down on my knees and help her put on her shoes. A customer is a customer.

One day I was delivering milk on Mount Pleasant. As with every other day, I saw people heading off in various directions, going about their daily routines. One guy was driving out of Mount Pleasant towards Chorley. He gave me a pleasant wave as he did every morning but on this day I had to flag him down as his flask and sandwiches were on the car roof.

In the same vicinity we had another customer who I will call 'Mrs Hall'. It is not her real name but close to it. She was not a good payer and was always behind with her weekly payments. To some extent I could live with that from a customer if they made an effort to keep up, but one thing I did not like was that she would leave the empties out dirty, without even rinsing them. What did that say about the state of her house? But there's one thing I'll always remember about 'Mrs Hall'. I was standing behind her in the butcher's and, as it came to her turn to be served, she asked for something very cheap, I can't remember what, and then she said, 'And can I have some scraps for the dog?' It was quite common that if a butcher had some scraps of fat or whatever, he would give them to customers for their dog. But at that moment her little girl looked at her and asked, 'Are we getting a dog?'

It cannot be a coincidence that customers who were bad payers (every tradesman had a percentage of these) also had one other thing in common – they all left their empties out dirty. They would also go days without leaving any out at all and then leave twenty or thirty out on one day. What must their houses have been like?

On the day that Jonathan was born I had a milk customer called Cyril Robinson, who was also a good mate of mine, so when I delivered his milk I told him the good news. Now at that time Cyril was big into making home-brewed beer, so he suggested he would help me to deliver the remainder of the milk then we could go back to his house to wet the baby's head. This we did and we got back to his house about midday, at which point I only had a dozen or so customers left to deliver to around the farm in the outlying area. The home brew went down well and the afternoon flew by, with all thoughts of the remaining customers only a dim and distant memory. Eventually, by late afternoon, I decided that I must leave and finish what I had to do.

Now this particular day coincided with The Yew Tree Inn reopening, as it had been closed for several months to convert it from a pub to a pub restaurant. The new manager, Stan Pollowski, went to a cottage across the road to ask the owner, Mrs Corless, if there were any milkmen that delivered in the area.

She replied, 'There is only one and that's Fred Smith.'

'How early does he deliver?' asked Mr Pollowski.

'Well he's here now,' said Mrs Corless, as I staggered up to the door, drunk, with a pint of milk in my hand. It was five o'clock. I somehow managed to get his custom and served The Yew Tree for several years.

One of my customers was Mrs Graham at 208 Babylon Lane, who was pregnant and had two pints of green top. One day I delivered the milk on the doorstep, got in the van and was setting off to the next customer when she opened the front door and called me back.

I assumed that she wanted an extra pint or maybe a dozen eggs, so I reversed to her door.

I was not prepared for what she wanted. 'I've started in labour. Could you take me to Chorley Hospital?' she asked.

What could I say? I couldn't refuse her, so I went and got her case and helped her into the van. To make matters worse, we had removed the passenger seat from the front of the van to make way for a wooden egg box, so that was her seat all the way to Chorley.

Chorley Hospital has never seemed so far away but we made it, thank God. That was one delivery I didn't want to make.

An embarrassing moment I had with a pregnant milk customer, of the better-fed fraternity, was when I asked her how long before the baby was due. She replied, 'I had the baby two weeks ago.'

Normally I am pretty quick at getting out of tricky situations but I just looked at her and said, 'Oh.' That didn't really get me out of trouble but it was all I could think of.

I went from carrying a dead man downstairs to bringing a new baby into the world, so I like to think I've done my bit at both ends!!

Talking of pregnancy, if an unmarried girl got pregnant in the 1950s and sixties it was a big disgrace and the families kept it to themselves for as long as possible, but strangely enough the milkman was always one of the first to know. The reason for this was because of something called milk tokens, enabling mothers-to-be to get free milk. It used to put people in a difficult situation; mothers didn't want anyone to know that their teenage daughter was pregnant but at the same time they needed the free milk, so they would come to the door on pay day looking very embarrassed and thrust the token book into the milkman's hand. The milkman would accept the book and neither of them would mention anything, except perhaps the weather. The mother was probably thinking, 'I hope he doesn't tell anybody!' Whereas I would be thinking, 'So your Jenny's got caught has she?

She has done well to get away with it this long. Wait till I tell the lads!'

I have vivid memories of delivering milk to two of my ex-school teachers, the Misses Maher, Margaret and Mary, who were very devout and lived in a lovely house up Shawes Drive with large gardens. They were both retired by then but to me they were still my teachers and had to be treated with respect. I still referred to them as Miss as I always did at school. Mary, the older one, looked after the house and also did a lot of baking while Margaret looked after the large gardens.

One day, Margaret saw me coming with the milk and told me that Mary had taken ill and that she had had to call the doctor. After that I didn't see her for a few more days and then, three or four days later as I was walking down the garden path after leaving the milk, I heard Margaret shout 'Fred, Fred!'

I turned round to see her following me down the path. When she caught up, she said, 'My sister Mary died at three o'clock this morning.'

I started to express my sympathies but she stopped me in my tracks. 'Oh no,' she said. 'It's not sad. It's marvellous. She is now in heaven. She is where we all want to be. She will be looking down on us right now. Isn't it wonderful?'

'Oh yes,' I said. 'Wonderful news.' Whilst trying to switch my expression from sympathy to delight. At least she didn't ask me to carry her sister downstairs!

In the years before I passed my driving test, and when I was still helping my dad on the milk round, we delivered to most of the houses in Rivington and also to Rivington Barn, a dancing and catering establishment that is still thriving today. We also delivered to a little cottage at the side of the barn where two old sisters lived. They were the Miss Wards, and I believe (like the Miss Mahers) they had also been schoolteachers. The year was around 1956, the time of the little black-and-white televisions with the twelve-inch screens. One Christmas

Day we stopped outside the cottage and my dad took the milk to the Barn and I took two pints to Miss Wards. As I was walking back to the van one of the sisters came to the door. 'Mr Smith,' she said. 'Come quickly!'

I hurried back and followed her into the house where she and her sister were sitting in front of a big coal fire with the television switched on. I did not have a clue as to why she had shouted me back but then she said, 'Her Majesty is about to deliver the Queen's Speech.' She had shouted me back because the Queen's Speech had never been televised before and she thought that it would be a great thrill to watch it.

I was fourteen years old and couldn't have been less interested but I wouldn't have dared to show it as that would be bad mannered, so I had to pretend to be very grateful. But I also had another problem: my dad had finished his delivery to the Barn and was back in the van and didn't know where I was. From where I was standing in the house, I could see him and, knowing him as I did, I could tell that he was getting irate. But still the two sisters sat glued to the television, in their minds witnessing history.

I couldn't take my eyes off my dad, now on his second cigarette and constantly looking round to see where I was. I was praying for the speech to end and not actually listening to a word of it but Her Majesty still went on and on, oblivious to my predicament. Eventually, offending the sisters or not, I just had to go.

When I got back to the van my dad exploded. 'Where the heck have you been till now?' he shouted. I tried to explain but it made matters worse. 'You've been what? Watching television? By the heck!' – which was always the expression he used when he was angry.

In later years, one of the houses that we delivered milk to was the Rivington Vicarage and at that time the vicar was Vicar Peet, who had a tasty daughter, Angela. But, moving on... His wife was a lovely lady who came to the vicarage door every Saturday morning with a bowl in one hand and a £1 note in the other to pay for the milk. The bowl was for a dozen eggs. This was an ongoing thing every Saturday morning but one midweek morning the vicar came to the door to tell me that his wife had died suddenly. She had been a very recognizable person, being very overweight with a head of thick silver hair, and she always dressed colourfully. Let's just say you couldn't miss her.

On Saturday morning, I went as usual with the two pints and a dozen eggs. I put the milk down on the step and, as I looked up, there was Mrs Peet with the bowl in one hand and a £1 note in the other! I knew that she had definitely died because all the villagers had told me, so I hadn't got it wrong. She was even dressed the same. 'Don't be alarmed,' she said smiling. 'I am Mrs Peet's identical twin sister. We've come up for the funeral.'

The aforementioned Rivington Barn was run by the Salmon family in the 1950s and, to the best of my knowledge, it still is. The father at that time was Billy Salmon, one of life's gentlemen. Billy was generous to a fault and a very genuine person. He was well liked in the area – although maybe he was not always as efficient as he should have been.

I remember one occasion when he had taken a booking for 150 for lunch on a certain day at a certain time. The staff had turned up, the meal was ready and they awaited the arrival of the party but no party arrived at the allotted time. One hour later, there was still no party. Billy rang the contact number that they had given him, only to be reminded that they had cancelled weeks earlier. Billy had completely forgotten. I never did find out what he did with those 150 three-course meals but, knowing Billy, I'm sure he wouldn't have lost any sleep over them!

Without doubt, the most complaining sector of the milk customers were the old-age pensioners. The young mothers with two or three children never gave the milk deliveries a second thought but the old people required their milk to be delivered on the dot, at the same time every day. One woman, Mrs Marsh, always got two pints per day. It was never a problem but then she started to complain that I didn't deliver early enough and asked if I could come earlier. She continued to complain and it got to the point where, as I was getting nearer, I could see her standing on the doorstep with a stern, black look on her face. She wanted her milk even earlier; one day I asked why, after all these years, she suddenly kept running out of milk. It turned out that her daughter and son-in-law had sold their house and couldn't yet move into their new one so had temporarily moved back in with her. I had to bite my tongue.

Another old lady, Mrs Leeming, lived on her own and every week I gave her some cracked eggs which I didn't charge for. Cracked eggs are just as good as uncracked except that you can't boil them, so I was giving her six perfectly good eggs every week, free of charge. One day I was a few minutes late and she had run out of milk so couldn't have a cup of tea, and she really let me know about it. So, no more free eggs. After a couple of weeks she asked me why there were no cracked eggs any more. I told her we had trained the hens to lay their eggs sitting down! 'Oh,' she replied.

In those days you could only buy cream from your milkman. Supermarkets were few and far between and small corner shops didn't stock it. One Christmas Day, a customer called Mrs Johnstone from Lees Road ordered four pints of milk and half a pint of cream as she had relatives coming from Scotland and wanted to make a trifle. But with it being Christmas Day I had an extra half hour in bed, thinking that no one was going to complain. I hadn't reckoned on Mrs Johnstone though; as I drew up in the van in front of her lounge window, I could see all her Scottish relatives looking out and, as I put the milk and cream down on the doorstep, Mrs Johnstone appeared in the doorway. She had some money in her hand.

'Oh good,' I thought. 'A Christmas tip.' I couldn't have been more wrong!

'I have been waiting all morning for this cream,' she said. 'I need to be making the trifle. Here's the money to pay for it and I'm not having any more milk from you after today!'

I thrust the money back into her hand. 'You're not having any more milk after yesterday!' I said, picked up the milk and cream and walked away.

'But what about my trifle?' she shouted.

'Sorry, not my problem,' I replied. I mean, I was thirty minutes late on Christmas Day and she sacked me – but at least I got a bit of pleasure from it.

One other incident that sticks out in my memory was when I was delivering milk in Rivington. I always left Rivington until the end, as the houses were scattered all over and deliveries were slow. As I was driving along one of the quiet country lanes, I saw a lady standing outside her car. As I got close to it, I recognised her as Mrs Davis, a customer, so I stopped to see if I could help. It turned out she had a puncture. Obviously there were no such things as mobile phones then so she couldn't ring anyone.

'Don't worry,' I said, 'I'll sort it out.' So I got the spare tyre out and jacked the car up but some of the bolts hadn't been undone in years, if ever, so it took some doing and it took a bit of time. Anyway, eventually I got it changed and she was very grateful and off she went and I continued with my deliveries.

About an hour later I arrived at her door to find her standing on the doorstep and she started complaining about me being late. She had wanted to make her husband a rice pudding for lunch and now she couldn't. I couldn't believe what I was hearing – the reason I was late was because I had stopped to change her tyre! Old folk – not good.

In those days on Sunday mornings, another milkman called Alan Bond and I had just about the only vehicles on the road in Rivington.

You would hardly see another. Today, on a sunny day you almost need traffic control as traffic through this once-sleepy village is now constant. I sometimes drive through Rivington and think, 'What have you done to my village?'

I think the year was 1971 when Britain converted from pounds, shillings and pence to decimalised currency and the price of everything had to be converted. Now some commodities made a direct switch from one to the other while others didn't, which meant that a decision had to be made. Did the supplier round the prices up, which would mean the supplier would win and the customer would lose, or did he round them down so the customer would win and the supplier lose? Milk was one of the commodities that needed rounding either up or down, so all the milkmen in Adlington and Horwich arranged to hold a meeting in Rivington Club to thrash things out and agree a strategy. I don't remember the date but I know it was a Thursday evening when we met. There were about thirty of us attending the meeting and everyone arrived between 7 and 7.30pm and stood around drinking. The club steward had opened the bar specially for us.

By 9.30pm no one had mentioned the price of milk then one fellow, I think it was George Ashworth, called order and reminded us all why we were there. He said, 'All those in favour of rounding the price down raise your hand.' Not a single hand went up. 'Right, those in favour of rounding the price up, raise your hand.' Every hand in the room went up. 'Right,' he said. 'Meeting closed. Next round barman!'

In total we were in the club around seven hours and the meeting had lasted about thirty seconds. The following day, the residents of Adlington and Horwich had very late deliveries.

Ali at Madison Square Gardens

In the 1960s and 1970s, I was a fanatical boxing fan. In 1971, after Ali had come back from his three-year exile because of his refusal to fight in the Vietnam War, it was arranged that he would fight Joe Frazier at Madison Square Garden for the vacant heavyweight title.

March's fight was to become the biggest world title fight ever. At that time my brother Roy, family friend John Winstanley and I were members of the British Boxing Supporters Club which chartered a flight to the fight. This flight was put on purely for the fight, and took just ex-boxers and boxing supporters. The cost for the tickets for the flight and seven nights in New York was £140.

In those days flying rules were not as stringent as they are today. In fact, there were no rules whatsoever. All the way to New York the plane was thick with cigarette and cigar smoke and people were walking about, talking to their mates, and drinking whisky straight from the bottle. I have no doubt that some of these people were unsavoury characters from the underworld. It was the kind of flight that I wouldn't like to make today.

On the night, as happens with most boxing matches, the arena didn't start to fill up until the main event was getting close. There was seldom much interest in the undercards, although on this occasion Ali's brother Rachman Ali, formerly Rudolph Valentino Clay (who'd swapped a name like that for Rachman Ali), was fighting the British heavyweight champion, Danny McLinden. That was a fight that I wanted to watch. McLinden won on points, although the fight was not inspiring.

On the way in I bought some programmes, intending to take them home. I think I bought ten for about a dollar each but, as the big fight drew close and the arena started to fill up, I can only assume they ran out. As I was sitting in my seat, with the programmes under my arm, a young popcorn seller came and pointed out a fellow at the front. 'That guy wants to know how many programmes you've got and how much you want for them all?'

I said, 'I've got ten and will sell them for $100.'

The young popcorn seller went back to the guy and I could see them talking. The fellow pulled $100 out of his wallet and the young lad came back, gave me the money and I gave him the programmes. I am convinced had I said $200 or $300 the man would still have bought them.

The Vietnam War was either still going on or only just over, but was still fresh in everyone's mind… As Roy, John and I were in the crowd outside to the venue, there was a devious-looking character going round the crowd who was supposedly collecting money for Vietnam War veterans. It was obvious the guy was a crook and I remember him vividly. He had a few papers in his hand, which he hoped would make him look official, and he had a cigarette in his mouth, which for some reason wasn't lit.

'Help the Vietnam Vets,' he said, as he stared and shook a tin at me.

'No thanks,' I said, trying to avoid his gaze.

Then he turned his attention to Roy and John. 'Help the Vietnam Vets, man.'

To which John, in a moment of false bravery or madness, asked, 'Yes, but who gets the money?'

The guy exploded. 'Who gets the money? The f*****g Vietnam Vets get the f*****g money, that's who.'

Nobody in New York that night got their money out faster than John. A very generous donation was made and off the man went – a job well done.

'Well, I think he made his point there,' said John, nervously forcing a laugh.

As the big fight grew closer the tension mounted and we couldn't take our eyes off the doors because almost everyone that came through was a celebrity. They were all there: Elizabeth Taylor and Richard Burton; Frank Sinatra and Sammy Davis; Robert Mitchum; Burt Lancaster, the lot. Sitting near me was a famous song and dance man of that era called Danny Kaye who for some reason was on crutches – maybe he had fallen during a routine.

And never mind all the showbiz celebs; if you were boxing fans (as we all were) the people there were beyond belief. All our boxing heroes were streaming in, heroes that we never thought we would see.

What made the fight even more intriguing was that both boxers were undefeated. That added greatly to the suspense as that night one of them had to lose their record.

It was said that by the start of the fight there was only one empty seat in Madison Square Garden and that was because the organisers had insisted that one seat remain empty in case the President turned up. That was how big the event was. Although I must admit I have never been able to get my head round that one seat thing; did they think he would turn up on his own? Anyway, who was I to argue?

After the announcements and introductions, the fight got underway. Although today, and in recent years, Ali was a worldwide hero, he wasn't so well liked in those days. His refusal to be drafted and his involvement with some unsavoury people led him to be despised by millions. Although he was still 'our' hero and we were desperate for him to win, the vast majority of the crowd were up for Frazier.

The fight was a classic and went fifteen rounds. They don't do fifteen rounds today, as twelve is the maximum. There was not one second when Frazier was not going forward (there never was in any of Frazier's fights). You could have put him up against a bulldozer and he wouldn't have taken a backward step. His nickname was 'Smokin' Joe', after a massive hurricane that had destroyed everything in its path.

49

At the end of the fifteen rounds, Frazier was declared the winner by a very fair unanimous decision. The next two fights between them were both won by Ali. The whole experience was one I will never forget – and I got it all for £140.

A couple of weeks after I wrote this, Ali died aged 74 on 4th June 2016. He had suffered from Parkinson's Disease for thirty-two years. God bless him, or should that be Allah bless him.

BUDDY BEAR

AS I WROTE earlier, one thing my dad used to do was take us to the pictures. There were five cinemas in Chorley so picking which film to go and see was a very important decision. My dad always loved a cowboy film and one week there were two cowboy films on: *Return of the Bad Men*, starring Randolph Scott at The Odeon, and *The Big Sky* starring Kirk Douglas at The Pavilion, or The Pav as everybody called it. It was decided that we would go to The Pav to see *The Big Sky*. That decision, although I didn't know it at the time, was to have a big influence on the rest of my life.

The film was about a Mississippi riverboat and the dangers that it encountered on its journeys, including bandits, Indians, rapids and mutinies. The boat had a captain and the captain had a bodyguard, a giant of a man played by an ex-heavyweight boxer named Buddy Bear. He was the brother of Max Bear, who had been the heavyweight champion of the world; incidentally, his son, also called Max, played the part of Jethro in the original *Beverley Hillbillies*. When I saw this huge man I was fascinated by him and for the rest of the film he was the only person I watched. By the time I came out of the pictures, I wanted to be like Buddy Bear. For years afterwards I never missed a film that he was in and collected every picture of him from film magazines.

In fact, I was so obsessed with him that my family and friends started to call me Buddy. Even though I was only about ten at the time, I did anything I could that I thought would make me stronger. Someone said that press-ups made you strong so I started doing them. Someone else said that drinking milk made you strong so I drank gallons of it.

At the time, we used to chop the turnips for the cattle and we had an old turnip chopper that you had to turn using both hands. It was a hard, backbreaking job and no one wanted to do it, so my brothers Roy and Barry, and farmworker Les told me that there was nothing better for making you strong, knowing that that it would make me want to do it and they wouldn't have to. What they didn't know was that I had studied the chopper and already decided that it would be a good exercise so I was determined to be the one to do it. When I saw them smiling and nodding to each other, thinking that they had tricked me, I was secretly smiling to myself.

I wrote fan letters several times to Buddy Bear but never received a reply, although I suppose the address I'd written on the envelope (Buddy Bear, America) didn't give the postman a right lot to go on!

I don't know if there is any connection, but Jamie Oliver has christened one of his children Buddy Bear. Surely that must be just a coincidence? I would just love to know.

GETTING INTO LIFTING

As the years went by, my determination to be strong never wavered. While the other lads at school had heroes like Stanley Matthews, Tom Finney and Nat Lofthouse, my heroes were strongmen and I never missed a Buddy Bear film. I remember there used to be a bedtime drink called Milo that my Mother got for us – I think it's still around. Milo was a mythical strongman who, legend has it, picked up a newborn calf, put it on his shoulders and walked around the field with it. The following day he did the same again and then the same again, each day carrying the calf round the field. He did not notice that the calf was getting heavier and heavier; eventually he was carrying a full-grown cow around the field on his shoulders. This appealed to me; I could see the logic in it and living on a farm there was no shortage of calves.

We had one calf, a Friesian about three days old. It was perfect, though what I had not taken into account was that even though Milo's calf was new born, Milo was already a grown man, not a twelve year old. Although I managed to get the calf on my shoulders and walk around the yard with it, after about the third day I decided there must be more conventional ways of getting strong. It didn't help that the calf was probably heavier than I was.

At the time I was at school, Adlington was definitely a village of two halves – the top road and the bottom road (or top end and bottom end) and they were two separate communities. Today the land between has been developed into one large community but back in those days most people didn't drive, so some people from either end never went to the other end. The top road was always seen as the posh end because most of the houses were semi-detached, whereas at the bottom end they were terraced. It was always assumed that the lads from the bottom end were tough nuts and the ones from the top end were big girls' blouses.

Because St Joseph's was the only Catholic school in the village, it drew in pupils from both ends. It became common knowledge that I was stronger than most of my mates and I started to get a reputation. One day there was a group of us in the playground discussing who could do what (as school lads do), when one of the lads, John Porter, said, 'There's a strongman lives on Park Road,' which was at the bottom end.

My ears pricked up. 'Who's that?' I asked.

'His name's Gerry Fairclough and he's a weightlifter.'

I hadn't realised – and didn't realise until years later – that if you wanted to be strong or be a good weightlifter there wasn't a better village in the country to live in than Adlington. This was down to Gerry Fairclough and his two brothers, Alan and Frank. In the early years Gerry was the most talked about because Alan and Frank both went away on National Service and, until they finished their two years, they spent little time at home. My passion had been roused and I loved to hear the stories about Gerry Fairclough from the lads from the bottom end of Adlington. It's possible that some of their tales may have been exaggerated as stories often are but no matter – I wanted to hear everything.

Then one Monday morning, Alan Fishwick, a mate of mine, came to school and said Gerry Fairclough was on the television that Saturday. I couldn't believe it – a lad from Adlington was on telly! You must remember that in those days television consisted of one channel so to get on TV you had to be good. In fact you had to be very good.

It was about this time that Gerry's brothers, Alan and Frank, came home from doing their National Service so now I heard stories about all three brothers. I was fascinated and could listen all day. By now I was almost fourteen years old and beginning to develop physically; my work on the farm, humping around hundredweight sacks, definitely made me stronger than most fourteen year olds.

CHALLENGING MY TEACHER TO AN ARM WRESTLE

ABOUT THIS TIME, St Joseph's School took on a male teacher whose name was Mr Wilson (up until then we had only had female teachers). He was an excellent teacher with a good sense of humour. He did a good job. Then, about a year later, another teacher retired and the school took on another male teacher, Mr Danson. He couldn't have been more different to Mr Wilson. I'm not criticising his ability as a teacher but, to put it bluntly, he was cruel.

Corporal punishment was accepted in those days, so to be slapped across the face or hit relentlessly on the hand with the flat of a ruler or a strap was not uncommon. Even being dragged out of your desk by the hair was a common occurrence if you pushed the teacher that bit too far, but Danson was in a league of his own. It was as though he enjoyed making you suffer. To give you an example, when any of the other teachers hit you with the ruler it was with the flat side but Danson hit you with the sharp edge so that it cut into you more.

Another of his party tricks was to get the blackboard duster and turn it upside down, make you hold your hand facing the floor then hit your knuckles with the wooden side. He would repeat this about ten times until your knuckles started to swell up. Usually by this point, the kid would be crying. Not surprisingly, lots of the kids lived in fear of him. Fear is not conducive to getting the best out of the pupils – not when they spend the entire day petrified of the teacher.

Anyway, I decided that he was not going to intimidate me. One day, when he was having a rare light-hearted go at me in front of the rest of the class about how strong I thought I was, I plucked up courage and also in a 'light-hearted' manner I challenged him to an arm wrestle. His face dropped, while all the other kids shouted, 'Go on, sir, arm wrestle Fred.'

'Get on with your work!' he snapped, with all the light-heartedness gone. Then he said 'Come and see me at playtime, Smith.' I assumed he meant for an arm wrestle.

Playtime came and, as all the kids went outside, I sat at my desk until the classroom was empty. I went up to see him, psyching myself up for an arm wrestle. Wrong! 'Look Fred,' he said. 'Arm wrestling proves nothing because the person with the shortest arm always wins.'

I was smaller so obviously I had the shortest arms, meaning that if I did beat him it didn't mean I was stronger than him – and that was a load of rubbish. He also said, 'It's just like saying, "Who's got the longest fingernails?"' That was another load of rubbish. I could sense the fear in his voice. What if I beat him? Would the class not be scared of him anymore? This was his fear so, after giving me several more reasons why it would prove nothing, he sent me out to the playground with no arm wrestle.

But I felt a moral victory had been won and the other kids agreed. Danson was scared. There is an old expression that one excuse is always more convincing than several, an expression that Danson had obviously never heard as excuses were rolling from his tongue like a conveyor belt.

SOUL SEARCHING AND CONFESSION

Both my parents were from Catholic families; Mum's family were devout Catholics and would never miss mass on a Sunday. That would be considered a mortal sin, and if you died with a mortal sin on your soul that meant eternal damnation.

I remember when I was about twelve years old and started to doubt what I was being taught in class. It was too fairy-tale like for me to believe but, because of what I had been taught by my family and the teachers, I felt very guilty and thought that I must be a bad person. How could I insult God like this?

So, after much soul searching (no pun intended) and much agonising, I decided that I must go and see the priest as he would help me. That was a very big thing for me to do at age twelve and I was scared, but felt that it was something I must do so I could become a good person again. The school and the church were side by side so at playtimes I kept a lookout for the priest as his house was only a short distance from the church and he made regular visits to and fro.

One playtime the opportunity arose and I saw the priest leaving the church. Our regular priest, Father Roskell, was away and this was a locum priest who I didn't know. That didn't matter and I left the school playground and met him outside the church. I was scared and nervous but I was also confident that he would help me and I wouldn't be a bad person anymore.

At twelve years old it was a brave thing to do. I told him my problem – that I was having doubts about the existence of God – and how guilty I felt about having these doubts, confident that he would take me under his wing and dispel my doubts. I couldn't have been more wrong. To be fair, he listened to what I had to say and offered some explanation of sorts but he didn't seem all that interested and, after a few minutes when he felt he had done his job, off he went. As I watched him walk away, I knew he wouldn't give it another thought and, as far as I know, he didn't. I was so disappointed.

Anyway, time went on and I convinced myself that my mother and my teachers couldn't be wrong so I settled down and tried to be a good Catholic. At this point I must say that when we were growing up, my younger brother Barry and I were very similar in looks and people quite often mistook us for each other. One Saturday night, when I was about fifteen or sixteen, I went to confession as I wished to go to communion the following day.

At St Joseph's the procedure for going to confession was that everyone knelt in the benches on the right of the church and would gradually move forward to the front as people went in and out of the confessional. Then they would kneel in the centre of the church to say their penance. Above the confessional there was a light; as long as that light was on, Father Roskell was still hearing confessions. He turned the light out on leaving. I eventually made my way to the front bench but, as I was just about to go in, the light went out so that was it: no confession.

I was about to get up and leave when I felt a tap on my shoulder. It was Miss Maher, my former headmistress. In her very commanding way she said, 'Now look, Fred, you must knock on the vestry door and tell Father Roskell that you are the only person left in the church and I'm sure that he will hear your confession.'

Even though by this time I had left school and started work, I would never have dreamt of not doing what Miss Maher told me. Nervously, and with my heart thumping, I went and knocked on the door. It was so embarrassing, as a confession is supposed to be a very private thing with the priest not knowing who he is listening to. To make things worse, I had also been seeing a lovely girl from Horwich named Olive and that made it even more embarrassing, as now the priest knew who I was. Also, we were always told at school that you could not miss anything out otherwise it would not be a proper confession.

Anyway, I managed to mumble my way through my confession and he gave me my penance of three Our Fathers and three Hail Marys and back I went into church to finalise the event. By now everyone had gone and I was the only one left in church. As I stood up to leave, Father Roskell came out of the vestry to lock up. As I passed him I said, 'Goodnight, Father,' to which he replied, 'Goodnight, Barry.' Yes! He had mistaken me for my brother. Result! I warned Barry that if I were him, I'd keep away from Father Roskell for a week or two.

GIRLS! GIRLS! GIRLS!

The topic of girlfriends was one you would never discuss with my dad. He was narrow-minded in that respect and very disapproving. I remember one year when I was fourteen and I received a Valentine's card from a girl from Lower Adlington called Alma. By the time the postman arrived at the farm, I had gone to school and my dad received the mail. As it was Valentine's Day and there was a letter for me, he had a good idea what it would be so he opened it, read it and immediately ripped it up and threw it on the fire. I never saw it and only found out about it when Alma's friend asked me if I liked it and told me the verse she had written, which went like this:

> 'I love you dearly, I love you almighty
> I wish your pyjamas were next to my nightie
> But don't be mistaken and don't be misled
> I mean on the clothes line, not on the bed.'

Was that so bad?

LIFTING AND BODY BUILDING

As I wrote earlier, at age seventeen I passed my driving test and this opened up a whole new world for me. Living in the country and having to walk everywhere severely restricts you, but once you can drive everywhere is within your reach. Dancing at Rivington Barn was a must for me on Saturday nights. One old school friend I used to see there was Anthony Higginson, who lived on the bottom road in Adlington. He knew the Fairclough brothers so, as you can imagine, I was always fishing for stories.

One Saturday night he said, 'Why don't you come down and I'll take you to the weightlifting club where they train?'

I was delighted; at only seventeen I was a bit shy of going myself, but now I had someone to go with. 'Do you know the bottom road?' he asked.

'Yes,' I replied.

'Well, I'll meet you at the bridge at eight o'clock on Monday night.'

Monday night came and I got to the bridge at about ten to eight, nice and early. Eight o'clock came, but there was no Anthony; 8.15, still no Anthony; 8.30, no Anthony. I was so disappointed but came up with possible reasons. Then at 8.30 another school friend, Peter Proctor, came past and stopped for a chat. I told him why I was there and after about five minutes he went. At nine o'clock there was still no Anthony.

By 9.30pm I reluctantly decided I must go home, as he wouldn't be coming. Just then, Peter Proctor reappeared on his way back from wherever he had been and couldn't believe I was still there. 'Are you sure you're waiting at the right place?' he asked.

'Yes,' I said. 'He told me to wait at the bridge.'

And then it dawned on him. 'It won't be this bridge – it will be the Bridge Inn on Park Road.'

Peter got in the van, saying, 'I'll show you.' And he was right. When we got there Anthony was waiting and thought I was the one who hadn't turned up!

None of the Fairclough brothers were there that night but it didn't matter. It was just the beginning; there would be many more nights over the coming years. And so there were, even to this day fifty-six years later.

Yes, that Monday night was the start of a very big part of my life. The five years from age seventeen to twenty-two, when I got married, I lived for weightlifting and bodybuilding. I wasn't the best in the world at either sport but very few people have had more pleasure from their sport than I did. Obviously after I got married, started my own business and had a family, it had to take second place but through all the years I still managed to train. I've even gone to the gym at eleven o'clock at night and three o'clock in the morning when work demanded it.

On the first night at Adlington Barbell Club there were three brothers from Chorley training there – Harry, Paul and David Ratcliffe. For two or three years I trained with them and we became good friends. Also they lived on't lane and went to Sacred Heart Church, so they were almost family. Mondays, Wednesdays and Fridays were training nights. One thing that I remember on training nights was coming in from milking, having a quick wash and change then, almost without exception, as I was going out of the door to go to the gym at eight o'clock, I would hear the *Coronation Street* music playing at the end of the programme. Even today, although I never watch the programme, when I hear that music it brings all the memories flooding back. That music is synonymous with me rushing off to the gym.

It was about 1962 and I was training with the Ratcliffes when Alan Fairclough came in. Alan didn't train the same nights as us but he used to call in on his way out for a pint. He told us that he'd entered us for a competition in Crosby, Liverpool. It was an Olympic competition, meaning a three-lift competition consisting of Press, Snatch and Clean and Jerk.

Until then we had never entered a competition and so the day came and we all met at the club on Park Road. Alan came with us; we were all excited and a bit nervous as this was a first for all of us. Everyone piled into the milk van which, incidentally, had no seats, so I had shoved in a few wooden egg boxes to sit on and then off to Crosby we went. None of us had been there before, but it wasn't difficult to find and we arrived just in time for the weigh-in. It's strange but when they called my name to be weighed in, it gave me a real thrill. I'd seen people on television being weighed in for various sports competitions and, all of a sudden, I was one of them. In my own mind, I had arrived!

I lifted reasonably well, doing 145 Press, 145 Snatch and 180 Clean and Jerk. I didn't win (not by a long way) but in my own mind I had made the transition from being just a lad who went to a weightlifting club (which loads did) to being a competitive weightlifter, which is what I had always wanted to be. Incidentally, at the weigh-in I weighed 11 stone 6lb, the lightest I have ever weighed in at.

As I was writing about *Coronation Street*, sitting in my caravan in the Lakes, the theme music came on the television in the middle of the morning. How strange. Then someone announced the death of Tony Warren, the creator. Spooky.

After that first competition I started to enter quite regularly, not so much on the Olympics but more on the power lifting and bodybuilding side as I found they suited my abilities better. I will never forget my first bodybuilding contest; it was for the Novice Mr North West Britain, held at The Houldsworth Hall on Deansgate, Manchester. It was a big competition, especially for my first one, and the show organiser, an ex-Mr Britain called Bert Loveday, told me there were more than forty entrants including some big names. That didn't worry me as I knew I wasn't going to win but I set my sights on being in the top twenty – that would suffice, I kept telling myself. When we were in the warming-up room I was silently weighing up the opposition (which everyone secretly did) and I saw no reason to change my mind.

It was a Saturday and the judging took place in the afternoon with the show at night, by which time the eight judges had made all the decisions. Evening came and, after one or two supporting items, it was time for the Novice contest.

The hall was packed with 700–800 spectators, almost all of them bodybuilders and weightlifters. A few of the Adlington lads had come to watch me, including Alan who always loved to see his gym members compete. I stood in the line-up, trying to make myself look as big as I could, completely forgetting that the decision had already been made in the afternoon. After everyone had stood on the podium and flexed their muscles, it was time for the placings to be announced. I desperately wanted to be in the first twenty, possibly even the first fifteen.

The announcer was a fellow called Oscar Hiedenstam, probably the most well-known name in British bodybuilding. He was also the editor of a magazine called *Health & Strength* and the organiser of the Mr Universe contest. He announced the winner, Tony Haines, and then the runner-up, I forget his name, and in third place FRED SMITH. I couldn't believe it! And as I walked over to take my place on the podium, the crowd gave a massive cheer.

This was all too much! I didn't realise I was so popular! I wasn't. Coming towards me, and also heading for the podium, was this huge guy. Would you believe he was also called Fred Smith? One look at him told me that I certainly hadn't beaten *him*! As he leapt on the podium and acknowledged his cheering fans, I made the very long walk back to the line up to take my place alongside the other losers, watched by almost 800 people. It's true to say that of all the things I'd imagined could possibly go wrong on the day, that wasn't one of them! To make matters worse, I didn't even make the top twenty.

In the coming years I got to know Bert Loveday quite well and entered most of the many contests that he organised. I remember one day receiving a letter from him (not everyone had a phone then) telling me that he was running another show at the Houldsworth Hall. He asked if I would be interested in competing then added that he was bringing a young bodybuilder from overseas to appear as a guest. 'You must come and see him,' he told me. 'He's only nineteen but quite sensational. When you see him, it will either make you train harder than ever or pack in altogether.' His name? Arnold Schwarzenegger.

Adlington Barbell Club, although only a backstreet club located in a small village, had a big reputation mainly because of the Fairclough brothers. But also others in the club, myself included, were beginning to make a name for ourselves and we were once asked to put on a show of weightlifting and bodybuilding for the Haslingden branch of the Blackburn Rovers Supporters Club, to be held at Haslingden Town Hall.

Once again we loaded everything into the back of the milk van and set off to Haslingden. Again the hall was packed with about 800 people and we gave various demonstrations of strength and power that seemed to go down very well.

To prepare to go on stage, we were given a room to warm up in. After the show, a group of autograph-hunting kids stood outside the door, as there were a few Rovers players there. At that time there was a Rovers player called Fred Pickering; some of the youngsters heard someone call me 'Fred' and assumed I was Fred Pickering. They all clamoured for my autograph. I duly obliged and enjoyed a few minutes of fame, false though it was.

About ten minutes after the autograph hunters had left, a lone youngster came up to me and asked for my autograph. I duly obliged but then forgot the surname. 'What did you say my second name is?' I asked.

'Pickering,' he replied.

'Oh yes,' I said. 'There you are, son.'

'Thank you very much,' he said and off he went, happy.

When we were ready to leave, with everything loaded back in the milk van, the man in charge came and gave us five pounds for the show. There were seven of us and we went to a local pub for a couple of hours; we still had money left at the end, which Alan gave me towards the petrol.

It's no secret that bodybuilders are some of the most egotistical creatures on the planet. They love to be noticed; they love people to look at them and stare and, over the fifty-plus years that I have been involved, I've met plenty of the worst cases.

At Adlington Barbell Club we had one lad with whom I trained for many years. His name was Peter Holding. Peter was definitely up there with the best of them in terms of ego but, in fairness, he was well aware of his ego trips and happily went along with it when we were having a laugh at his expense. He even joined in and took the piss out of himself. He once said that some people get infatuated with themselves, 'But not me. With me it's the real thing!'

In bodybuilding terms, Peter had a very good upper body and won some good titles but he was a bit light in the leg department. He had to put in a lot of leg training to try and bring them into line with his upper body but, no matter how much work he put in, they remained his weak link. Despite his humour, Peter was a touchy kind of person and a negative comment could lower him into a depression that would last for days.

No one was more aware of this than his wife, Cath. If she and Peter were having a 'domestic', she always knew an easy way to get to him and win the argument. 'You call them legs?' she would scoff. 'I don't know how you bloody well stand up on them!' And that would be it, argument lost; Peter would just clam up.

He was also fanatical about his diet; one of his favourite expressions was: 'You are what you eat.' He lived by that philosophy until one night when he was leaving the house to go to the gym just as the ice-cream van pulled up. In a moment of weakness, he bought a large cornet that he ate with relish. Then the guilt descended and, instead of carrying on to the gym and working it off, depression set in and he went back into the house and sat on the settee, distraught. He didn't go back to the gym for a couple of weeks.

On a good day though, Peter could be great company and very entertaining. There was a rumour going round the gym that Peter was so in love with himself that when he was having sex he used to shout out his own name!

I suppose that when it came to egos I wasn't completely innocent myself – in fact I was as bad as all the rest. One summer night, when I was in my late teens, I was on Southport Pleasure Beach wearing my tightest T-shirt, walking past all the stalls and sideshows. The stallholders were all trying to separate you from your money and, as I walked past one stall with a young stallholder (SH) aged around thirty, he began giving me the spiel. The dialogue went like this:

S.H. Excuse me sir, would you like to throw some darts at the bull?

Me No, thank you.

S.H. Guaranteed a prize every time.

Me No, thank you.

*S.H.*One throw for free.

Me No, thank you.

*S.H.*Excuse me, sir, are you a bodybuilder?

Bam! That was it, a lightning 180-degree turn and back to the stall. 'Well, yes, I work out,' I said.

'I thought you did,' he said. 'How often do you train? Oh, would you like a throw while we talk?'

'Why not?' I said. 'How much?'

'Two shillings a time, sir.'

'Here's ten shillings, I'll take five throws,' I said. Five minutes later, still deep in conversation, I said, 'I'll take another five please.' Then another five, while he showed a great interest in my bodybuilding career. Eventually I came away skint; I'd blown all my money on that stall while he kept asking about my bodybuilding.

These days, every time I watch Arkwright on *Open All Hours* I think about the guy on that stall. He could teach Arkwright a thing or two!

I was recently reading some old *Health and Strength* magazines and I came to the conclusion that adverts must not have been regulated in the 1960s because some of the things they promised just could not have been delivered. One of my favourites was: 'Be taller, increase your height by three to five inches in six weeks or money-back guarantee. Send postal order for ten shillings to…'

Can you imagine? Increase your height by five inches in six weeks for ten shillings? I could have been six feet three for a pound! I also assume the endorsements from so-called 'satisfied customers' were false. For example: 'I used to be the shortest among all my mates and felt very self-conscious but then I took your course and now all my mates admire me and I feel much more self-confident.' I thought, let's hope your mates don't decide to take the course as well or you'll be back to being the shortest again.

Then there were the Charles Atlas courses claiming: 'You too can have a body like mine in six weeks,' which were advertised with a photograph of Charles Atlas, Mr World. No, you can't – and why did every course take exactly six weeks? These ads reminded me of the one I wrote about earlier by Horace Batchelor, who claimed that he could show you how to win the football pools every week. These people advertised for so long, I can only assume that people kept sending them money.

We had a lad who trained at Adlington Barbell Club called Tony McHugh. Tony was one of the most fanatical trainers I met in all the years I trained. Apparently, years earlier he had trained at the house of a mate who had rigged up a gym in his cellar. Tony went round three nights a week; one night when he went round there had been a flood and the cellar was a foot deep in water. Tony went back home and got his wellingtons, then headed back to his mate's house. He did his entire workout standing in muddy water.

Around 1967 we were told that we had to leave the gym on Park Road (at the back of the Bridge Inn) as the brewery was knocking the building down to make a car park. We acquired an old building on Oxford Street, about half a mile away, where we still are today. On the night of the move we did it all in an old wagon; all the lads sacrificed their training to help with the removal, trucking to and fro between the two venues. All except for Tony, who continued training till it got to the very end – Tony training on his own with two dumbbells. He put the dumbbells on the back of the wagon and got into the cab until we got to the new venue. When he got out of the cab, he grabbed the dumbbells, went into the new gym and carried on exactly where he had left off.

This may seem very selfish on his part, but this was how his mind worked. Nothing was allowed to get in the way of his training.

The main reason that my dad objected to me training was, in his words, 'If you've got enough energy to go weightlifting after a day's work, you've not done enough work.' Another of the put-downs he used to throw at me was, 'Wait till you're forty and see what good your weightlifting has done you then.' Well, I'm seventy-three now and still training.

One Sunday in the late 1960s, I entered a power lifting competition in Rochdale. At that time, we had a neighbour called Dr Garton who took a great interest in my power lifting career. On the Thursday after the competition, my dad was driving past his house on the tractor when Dr Garton came out and flagged him down.

'How did Fred get on in the competition?' he enquired.

'I don't know, I've never asked him,' my dad replied, and then possibly feeling guilty he added 'I suppose I should do.'

'Yes, you should,' said Dr Garton in disbelief. End of conversation.

I remember winning my first trophy when I was about eighteen years old. Up until then it had started to get embarrassing as I kept entering competitions and going home empty-handed, but on this occasion I had lifted well and came third. I couldn't wait to get home and show them my trophy. My dad picked up the trophy, looked at it and said, 'It's not so big,' and put it down. It was never mentioned again.

However, no matter how all this sounds, I was told by a milk customer, Bob Atherton, that he had been in the village's barber shop when my dad was in. My dad was telling the other men how strong I was and how much I could lift. So, maybe he was proud of me after all.

I remember my dad talking to another farmer about what a waste of energy training was. The other farmer, Jimmy Dodd, was in total agreement and said, 'If they gave it another name and called it work, they wouldn't do it.' Yes, criticisms and put-downs were in plentiful supply.

Kick-Start To My Social Life

Passing my driving test at seventeen didn't just kick-start my weightlifting career, it also kick-started my social life. I no longer needed to walk miles to catch a bus. Many more options and venues presented themselves. One of the first things I did was join Chorley Young Farmers' Club, which brought a whole new social life. As well as the weekly meetings, there were social nights, dances and organised trips. These were all good opportunities for farmers' sons to meet farmers' daughters. One of the main topics of conversation was driving because a many of the members were about the age when they could learn to drive.

I had occasional dates with quite a few of the girls – Barbara Topping, Jenny Nolan, Barbara Williams, and one or two others – but there was one who stood out from all the rest. I never asked her out simply because I put her in a different league. I was convinced she wouldn't be interested in me and I didn't want to aim too high. Her name was Margaret Ormisher.

The format of the weekly meetings was as follows: for the first half we had a guest speaker, mostly speaking on farming topics, then we had a tea break, and then went through any other business. It was always the girls who did the refreshments and then the washing up. Looking back, it was very politically incorrect but that's just how it was. One night, the two girls who were doing the washing up were Barbara Topping and Margaret Ormisher.

The tearoom was just off the main room and, for some reason, Margaret was standing in the passageway in the main room between the two groups of members. The chairs on either side of the passageway were six deep and I was sitting on the fourth chair in. Margaret had the tea towel in her hand and was talking to the person on the end chair. I was looking at her, secretly admiring her, when someone suggested that maybe some of the lads should do the washing up for a change. Margaret was in full agreement and threw the tea towel to me.

Now that might not seem like the most romantic gesture in the world, and I'm sure it wasn't meant to be, but as I drove home that night the thing that kept going through my head was, 'Why did she single me out to throw the towel at? There were three lads between me and her, why didn't she throw the towel to one of them?' All the way home one half of me was saying, 'Don't be stupid,' but the other half was saying, 'Although she's never spoken to me, she's obviously noticed me. Hmm, maybe, just maybe...'

Whatever the reason, it made my night!

A couple of months after I joined the Young Farmers' Club, their Annual General Meeting was held and, although I had only just joined and was only seventeen, I was elected Vice-Chairman. At seventeen I was the youngest Vice-Chairman ever for Chorley Young Farmers' Club. At the next Annual General Meeting, the Vice-Chairman automatically moved up to Chairman. I enjoyed my year as the Vice-Chairman and stood in for the Chairman on a few occasions.

I recall a farmer coming into the room one night whom I didn't recognise. He looked a typical farmer, with a trilby and brown boots. The meeting was over and we were all standing around talking. He stood in the centre of the room and said, 'Who's the Chairman?' Someone pointed in my direction and he came over and introduced himself. 'I'm Dick Ormisher,' he said. 'I've come to pick up my daughter.' I shook hands with him, little realising that in a few short years he would become my father-in-law.

I don't know whether the tea-towel incident meant anything or not (and to this day Margaret denies it ever happened) but after that the ice was broken and we became quite chatty, much to my delight. And then, the big breakthrough. One Saturday night a few of us were at Rivington Barn for the usual Saturday night dance, which in reality should have been called the Saturday night crush because everyone, every week without fail, was just shoulder to shoulder. Those numbers would never be allowed today but, as with so many things, things were much more relaxed then.

I asked Margaret for the last waltz and she agreed. As we danced I thought, 'I'm going to ask if I can take her home.' In those days, every dance consisted of three songs and through all three songs I was trying to pluck up the courage to ask. As we came to the end of the last song, I desperately tried to sound casual and said, 'Can I give you a lift home?'

'Yes, alright,' she replied. I couldn't believe it. I couldn't wait to tell my mates!

Along with everyone else, she went to get her coat from the cloakroom while I waited at the door, feeling like the cat that had got the cream. I was in a Commer van that night and she had to tell me where she lived; I remember driving along the A6 through Whittle-le-Woods hoping I could find my way back home. At that time, it was further than I had ever driven before. I dropped her off at the front door of Manor House and, after a brief chat, I got a quick kiss, nothing passionate, which is exactly how I expected it to be, then drove back home.

Not able to believe my luck, I remember seeing a couple of mates a couple of days later and mentioning that I'd been to Rivington Barn the previous Saturday. 'Yes, yes,' they both said. 'We know all about it. You took Margaret Ormisher home.' It was a talking point for everybody and I loved it. My street cred went through the roof, and rightly so. To me, all my mates had to settle for second best.

It was shortly after this that I realised that being a member of Chorley Young Farmers' Club was making my weightlifting training difficult. I used to go to the Young Farmers' Club then rush off to the Adlington Barbell Club to train but it wasn't working out well, as I was getting to Adlington too late. I made the decision to pack in the Young Farmers'. By now I was seeing Margaret on a more regular basis; she, too, wasn't making it to the meeting every week as she was training to be a nurse at Preston Royal Infirmary. So I quit and concentrated more on training.

Although Margaret and I first went out when we were seventeen and got married at twenty-two, we did have a three-year break when we both lived our own lives We eventually got back together when we were about twenty and married two years later. By this time, Margaret had qualified as a State Registered Nurse at Preston Royal Infirmary.

The years from seventeen to twenty-two were five good years spent training, going out with the lads – and plenty of girls – and expanding the milk round. It was a good time to expand as there were a lot of new housing estates being built in Adlington: the Rivington Avenue estate, Grove Crescent, Sutton Lane, Beech Avenue, The Asshawes and Lower Hill Drive, totalling a couple of hundred houses or more.

I always kept an eye on houses that were nearing completion and, once they were finished, at night and on Saturday and Sunday afternoons I went round the estates to catch people going in to clean them, ready to move in. I would knock on the door, introduce myself and offer them a week's free milk. More often than not, bang – I had another new customer! In a short time I had increased the daily sales from forty-five gallons to sixty-eight gallons. Word got around the other milkmen that I was giving a week's free milk so they started it as well; I increased it to two weeks and so did they, but that was as far as I was prepared to go. I understand that years later some were giving twelve weeks free milk, which was crazy.

In 1969 the M61 was completed and, as I was setting off on the milk round every morning, I had to drive across the motorway bridge. As I crossed, I used to look down at the traffic using the motorway and really envy the motorists. Where were they going? What was their destination? My day was just about delivering milk then trudging back to the farm to wash bottles ready for the next day. I was intrigued by the occupants of those cars. Why couldn't I have a more exciting life like them? In reality, their lives were probably as boring as mine but that's not how it seemed to me at the time. These people were using the motorway, so they must be important people. Little did I know that, years later, motorways would become a bigger part of my life than farming ever was.

During this period I got friendly with another farming lad from Horwich called Richard Owen. We became good mates – in fact, I was best man at his and Bernadette's wedding in 1963 at St Chad's, Wheelton. But in the years when he was single, we got about a bit; among our many dancing haunts were Rivington Barn, The Tudor at Chorley, Blackburn Mecca and Highways Hostel. One night at Highways Hostel, we bumped into another lad we knew called James Collins. The night was slow and boring until James mentioned there was another Young Farmers' dance on at Great Eccleston. We decided to leave Highways Hostel and go there but none of us knew where Great Eccleston was.

We started making enquiries and James went off to ask someone he knew. Meanwhile, Richard and I spotted two tasty-looking girls and they accepted when we asked them for a dance. While we were dancing, they said they had to leave to go home early so we asked if we could give them a lift home in the car. They agreed and we told James (who, I've got to say, was the most boring person on the planet) that we would be back in half an hour while he continued making enquiries.

Well, it turned out that, unlike James, the two girls were anything but boring! The half hour flew by, as did the next half hour and the next and the next, and all thoughts of James and Great Eccleston were long gone. Eventually the girls went home and we also headed home comparing notes, as you do.

As we drove past Highways Hostel, we saw a lone car on the car park. It was James in his Ford Prefect, shining a torch on the map. We thought we should stop and explain, as it was now well past midnight and Highways closed at 10.30; he had been sitting in the car park for an hour and a half. We mumbled some kind of apology and all James could say was, 'I managed to get hold of this map, so if you still want to go I can take you straight to it.'

'Oh,' I said. 'Thanks, James, but we've both got to be up early in the morning. Sorry.'

He didn't mind and was just happy that he had found out where Great Eccleston was. We were even happier that we hadn't.

It's strange, but a few weeks later I was at another dance at Highways; although it wasn't a Young Farmers' dance, there were many young farmers there. Amongst them was an absolutely drop-dead gorgeous girl. She was a farmer's daughter called Christine Fishwick from White Coppice, who I knew vaguely but not well. She was just sixteen. During the course of the evening, she accepted my offer of a dance and when it was over I was going to walk her back to her seat but the hall was packed and her seat had gone.

'It appears there are no empty seats,' I said.

'There are two in the back of your car,' she replied. I couldn't believe what I was hearing! The one girl in the room that everybody was looking at was propositioning me!

'Yeah, alright,' I said calmly, while trying desperately to stop my chin from trembling.

We headed across the car park and spent a pleasant half hour in the back of the car. By today's standards what we got up to would be regarded as pretty tame, but that didn't matter. After that, we started to see each other on regular basis. I suppose you could say that, apart from Margaret, she was the nearest I got to having a steady girlfriend. I used to go to her home quite often and got to know her parents pretty well. Her dad, Ernie Fishwick, was a gentleman and much respected in the farming community, and they lived at Causeway House Farm, White Coppice.

One night, after being together about six months, I went to pick her up to go to Rivington Barn. I don't know why but, although she was still pleasant and smiling, I noticed a change in her attitude – she wasn't as warm. We got to the barn, parked up and walked in holding hands. We were looking round, as you do when you first go in a crowded room, and we spotted another couple coming towards us. They were old friends of Christine's but I'd got to know them through her. What she did next was quite weird: she let go of my hand and stood with them, facing me, and chatted to me as though we weren't together.

When they left, she came back and spent the rest of the evening with me as usual but I was now in no doubt that this was going to be our last night together – and that's how it turned out. When I took her home she said that she wanted to end it. She didn't offer any explanation but she was quite pleasant and I only have fond memories of her. Strangely, I don't recall ever seeing her again after that night…

We had a customer called Mrs Winstanley on the milk round who lived in a cottage across from the Yew Tree. In fact, her son John, a lifelong friend of our family, still lives there. Mrs Winstanley was always interested in my love life and, every Saturday when I went to collect the milk money, she always wanted an update. After Christine had finished with me, I knew she would ask. I had my story ready and was expecting something along the lines of 'Don't worry, she'll be back' or 'Don't worry, you'll find someone else.' At least I expected to get a sympathetic ear.

When she came to the door with the milk money, the first thing she said was, 'Well, how's Christine?'

I put on a mournful face and said, 'She's finished with me,' to which she replied, without hesitation, 'Well, if you can't keep 'em, you don't deserve 'em!'

Another farmer's daughter of a 'friendly' disposition was Elsie. Now, Elsie had been out a time or two with my mate Richard, so I had an idea that the odds were for an entertaining evening. One night we were at a dance at The Empress Ballroom, Wigan, and I gave a few friends a lift home, one being Elsie. We got on very well and chatted a lot but she was not the last to be dropped off, so there was to be no hanky-panky that night. I asked if I could see her again and she agreed, so the following week I picked her up in the milk van and we went for a ride around Rivington, eventually finding a nice secluded spot and an opportunity to get to know her better – much better.

The milk van had three individual seats across the front and I somehow managed to position myself sat on the middle seat with Elsie lying across me facing the roof, her head up against the driver's window and her feet pressed against the passenger windows. Her panties were draped over the steering wheel, her skirt was pulled up, and I was happily helping myself to the goodies, in a world of my own.

This had been going on for ten minutes or so when I happened to glance up at the van roof and was shocked to see smoke swirling around. 'What's on fire?' I thought, and stopped playing the piano, so to speak, for a few seconds while I looked around. I could see nothing. 'Can you smell smo…?' I began, but I stopped in my tracks.

Would you believe that, while I thought I was sending her to heaven, she had lit up a fag and was having a smoke? I've heard of people enjoying a cigarette after but Elsie didn't even wait that long!

Many years later, when both Elsie and I were married to our respective partners and those teenage years were long gone, my mother held a Tupperware party – and who do you think was hosting it? Yes, Elsie. And she had driven up to Blindhurst on her Lambretta scooter with all the Tupperware tied with string to the sides and the back. Elsie rode, still with a cig in her mouth, and she also conducted the entire party whilst smoking. Nobody was going to separate Elsie from her Woodbines!

In those days, if you saw a girl that you fancied you would ask her for a dance. If she agreed, it didn't automatically mean she fancied you but you knew that (at the very least) you didn't repulse her. It was not uncommon to be refused then to try again later in the evening. If she accepted, you were cooking on gas! So, come the last dance (which was always a slow smoochy waltz), you would go in for the kill and ask her again. It was this dance that paid the rent because it was when you got the chance to dance cheek to cheek, ask if you could walk the girl home and then ask, 'Can I see you again next week?' Yes, the last dance was the one that mattered. Don't tell me that internet dating is better than that.

I remember one night I asked a girl for a dance at St Joseph's Youth Club, which led to the biggest put-down I'd ever experienced. She quite happily got up with me and I started with my chat-up lines. I can't remember what I said but whatever it was didn't impress her and she must have decided that she wasn't going to get up with me again. I was totally unaware of this and thought I had her eating out of my hand, so at the end of the dance I walked her back to her seat and decided she was the girl I was taking home that night. As she sat down I said, 'Can I have the last dance with you?' to which she replied, 'You've just had it!'

When you got a girl that you didn't know up to dance, you always tried to engage in conversation, making small talk to break the ice. 'Do you come here often?' was the most tried-and-tested icebreaker but my yardstick was to ask them their name. The girls would usually tell you. Some would just tell you and leave it at that but, if they told you and then followed it up with, 'What's yours?' I would immediately think, 'Result! This is going places – she's interested.'

On the other side of the coin were the wallflowers, the ones that never got asked, who would sit with their backs to the wall all night. Sometimes you would ask one of these girls out of sympathy but that could come back to bite you if she refused. That would get all your mates laughing, as they were nearly always watching you from the other side of the room. Then, of course, there were the times when the wallflower would refuse you just to impress her mates, when she was actually desperate to have a dance. There were also those wallflowers who would see you coming towards them and come to meet you, just in case you spotted something better on your way across!

In the years that I used to go dancing, I had a mate called Derek Brown. It's true to say that the nights that I went out with him were probably the best nights ever, certainly in terms of picking up girls. Brownie could pick up girls like nobody else I knew. Her looks, age, size and marital status mattered little to Derek – a female was a female, and that's all that mattered – a pulse was his only requirement. That's not to say that all the girls he picked up were rough. Oh no, he often had some tasty chick – but first and foremost sex was the motive and looks took second place.

I once remember him telling me about a girl he was seeing who was sex mad. Without going into too much detail, as far as sex was concerned, Brownie had no limitations: nothing was out of bounds and nothing was taboo. This particular girl was right up Derek's street – in fact, she may even have been in a different league! Apparently while they were 'at it', she kept shouting at him, 'You can do anything, you can do anything! Do you hear what I'm saying? You can do anything,' which you might think was music to his ears. But it was just frustrating him. All he could think was, 'What the hell am I not doing? What is it that I can do that I'm not doing?' Sometimes he used to lie awake in bed trying to work out what it was she wanted him to do – what else *was* there to do? I never discovered if he ever found out...

At that time, Derek was a self-employed joiner and property repairer and if he went to view a job he also took the opportunity to view the lady of the house at the same time. One day, I was delivering milk to a customer and he was there fitting new windows. Apparently he was fitting new windows to the back and the front of the house so I saw him each day. It goes without saying that he had tapped up the housewife and let's just say that not all his time was spent fitting windows!

Then one day I went and he wasn't there. In fact, even though he hadn't finished, I didn't see him there again. A few months later I bumped into him and he told me the husband had sacked him as he had become suspicious in the most hilarious of ways. Apparently, the husband had been in bed with his wife one night and had obviously been getting a bit frisky. He had slipped his wife's nightie over her head and started to fondle her breasts then suddenly sat up in bed and said, 'Your tits smell of putty!' Get out of that! Derek, you should have washed your hands…

By then I had been playing the field for three years or so and my mind kept wandering back to Margaret Ormisher. Everyone else was just entertainment and a stopgap. One night Richard Owen and I went to Blackburn Mecca and I was secretly hoping that Margaret would be there so I could ask her for a dance. Who knew what else would happen? After looking round for about an hour, I accepted that she wasn't there and there would be no dance that night. However, I spotted her sister Jennifer across the room, so all was not lost. At least I could get some inside information, like what she was doing and if she was seeing anyone. Anything that would maybe help me plan a strategy.

I went across and I asked Jennifer for a dance. Well, she got up but that was the nearest she got to being friendly. I couldn't get two words out of her. Everything I asked her got a one-word answer and, to make matters worse, she never looked at me. She just kept looking straight past me and then, after one song, she walked off and went back to her seat. Thanks a lot, that was a great help, I thought!

Over the coming months, Margaret and I did get back together again and settled down to what, in those days, they called 'going steady'. Just as it was the first time I took her out, I felt like I was the envy of all my mates.

I recall one night at the weightlifting club when I was training with a lad that I hadn't seen before. Throughout all the years that I trained, lads came to the club and lasted for a few months then you wouldn't see them again. Anyway, this lad said that he worked on a farm in the Whittle-le-Woods area, at which point I said, 'Oh, my girlfriend lives on a farm in that part of the world.'

'Does she?' he replied. 'What farm is that?'

'Ormishers,' I said.

'Are you going out with an Ormisher girl?' he asked in amazement.

'Yes, Margaret,' I said.

'I don't know which is which,' he said. 'But if you're going out with an Ormisher girl, you're a lucky bugger!' That was the high esteem in which they were held.

After two years of going steady, we eventually got married at St Bede's Church, Clayton Green, with all her four sisters as bridesmaids and my younger brother, Barry, as my best man. The date was 2nd May 1965, and we were both twenty-two. The reception was held at the Royal Oak, Chorley, and we were one of the first couples to have a proper, hot, three-course meal with wine and champagne. In those days ninety-nine per cent of wedding meals were soup, boiled ham salad followed by apple pie and cream. The guests couldn't stop talking about what a fantastic meal they had. People weren't used to eating out and the manager of the Royal Oak, a fellow named Fawcett, was a man who knew his job and ran a good ship.

We went to live in a rented terraced house in Horwich, 3 Rawlinson Street, which we got through Pat Kelly, the man who had bought Nabs Farm from my dad. Kelly's were the main estate agents in Horwich. It cost us £4 per week with an extra ten shillings (50p) to rent a lock-up garage. Margaret gave up her job at Preston Royal Infirmary and got a new position at Bolton Royal Infirmary. We lived there for a year before moving into 169 Chorley Road, Heath Charnock, into a brand-new, three-bedroomed detached house that we bought for £2,800 from Stan

Fairclough Builders.

When our first baby, Richard, was born we lived on Chorley Road. As we didn't have a car, Margaret used to travel to Chorley by bus, as most people did back then. Someone who used the same bus was a gentleman called Mr Blackburn. He was a real gent and was married to one of my old schoolteachers. He was also a milk customer and, whenever I saw him when I was delivering their milk, he used to say without fail, 'Your wife and baby would win any mother-and-baby contest going.' I couldn't argue with that.

During the next five years, from 1965 to 1970, I concentrated on increasing the retail side of the milk sales and also the semi-retail sales. I purchased a large milk round in Horwich and a small one in Adlington. On top of that, I negotiated supplying other milkmen with their milk, people like Richard Owen, Les Martin and John Garlick. By now, most of the milk was being sold at a price much better than wholesale and this remained the case over that five-year period.

Although everything was going well and the farm was very profitable, it was always in the back of my mind that being a milkman was not my destiny. This was not what I wanted to do for the rest of my life; there must be something else out there. And although I didn't know what that something was, I was – and still am – a great believer that opportunities come along and your future sorts itself out, providing that when the opportunity arises you have: (1) the ability to recognise it, and (2) the guts or confidence to go with it.

One summer day in 1966, that opportunity presented itself. It's true to say I had no idea at that time where it would lead – I just saw it as a good idea. I had a training buddy, a lad called John Baker who worked for Lancashire County Council in a department called Rural Studies (in other words, he worked in the Parks Department as a gardener). As I stated earlier, it was a decade when lots of housing developments were taking place and these new houses had new gardens, thus creating an

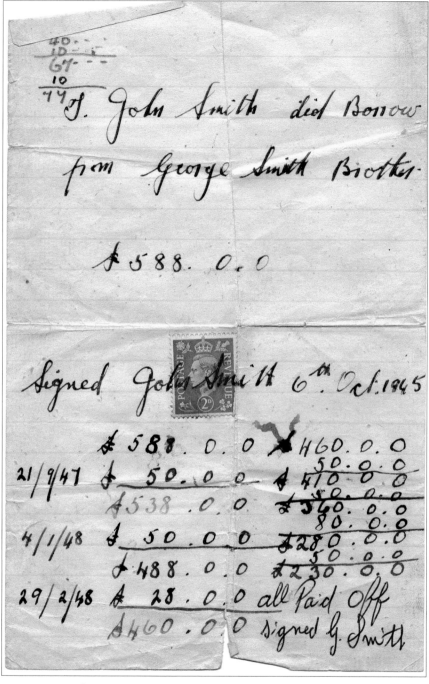

1948. *This page and following 2 pages,* the loan agreement between Uncle George and my Dad. Who needs solicitors? Just a slip of paper and a handshake (and I'm not even sure about the handshake).

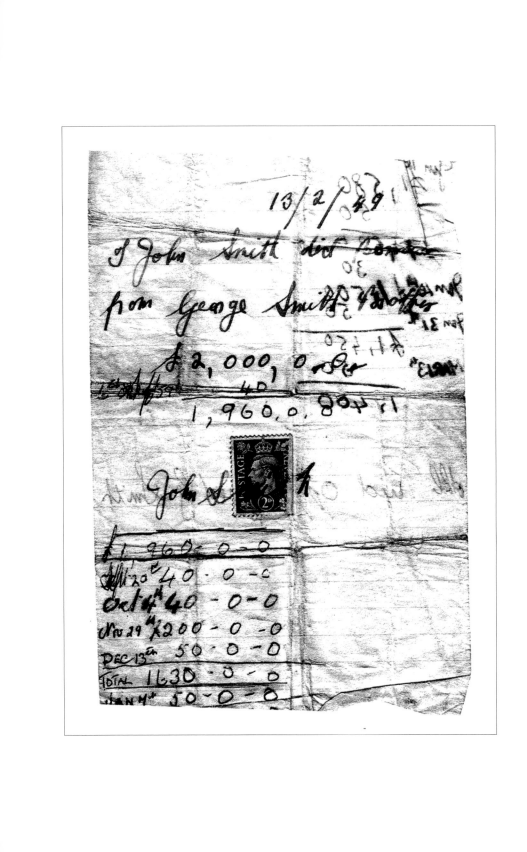

13/2/49

J John Smith did borrow
from George Smith...

£2,000, 0...

1,960, 0, 80...

John S...

£1,960 - 0 - 0
20th 40 - 0 - 0
Oct 4th 40 - 0 - 0
Nov 29th £200 - 0 - 0
Dec 13th 50 - 0 - 0
TOTAL 1,630 - 0 - 0
Jan 4th 50 - 0 - 0

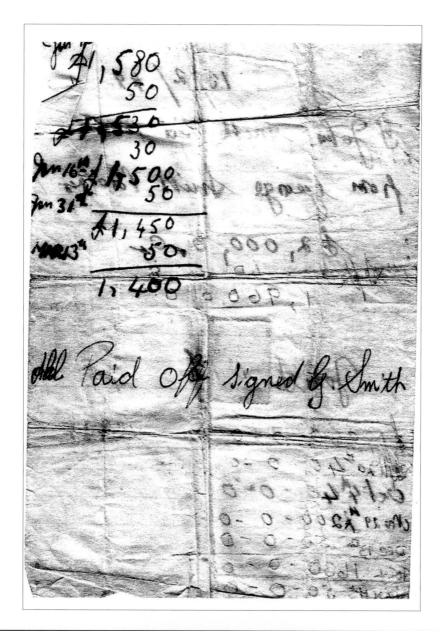

£1,580
50
£1,530
30
Jan 16th £1,500
50
Jan 31st
£1,450
50
Mar 13th
1,400

All Paid Off signed G. Smith

A GUIDE TO
RIVINGTON & ANGLEZARKE

1980. Shaw Place Farm to the right, Blindhurst to the left. An excellent photo on a Rivington & Anglezarke leaflet.

1974. This photo portrays why my Dad was held in high esteem by the Grassland Society.

1974. Our lodger Egon with my mum on the right and Aunty Jenny on the left. His year spent with us was very important to Egon, as it was to us.

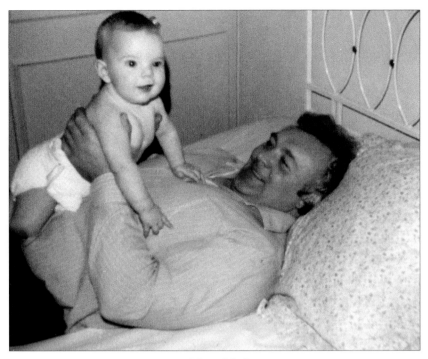

1983. Me with Ben.

1967. Margaret and Richard – you can see why
Mr Blackburn commented as he did (*page 82*).

1972. Adlington Carnival where Smiths Farms won the tug of war, with Miss Adlington Carnival Queen.

1975. Taking delivery of my second trenching machine (with Eddie Whielden), which was to launch us in to street lighting. This channelled my life in a direction I had never envisaged.

1992. Dave Joice backfilling cable trench on the M63 (now M60).

1997. Me, Jonathan and Richard at Hale Motorway Maintenance Depot.

1997. Rod Eccles operates the crane as the "Big Lamp" is erected. The "Big Lamp" is an iconic feature of Chorley town centre. This lamp replaced the original which had stood in that spot for over 100 years. In fact the whole area is known locally as the "Big Lamp".

opening for anyone prepared to bend their back. John picked up a few weekend jobs, using the Parks Department equipment.

One day he asked me if I would do him a favour the following Saturday and pick him up at his house after I'd finished the milk rounds. So after lunch I got in the milk van and went to his house, having no idea what he wanted me to do. We went back to his place of work, which at that time was on Duxbury Park (now a golf course).

I drew up where he told me to and he got out and loaded a very small rotavator into the back of the van. It was so small he could just pick it up, and he lifted it in and directed me to a house on St Paul's Close, Adlington. He lifted the rotavator out of the van, wheeled it onto the garden, started it with the starter cord and began to dig up this small front garden. The machine bounced about a bit the first time but the second time started to dig a bit deeper and by the third time produced quite a fine soil surface. He got a garden rake and raked it level then proceeded to scatter lawn seed over the soil.

The garden itself was quite small and the whole operation took about one-and-a-half hours, at the end of which the lady came out. She said how much better it looked and paid him £10. I know that £10 today doesn't seem much but in 1966 it was a lot of money. In fact, I had a young milk lad working for me who didn't earn that in a week. John loaded up the rotavator, we took it back to Duxbury, dropped it off and then I took him back home. As he got out of the van he thanked me and went.

I thought he might have offered me a couple of quid – after all I had given up my day – but he didn't. It was a trait that he carried with him throughout his life. In fact, if I can digress a little, I remember the early years of training behind the Bridge Inn. After training, some of the lads used to go in the Bridge for a pint and, although I didn't drink at that time, I often went in and had a soft drink as I loved the training atmosphere that prevailed around the bar.

One particular night as I went in John was about to leave but I said to him, 'Do you want a drink?'

'No thanks,' he said. 'I'm just leaving.' Then he had a change of mind and said, 'Oh yes, I'll just have a bottle of brown ale.' The barman put it on the bar. 'Oh, and I'll have a packet of crisps,' John added. He put both the bottle and the crisps in his pocket and said, 'These are for the wife,' and went! Yes, throughout all the years that I knew him he had deep pockets and short arms!

MILK AND GARDENS

Whenever we went to weightlifting and bodybuilding competitions we all chucked in but, without exception, John managed to pay a bit less than everybody else. Anyway, in the great scheme of things that's not important. What was important was the fact that what I had watched him do that afternoon had given me the idea for something to do myself after morning milk deliveries. Until then, my afternoons were spent washing bottles and refilling them ready for deliveries the following day. All I needed to do was to get someone to work part time in the afternoon thus freeing me up to go round knocking on the doors of new houses that needed their gardens sorted. Surely with my own van, rotavator and a few basic gardening tools I could earn more than I needed to pay a part-time dairy worker?

And so it turned out that I was earning a much better than average salary on the lucrative milk round, and repeating the earning process in the afternoon. I don't remember the exact amount but I think I paid the part-time dairy worker about £12 per week and I was earning between £12 and £20 per afternoon going from house to house, knocking on doors and offering to rotavate gardens and generally tidy them up. The man who did my dairy work was always known as Pedro. That wasn't his real name but he was a keen fisherman so was named after the song 'Pedro the Fisherman'.'

At a time when the average wage was less than £20 per week, I was earning between £140 and £180, but it goes without saying that the working days were very long. I had to be up by 5am to start the milk round, would finish around lunchtime and unload the van ready for Pedro to come in the afternoon. Then I'd go home, have some lunch, load the rotavator and other tools and go out on my second day job. Sometimes I would get a mate or my brother-in-law Norman to come with me so we could quickly polish jobs off and move on to the next one. There was never any shortage of work.

Apart from getting jobs through knocking on doors and by word of mouth, I had also started to advertise in the landscape section of the *Chorley Guardian* and this provided a steady flow of new work. I found that if I took a mate with me to help it made a tremendous difference in the speed that we could get through the work – and on one occasion this almost caused me some embarrassment.

I had got a job to rotavate and turf a small front garden at Blackrod, for which I had quoted £25. Me and my mate, Cyril Robinson, arrived to start the job just as the lady of the house was closing the door to go to Chorley shopping for the afternoon. She apologised for not having the cash on her but said that she would get it while she was out and pay me when she got back later. She walked to the bus stop at the end of the street and Cyril and I got stuck in, me rotavating while Cyril barrowed in the turf.

The garden was about the size of a postage stamp and we were done in no time, so we swept up. We were about to load up, drive away and come back for the money later when we noticed that the lady was still at the bus stop. We had finished the whole job while she was still waiting for the bus – and she could see us clearly from where she was standing. We went back to the garden and started taking up strips of turf, put each one back in the same place, then took up the next one and did exactly the same again until the bus arrived. Once she was safely out of sight, we loaded everything back into the van and headed off to the next job.

I carried on working at both jobs for about three years, during which time I invested in a second-hand ex-Army Land Rover for £250 and bought a second-hand trailer for £25, thus removing the need to use the milk van. By now, my wife and I had three children, Richard, Carmen and Jonathan, and we had moved from 169 Chorley Road to Stonyhurst, Lees Road, for which we had paid £8,500. It was a beautiful house that we loved and thought we would never leave. The year was 1970 so the house was very expensive. By then, predictably, the range of work that I carried out to the gardens had increased dramatically. Originally I had limited the work to rotavating and turfing but now I was being asked to carry out full landscape requirements – fencing, flagging, draining, rockeries and planting.

SELLING THE MILK ROUNDS

I REMEMBER ONE day, as I was delivering milk in Adlington, I was standing at a zebra crossing with an eight-pint milk carrier in my hand, waiting to cross the road to deliver someone's milk, when a beautiful Volvo stopped to let me cross. I nodded to the driver in appreciation – and oh my God, the driver was a landscape client from Euxton where I should have been working. It was embarrassing. I didn't show any sign of recognition but he had a good look at me. I knew it couldn't go on.

I decided that running two businesses was becoming more and more difficult and I made the decision to sell the milk round and concentrate on building up the landscape side. Also, I felt the landscape business held the greater prospect of opening up doors to other opportunities. In addition, it was becoming embarrassing; as the jobs became bigger and more involved, customers were beginning to wonder why I only ever started work after lunch. I didn't want them to know that the person that they were trusting their very expensive landscaping to was in fact a milkman. So the milk round was sold for £4,000 to a lad from Chorley called Tony Clarkson who I still see from time to time.

When I sold the milk round, I thought I'd finished with delivering milk. In a way I had but also I hadn't because of one totally unexpected phenomenon – a recurring dream. It's over forty years since I sold the milk round but I still dream that I'm delivering milk and, sadly, the dreams are never pleasant. I'm always under pressure; maybe I've run out of milk and there's none left at the farm, or people aren't paying me and I don't know how much they owe, or I'm very late and I can't catch up. Sometimes the dreams are so vivid that I just accept them – in my dreams I've still got the round and always will have. Weird.

I remember that when I told my dad that I was selling the milk round to concentrate on the landscaping he was very supportive and didn't try to talk me out of it, but he did ask the same question that everybody asked: 'What are you going to do in winter?' The short answer was that I didn't know, but I did know that I would do something. I had no idea what that something would be but, as I said earlier, I am a great believer that things come along and you get through. I am not one of those people who think everything through and weighs up all the pitfalls and the risks, because if you do that you'll never do anything. I honestly believe that you have to trust to luck and go for it, although I've got to admit that not everyone can cope with the problems that that attitude can bring and maybe for those people caution is the best option. I'm glad to say that my children also seem to have the 'go for it' attitude, within reason of course, and it has paid off for them too.

Around 1970, I sold the Horwich milk round to David Thistlethwaite, the brother of Norman. On occasion, when he had finished the milk round in the morning, he would work on the farm in the afternoon. One spring my dad bought a new muck spreader. It was what they called a side spreader as it threw the muck out from the side as opposed to previous spreaders that threw it out from the back. It was agreed that David would go muck spreading in the field opposite the Yew Tree Inn so he loaded up the spreader and off he went with the first load. He drove to the top of the field, put the spreader in gear and set off down the field, spreading as he went. Now I don't know whether it hadn't occurred to him, or whether he had misjudged it, but when you are spreading muck with a side spreader it's not very bright to set off at the side of a white house. David did. The house belonged to Mr & Mrs Ashworth and it got absolutely covered in cow muck. The next thing, Mrs Ashworth was down at Blindhurst playing hell with my dad, who had to take a ladder, bucket and mop and spend all afternoon washing the side of her house as she was determined that there was not going to be a speck left on it.

That did not help neighbourly relations, but things were to get much worse.

The following week my dad went to bring in the cows for milking. They were in a field further on than the Ashworth's house. He went up in the van, as he always did, and when all the cattle were out of the field and on the road, he followed them driving slowly in the van. As he was passing the Ashworth's house, Mrs Ashworth's little dog (I think it was a Jack Russell) ran out yelping and barking at the cows. This was no big deal as it happened every night; the cows were used to it and it didn't bother my dad. But on this particular night the dog must have either been stood on or kicked by a cow, and it rolled under the van wheel and was killed instantly. My dad had the unenviable task of picking it up and taking it back to Mrs Ashworth. She went into meltdown, becoming hysterical and accusing my dad of killing the dog on purpose because she had made him wash the side of her house. Obviously he hadn't, but Mrs Ashworth was having none of it.

Anyway, back to 1971, and I remember getting up the first morning with no milk to deliver and £4,000 in the bank – what a lovely feeling! And just for one day I decided to wallow in it and have a day off work.

Full-Time Landscaping

The first job I did as a full-time landscape contractor was to turf the front gardens of a housing estate in Blackrod. The builder was Stan Fairclough, who had built 169 Chorley Road. I have never seen houses built so steeply. As you drove up the road, the houses on the left were on a downward slope and the ones on the right were on an upward slope. On the first day of turfing I had to get some pieces of wood and chop them into pegs then, as I laid each roll of turf, I would hammer the pegs into the turf then into the ground. If I hadn't, the turf would have all slid to the bottom of the garden; that's how steep they were. While I was laying the turf on the first morning on the upward slope, I heard a nasty crunching sound and I turned around to see a new resident on the downward slope attempting to drive his car out of his drive. When he'd got to the top, the car balanced on the footpath and was literally rocking. Some of the building lads and I had to go and rock the car off the drive and on to the road.

It was while I was working on this site that I met an Irish lad who was doing the groundwork. His name was Pete McGowan and, as well as being in the construction business, he was a professional wrestler. Over the time we worked together we got on well, especially as we had training in common, and we would discuss it at length. One day, at around three o'clock in the afternoon, Pete asked me if I would rotavate the back garden of his house after work that night.

Pete lived in Weldbank Lane, Chorley, in a new detached house. After work, I loaded up the rotavator and went to his house. He showed me what he wanted me to do then put on his tracksuit and went to do some roadwork. He got back about an hour later as I was nearing the end.

'That's great,' he said. 'Have you had a drink?' I hadn't. 'I'll get you one,' he said and went into the house, coming out with two glasses – one each. By that point it was around 8pm and I hadn't eaten since lunchtime. He gave me one glass and kept the other. 'Cheers!' he said and we both took a drink. It was neat whisky! I couldn't believe it – there was so much in the glass I had assumed that it was a long drink. I think the rotavator finished the job off on its own, dragging me with it!

After the site in Blackrod was done, Pete and I lost touch for a long time but our paths were to cross again years later. I was working on a site in East Lancashire, I can't remember the contract, but Pete was there doing the groundwork. It was good to see him again and, of course, talk soon got round to training. After a bit of banter, I challenged him to an arm wrestle, a challenge that he accepted. We chose the bonnet of my van to use as the table. I realised that the van was on a slope and that I would be pushing uphill while Pete would be pushing down, but no matter, I was sure I would win anyway. I had never been beaten. This was a mere detail but of course Pete was not your average Joe – he was a professional wrestler and very strong.

After a very long and close battle, he eventually won. Years later, it transpired that he too was very proud of that win and that made me feel proud (there's always a positive if you look for it).

As the landscaping business grew, we started to get work from the local councils building children's play areas. Some of those contracts I could make good money on and on others I made no money at all. Well, you know what it's like with children's play areas, it's swings and roundabouts! Joke...

Probably the most required aspect of landscaping was turfing. This was a very simple procedure. You rotavated the area consistently till the soil became a fine tilth, then raked it level and laid the turf. Sometimes, if it's an area where the ground mainly consists of clay, it is almost impossible to break down fine enough to lay the turf; on these occasions I would order a load of sand or fine ash to spread on the surface to obtain a good level.

One day I was talking to another landscape contractor about this problem when he told me that, although it doesn't sound pleasant, the best thing to use is sewage waste. He explained that the waste has been left to rot over many years and has no smell or anything unpleasant about it, and that it is also very nutritious for the ground.

I decided to give it a try and on my next turfing job (in Euxton) I ordered twelve tonnes. It was duly delivered, and (as my friend had said) it did a good job, with no smell or anything else unpleasant. I completed the job and the customer was very pleased with the end result, which was a complete transformation of his garden.

I heard nothing more until about three months later, when I got a phone call from the householder who had just got back from a long holiday. He asked me to go round and look at their lawn. I was somewhat puzzled but got in my Land Rover and went to his house. Before I had even pulled up I could see why he had rung. I was met with the sight of the most fantastic crop of juicy, plump, red tomatoes that I had ever seen. How the hell did that happen? Then it slowly dawned on me. It was the sewage waste. Sewage comes from people, people eat tomatoes and tomatoes have seeds. You do the maths!

Obviously I had to pull out all the tomatoes and re-turf the area. I offered the tomatoes to the customer but no way was he going to eat them, knowing how they had got there – and neither was I. However, a wicked smile flashed across my face. I had a 'friend' who was always borrowing my Land Rover and trailer to do little jobs for himself and he never offered to put any petrol in. The tank could be full when he took it and half empty when he brought it back, but he never offered to reimburse me. This used to make me mad. He was a freeloader so I felt sure that a freeloader would appreciate two or three pounds of beautiful, *home-grown* tomatoes and indeed he was a grateful recipient, bless him. That'll teach the bastard!

Around that time I got a job at Lostock, near Bolton, on an exclusive housing estate called The Whinns. I was working for an insolvency accountant, to whom money seemed no object. On his first interim payment, which was for £1,000, I realised why: on the bottom of the cheque it said 'Client's Account'. He was paying with money from his insolvent clients' accounts!

I'm the first to admit that I was not a gardener and knew nothing about gardening but I seem to have made a career (in fact, several careers) in building up businesses that I know nothing about. Anyhow, on this job it came to the time, after all the spadework had been done, to start the planting. This was the part that changed the look of the garden, a bit like when you've baked a cake and it's time to put the icing on. Off I went to the garden centre to choose things that I thought would look good. The client who, incidentally, drove a beautiful Rolls Royce, left it to me to plant it up as I wished – after all, I was the professional gardener. I got an assortment of plants, shrubs and flowers then I pushed the boat out and bought some very expensive miniature conifers which he was very pleased with as miniature conifers were very rare and not easy to acquire (or at least that's what the lad at the garden centre told me).

These days, I drive past the house a lot taking my grandson Charlie to Bolton School, and I always get the urge to put my foot down a bit going past the house in case he still lives there, as the miniature conifers are now about forty feet tall and completely dwarf the house.

At the time that this work was going on, at the house next door there were two fellows doing a similar job so naturally we got talking and used to have a brew together. The boss of the two lived in Bolton and his mate, Ernie, lived in Aspull which was practically on my way home. Each night

I gave him a lift to save his boss having to take him. One night he confided that work was slow and he thought that he was going to be laid off. At the time I had more work that I could cope with and I thought, with his experience, he could be an asset to me so I offered him a job, which he accepted. The down side was that he didn't drive but as he would be working with me most of the time I didn't see that as a massive problem, and he started for me the following Monday.

It's true to say that I have never met anyone like Ernie. He has got to be the funniest person I have ever known. He was joking from picking him up in the morning to dropping him off at night, and he was genuinely funny. I remember hearing one lady customer ask him if he had always been a gardener, to which he replied, 'No, I used to wring out for a one-armed window cleaner.'

'Oh,' she replied, and didn't push it any further.

If that was the upside of Ernie, there was also a downside which, in fairness, there is with most people. I soon realised that he was not as capable as I thought he would be, and apart from basic labouring jobs, he was really no asset at all. Also, as with a lot of people, if I wasn't there production was almost non-existent. A smoke and a brew was all that he was interested in. I realised that him having no driving licence was a bigger burden than I thought it would be. For instance, if I had to leave the site he had no way of getting home, so I was tied to being with him all the time and this was just not possible. He had to go, so the parting of the ways was inevitable. However, I sometimes look back and have a laugh.

The next lad I took on was a different ball game altogether. He was an Adlington lad that I'd known most of my life. His name was Frank Higginson and he was a joiner by trade. I can't remember why he was available to work for me but he was and I took him on. Although Frank was a bright lad in many ways, could get jobs done and was good at solving problems, sometimes I couldn't believe the simple mistakes that he made. Although he was a very intelligent lad, he was not great at reading and writing, something he had no problem admitting.

We were on a job in Chorlton Cum Hardy where we were laying a water main, and Frank was attempting to fix the pipe joints. I was working further up the site and I could see him reading the jointing instructions, which seemed to be taking him an extraordinary length of time. Eventually he walked up to me with the instructions in his hand and said, 'Fred, I can't make head nor tail of these instructions. See what you think.' I took the papers from him and realised that they were printed in both English and German – and Frank was trying to read the German version.

Frank liked to do a bit of shooting. All the years I knew him, he owned one or sometimes two guns. One summer, he and one or two of his mates went to Perth in Scotland to shoot. On the Thursday morning, Frank did something that only Frank could do: he went into the local newsagents and asked them for a *Chorley Guardian*. In Scotland!

At the time that he worked for me, we lived at Stonyhurst in a very imposing house which had a large double garage as well as a drive-through garage, as the house had an entrance at the front and a drive round the house. You could go through the drive, through the garage and out through the bottom entrance but the first set of doors in the garage were in a bad state and needed replacing. Although money wasn't plentiful at that time, I eventually agreed that we should invest in a new pair of doors. I rang my mate, Derek Brown (the putty man), and got him to make us some bespoke doors which, I've got to admit, completely changed the look not just of the garage but also the immediate area around it.

At that time, we were about to start a flagging job at Brinscall. On the Friday before we started, we went to the builders' merchants and loaded up the trailer, ready to start the new job on Saturday. Rather than bring the loaded trailer back to Adlington, we parked it overnight at my in-laws at Manor House Farm, which was much nearer to Brinscall. On the Saturday morning we went for the trailer, hooked up and set off for

Brinscall. We got as far as the Top Lock at Wheelton when somehow (don't ask me how) we got talking to a man who worked on a pleasure boat called *The Lady Mary* on the canal. After chatting to him for about ten minutes, he invited us on it to have a look.

Now in those days nobody enjoyed a pint more than Frank and, while the man was showing us around the boat, he said 'Do you fancy a drink?' The answer was obvious so he pulled us a pint each and would not take any money. Despite it being early in the day, it went down very well so, when he asked us whether we fancied another, we gratefully accepted. This was followed by the offer of a third but by now I could see that Frank was beginning to get a taste for it so I declined the offer on behalf of both of us, a decision which Frank reluctantly went along with. We got back in the Land Rover and set off towards Brinscall to start the job.

As we were approaching Brinscall, we could tell that this was not an average Saturday as the traffic was queuing all along the roads. Would you believe it, it was Brinscall Carnival Field Day. There was entertainment, sports and, of course, a beer tent; to put a top hat on it, the house that we were going to work at was right on the road that was chock-a-block with traffic. That was it, the decision had been taken out of my hands; no way could we start that day. We found a bit of spare land and parked up before making our way to the beer tent for another couple of pints. I've got to say that I wouldn't do that today but nobody had heard of breathalysers then and nobody bothered.

After another couple of pints, we left the tent and walked back to the Land Rover. We unhooked the trailer and headed home but we were only a mile into our journey when we came to a halt sign. I put my foot on the brake and shock, horror! – I felt a snap and my foot went down to the floor. The brake cable had snapped. As we headed towards the halt sign we were going faster than ever. I knocked the Land Rover out of gear and pulled the hand brake on. Fortunately there was a wide grass verge that I managed to mount and bring the Land Rover to a standstill. All we could both think was, thank God! We unhooked the trailer loaded with flags. I don't know how I managed to get back from Brinscall to Adlington with no foot brake but I did.

As we were passing the Bay Horse at Heath Charnock, Frank wanted to stop for a drink but there was no way that I was stopping, especially with no foot brake. I dropped Frank off as he knew that some of his mates would be in, and I went home.

When I got in, the house was empty as Margaret had gone out with the children. I sat on the settee and turned on the TV but, after four pints, I was asleep in seconds and I knew nothing until sometime later I heard the doorbell ring. I managed to open my eyes, answer the door and there was Frank. After a few more pints he had left the Bay Horse and come to pick up his van but my Land Rover was blocking him in.

'Can you move the Land Rover and let me out?' he asked.

'Yeah, no problem,' I replied. I grabbed my keys, climbed into the Land Rover and drew it up, completely forgetting it had no brakes! The next minute, CRASH! It went straight through the beautiful new garage doors that were less than a week old!

I remember sitting in the Land Rover inside the garage, looking at the doors lying across the bonnet, but the over-riding memory is Frank's face looking at me. He didn't know how to react; he literally didn't know whether to laugh or cry. He wanted to laugh but also realised the seriousness of the situation and didn't want to upset me.

It's ironic that the landlord of the Bay Horse, Graham Beeby, who was later to ban Frank from the pub, was also to become his father-in-law as Frank married Graham's daughter Maxine – and they are still together today.

Frank used to arrive at my house each morning at around 7.30am, about the same time as the postman. I always liked to read the mail before I left in case there was anything that needed attending to. One morning Frank arrived before the postman and, as he always walked to my house,

I asked him if he had seen the postman anywhere.

'No,' replied Frank. 'But to be honest I don't know him.'

Now I'm not being clever, but I didn't realise that you had to know the man to know that he was a postman. I thought maybe the uniform, the bag on his back and the fact that he was pushing letters through letterboxes may have been enough of a clue.

In the early days, when Graham first moved into the Bay Horse his dad, old Mr Beeby, used to stand near the bar every night in his flat cap and talk to the locals. One of them was a lad I used to know called Bill Harris, a young man in his thirties. He was a very likeable chap. One night I went in and old Mr Beeby said to me, 'Have you heard about Bill Harris?'

'No,' I replied. 'What about him?'

'He's dead' he said. I was shocked and he continued. 'They took him into hospital at six o'clock last night and he was dead by eight.'

'That's terrible,' I said. 'What did they take him into hospital with?'

'I don't know,' he said. 'But it were nowt serious.' Well, thank God for that!

Now that I was in business on my own I needed an accountant to help with my tax affairs; the obvious choice was John Goulding & Co, St Thomas's Road, Chorley, as they were accountants for the farm. We had dealt with them for many years and they held our account in high esteem, so I was convinced that they would welcome me with open arms as I would be a young and new account for them. Unfortunately, they didn't seem to see it that way; I was placed in the hands of one of the partners, Donald West, and it soon became clear that the only reason that they had taken on my account was because of who my dad was. They didn't want such a small account. I was probably more trouble to them than I was worth but I didn't realise this and, as time went on, the minutes that he afforded me on each visit became shorter and shorter until it reached the ridiculous situation where he conducted our entire meeting in the hallway. The final insult was the day I went to see Donald West and he held the meeting on the outside step while I stood on the tarmac looking up at him. When we had finished I walked away and, as he shut the door, I thought, 'I need to find another accountant,' which was probably going through his mind too.

I did find another accountant, Paul Rotherham from Preston, and he wrote to Gouldings to tell them of my plans. I will always remember their reply. They acknowledged receipt of Paul Rotherham's letter that I would be moving my account and put in block capitals: 'OBVIOUSLY WE HAVE NO OBJECTIONS WHATSOEVER.'

I think maybe my suspicions were well founded. I believe Donald West later suffered from dementia and, I must admit, I found it hard to feel sorry.

LODGERS

During these years, Margaret had an Aunty Doris who lived at Clayton Green. She lived in a very nice semi-detached house near The Halfway House. To Aunty Doris, money was everything. She certainly wasn't short but in order to make more, she used to do bed and breakfast. Although I am confident that the accommodation was spotless, I doubt whether any guest ever gained weight while they were there.

Anyway, if she couldn't accommodate someone she would phone Margaret and ask if we could put them up. That was actually very kind of her, and Margaret was only too happy to take them in as the money was very useful to us. If I remember correctly, she charged £6 per night, which was good money for us at the time and very welcome.

One day Aunty Doris rang and asked if we could take a young German boy for three nights while he looked for something permanent. He was twenty years old and in England to study at Runshaw College.

'Yes,' said Margaret. 'That would be fine.'

So Aunty Doris drove up to our house in her car while the German boy followed behind in his. When they arrived, she came in with him and introduced him to us. His name was Egon Schwebig.

Rather than stay with us for the three nights, he actually ended up staying for over a year and became one of the family. When he returned to Germany he kept in touch and sent other students to stay with us, which helped their English (he was an English teacher by now) and also helped our finances, so everybody won. We still keep in touch today and Margaret is godmother to Egon's eldest child, Maximilian. Egon is married to Petra and they also have a daughter, Christina.

When he stayed with us, Egon would quite often sit and talk to other paying guests. I remember, with part hilarity and part horror, when one night we had some other German guests staying who didn't speak English. Egon was a godsend. We didn't have a strict tariff and we used to ask for what we thought we could get. Egon was aware of this, so he was chatting to the people and also weighing them up to help us decide what to charge.

They were sitting in the lounge when Margaret came in and Egon said to her, 'They are stupid. Charge them as much as you like,' but forgot to change his language back to English and said it in German! Oops!

Many years later, Margaret and I were visiting Egon's family at their home in a place called Burgh in what was then East Germany, around twenty miles from the Polish border. We had been out with them this particular day and were due to fly home the day after, so when we got back to their village I asked Egon to drop me off at a bar about a mile from their house.

Egon walked into the bar with me and gave the barman his telephone number so that when I was ready to head back the barman could ring Egon and he would come to pick me up. Egon knew that at the time I was drinking Jack Daniels and Coke and in Germany (as in many other countries), you don't pay for each drink as you go but you build up a tab and pay at the end.

As he was leaving, Egon looked at the part-filled bottle of Jack Daniels behind the bar and told me to take note of my bill as these people often put drinks on for themselves. There was an international football match on TV so I sat on my own, enjoying a drink and watching the football. The barman kept an eye on me and filled up my glass whenever I was ready, until eventually I asked him to ring Egon.

When Egon arrived, the barman was just giving me the bill. He looked at the bill and shook his head; I think Egon said it had come to about 120 Euros. That couldn't be right; not enough whisky had gone out of the bottle to come to that much! The barman replied that it was not the same bottle and that I was onto my second. Egon shook his head in embarrassment. 'Pay the man,' he said.

Trenching

It was in the 1970s. We were living at Stonyhurst, my landscaping business was providing us with quite a decent living and I now employed three or four men. Work was pretty constant; as a family, we weren't catching any harm but, as with the milk round, I realised that there was not a fortune to be made. Also like the milk round, I didn't see gardening as my job for life. If I was to make any serious money I needed something else, but what?

Landscaping was only a stepping stone – but for what? As I said earlier, I am a great believer in fate and I always felt confident that something would turn up. Also, as I wasn't a qualified gardener, I spent most of my working life bluffing my way through. I didn't like that. The majority of jobs that we could make good money from – turfing, seeding, fencing, flagging etc. – were all jobs that you could get stuck into, get finished and move on to the next.

But one thing that wasn't easy to make good money on was garden drainage. Yes, the job itself was easy enough but what you could reasonably ask people to pay didn't leave a lot of profit because it was slow work. I discussed this with my brother-in-law, Norman Thistlethwaite, who suggested that I buy a small trenching machine. I didn't know such things existed but we agreed that we would go to the dealer in Uttoxeter to look at one. The rotavator and the trencher, minor as they were, were two purchases that were to eventually change not only my business but my life and my family's lives too. There were to be more of these decisions in years to come.

Again, as I knew being a milkman all my life was not my destiny, being a gardener all my life wasn't going to be my destiny either.

Norman and I went to Uttoxeter to a company called Trenchex on Dove Fields Industrial Park and they had a little Davis 500 trenching machine for sale for £1,200. It was only a small machine, which is just what I wanted for getting into back gardens through narrow paths and back gates. We did the deal with the Trenchex rep, a lad called Eddie Wieldon, but when the bill came I had a shock as it was for £1,320. I rang Trenchex to ask why this was, only to be told that the additional £120 was VAT.

VAT had only just been introduced to replace purchase tax and I wasn't registered. This bill was what prompted me to become VAT registered and in the process to break a British record. I became the first person in Britain to be fined for sending in a late VAT return – so no surprise there then!

The VAT Office must have thought that I was a total dipstick as, when you apply to register, they send you the relevant forms and enclose a dummy VAT return with fictitious figures and details to let you see what your completed form should look like. Would you believe the fictitious name on the fictitious form was Charles Frederick Smith? I couldn't help wondering if they thought I'd copied their dummy name down?!

The little Davis trencher was fine and did its job, meaning that digging a drainage trench now took a fraction of the time and we therefore realised a decent profit. The only problem was that not enough gardens needed to be drained to keep it going, so I put an advert in the *Farmers Guardian* in the hope of getting more work. The advertisement worked well and more jobs started to come in – but this brought its own problems. Obviously, draining a farmer's field was a much bigger job than draining someone's back garden and it soon became apparent that my little Davis 500, whilst fine for draining gardens, did not cut the mustard when it came to draining a twenty-acre field. So, where did we go from there? Well, it was obvious that a bigger machine was needed.

By this time I had heard of another trencher dealer much nearer to home at Tarporley in Cheshire, so Norman and I set off to pay them a visit. It was a company called MK Dynamics, MK being the initials of the owner, Michael Kukla. MK Dynamics was a very appropriate name for the company as Michael was a very dynamic person. He was only twenty-six years old at the time and I think the description 'whizz kid' fitted him to a tee. He was somewhere between Del Boy and Arthur Daley, a real high flyer and go-getter, and his premises were also out of this world: a large office complex and workshop set in the Cheshire countryside. Apart from his red BMW, he also drove a fantastic Aston Martin, which someone said he had bought from Elton John's manager. Maybe, maybe not – who knows? He was the kind of person who, when he could sense a deal was in the air, refused to miss it no matter what.

The trenchers were called Ditch Witch and were made in America. On the first day we met Michael there was an American fellow over called Gene Brigge, who was a very likeable chap and a director of the American firm. The first thing that Michael Kukla said after introducing us to Gene Brigge was, 'Jump into the BMW, I'll take you out for lunch.' So, off we went to a lovely country pub.

After the meal, we started to talk business. I had already made my mind up that if we did a deal, the Ditch Witch R65 model was the one that I would go for. It was the biggest one they made and looked capable of any job that I would need it for. It looked like a machine that you could have confidence in. The only doubt in my mind was that it was on wheels, not tracks, and a lot of the work would be on wet ground. I was assured, however, that as it was a four-wheel drive this was not a problem and that no Ditch Witch owners had ever complained. This went some way to putting my mind at rest. Note I said 'some way', as it did not entirely reassure me.

Back in the pub it was time to talk business and my intention was to trade the Davis in against the Ditch Witch. I can still see Michael, a very self-confident young man, sitting with his legs crossed and constantly smoking, as almost everyone did in those days.

'Alright Fred,' he said looking directly at me. 'How much did you pay for your Davis 500?'

'£1,200,' I said.

'And how much do you want for it?' he asked.

This question rather took me by surprise, as salesmen don't normally ask you to name your price, so I thought I'd be cheeky; you can always come down but you never go up. '£1,200,' I said, expecting an outburst of laughter.

'I'll give you £1,500 and a free week in America to visit the factory.'

Suffice to say, we did the deal there and then and I became the proud owner of a Ditch Witch R65 but I never got the trip to America as the R65 turned into a nightmare.

My original fears about rubber tyres proved true. I don't think I ever did a job where I didn't get stuck and when the client is watching this can be very embarrassing, not to mention costly. So, my perfect relationship with Ditch Witch didn't last very long. I later learned that Michael Kukla was being financed by a wealthy local but things didn't go well and MK Dynamics went bust.

By that point, however, I had realised that there was a living to be made with a trenching machine not just by digging trenches but by the work associated with trenches, i.e. water, gas, electricity, etc. I decided that I must persevere with trenchers and exploit the doors that one could open, so I swallowed my pride and went back to Trenchex in Uttoxeter after having told them that I was getting rid of the Davis and going for a far superior machine. Swallowing my pride comes easily to me and is no big deal. I purchased a Davis 1000 for £8,900, which was then an enormous sum of money bearing in mind a new semi-detached house was around £3,000 at that time.

I couldn't afford to pay for it outright so I put down a deposit (I can't remember how much) and bought the machine on finance from a company called Forward Trust. I remember telling John Young, my bank manager at the RBS (or whatever it was called in those days) how much I'd paid for it, and he almost collapsed. I will always remember his comments, and even today Margaret sometimes reminds me of what he said: 'If you ever pay for this machine in full, I'll consider you a financial genius!'

I don't think that this was meant as a compliment, more as an expression of his concern. The monthly repayments were £247, while the mortgage on Stonyhurst, a beautiful house in its own grounds was only £65 per month.

Not only did I pay for it, I also bought another slightly smaller trencher for £7,700 and paid for that as well. By the time I'd paid for them, John Young had moved to another branch and I never saw him again so unfortunately I never got to hear him refer to me as a 'financial genius'!

On the day that I made the last payment, Margaret and I took my mother, Aunty Jenny and Uncle Bernard out for a meal to celebrate. We went to the Blue Anchor at Wesham, which is now a residential development. It was a memorable night and I felt like enormous weights around my neck had been removed. I looked forward to keeping some of the money that the machines were making instead of handing it all over to Forward Trust.

The Davis 1000 trenching machine was the only one in the area. In fact, I didn't know anyone else that had one and (what was even better) customers thought that it was something special and were willing to pay over-the-top hire rates for it. They thought it could outperform the usual excavators. In fact it couldn't, but we didn't worry about that. I also started to get a lot of hire business from Lancashire County Council to work alongside their own staff.

Although I was only on an hourly rate, because of the regular tea breaks and restricted hours on motorways for the council workers I was getting paid for eight hours but only working for about three as the men didn't want me to get too far ahead of them when they were laying the cable in the trench behind me.

One job that I did for Lancashire County Council was on the M58, to assist the council in planting trees. The manager said that a shallow trench would be better than digging holes because when the trench was backfilled, the air would filter through the trench and allow the saplings to breathe. That was his theory and I found no reason to argue; he only wanted the trench to be eight inches deep, a trencher driver's dream and money for old rope, but at the same time we were doing a good job for Lancashire County Council. Ironically, the two bosses in charge of the job were Mr Oaks and Mr Birch, two good names to be in charge of a tree-planting job.

One man from LCC who was delegated to oversee our work was a chap named Sam Pickford. Sam was a likeable guy but made a lot of noise. He talked very loudly and was, as they say, 'full of himself'. He liked to throw his weight about and show his authority.

One day we were measuring the length of a cable trench using a trumeter measuring wheel that you pushed along the ground so that I could submit an invoice. We were walking along the road parallel to the trench when we came up to a big wagon parked on the road. Sam continued to walk along the road on the inside of the wagon but I deliberately walked round the outside of it to fiddle a few extra metres. As I got to the front of the wagon, Sam realised what I was doing and told me in his very loud voice to get back and measure it on the inside.

I turned round and went back but didn't switch the wheel off – and I measured all the way back as well. Thanks to Sam, I'd fiddled twice as many metres as I'd set out to do. 'Don't try pulling a stunt like that with me again,' Sam said proudly.

'Sorry, Sam,' I replied.

CARMEN'S PONY

IN THE EARLY 1970s, Carmen had developed a love of horses and one Christmas our Roy bought a pony as a present for her and my two nieces, Debbie and Carol, to share. We had no idea that he was going to do that. On Christmas Day we went to visit my mother at Blindhurst. Roy got us all to congregate in the yard then went into the shippon and came out with this little pony. I will never forget Carmen's reaction – it was not hysterical screaming, it was more staring in disbelief, almost ecstasy. I just gazed at Carmen; I knew how much she had always wanted one. The pony's name was Reno.

Carmen loved Reno and spent a lot of time with him but eventually she needed to move on to a more experienced pony, which we acquired for her. I can't remember its name but we decided that it should be kept at Manor House Farm. This meant that every time Carmen wanted to ride her pony, she had to get the bus at The Ridgeway, Adlington, and travel to The Pines, Clayton Green. She was only about ten years old at the time and Margaret and I were a bit uncomfortable with this, especially as she had to carry all her kit with her.

At this time, Margaret's dad was selling Town House Farm in two lots. Lot 1 was the house and buildings and a four-acre field, and Lot 2 was about forty acres of land. I was interested in the first lot, mainly for the pony. However, I was anxious not to overstretch myself financially, as the previous years had been difficult. I was now getting on my feet and didn't want to put myself back to being financially stretched again. So, it required some serious thought.

Eventually I decided to bid, partly because of Carmen and her pony and partly because the boys were keen for me to have a go. In advance of the auction, potential buyers were allowed to put offers in. I remember my father-in-law ringing me a day or two before the auction and saying, in a very matter-of-fact way, 'Right Fred, can you come up with £54,000? If you can, the farm is yours.'

Now, you might assume from that, that he had been made an offer of £54,000 and if we could match it he would sell the farm to us. In actual fact, the best offer he'd had was £44,000 and he was trying to get an extra £10,000 out of us! I went to the auction later and bought it for £44,000.

The year was 1978. Although we loved Stonyhurst and never wanted to leave, I knew that long term this was the right move. All credit to Margaret; even though she loved Stonyhurst perhaps even more that I did, she didn't complain and just looked forward, not back. For the next three years we lived in a caravan until we could raise the money to renovate the house.

As is commonplace in contracting, work can either be a famine or a feast. Eventually, although I still had some landscaping work, the trenching work dried up. I desperately needed to keep the trenchers working so I could meet the monthly payments.

I remember sitting in the dining room at Stonyhurst (which doubled as my office) one day. It was pouring with rain and I was sitting there, staring at the rain through the window, wondering how I could drum up some work for the trencher, when I suddenly remembered being at an open day for Ditchwitch trenchers. I'd begun talking to one of the staff who had asked me, 'Do you ever do any work for Cohen brothers?'

'I have never heard of them,' I'd said. 'Where are they from?'

'Preston,' he replied. 'They are quite a big street lighting company.'

I found their number and rang them. I asked to be put through to the contracts manager who was a Mr Northwood. The girl put me through and I remember vividly the opening lines. 'Can I help you?' Mr Northwood said.

'Yes,' I replied. 'My name is Fred Smith and I have got a Davis trencher.'

'So have we,' he replied. 'And I don't want another.'

He was about to put the phone down when I said, 'I am not trying to sell it, I'm looking for hire.'

'Oh,' he said. 'That's different.' We had a long discussion and he arranged for me to go to their offices and meet one of the directors, Mr David Linnington. I duly went a couple of days later and had a very productive meeting with him, which started what was to become a very long, happy and successful working relationship for both parties. I often think about how close Mr Northwood was to putting the phone down, and how all the incredible things that that phone call led to would never have happened if he had.

By now, I had about six men working for me and Cohen's became our biggest client. Whenever they won a street-lighting contract they always sub-contracted the trenching and cable laying to me. I realised that the landscape gardening part of the business would have to go as trenching and cabling were much more lucrative. Also, that is where most of my investment was tied up, so it made sense to concentrate on that side of the business.

One contract that we did for Cohen's was the Queensferry Flyover in North Wales. As you can imagine, it involved a lot of driving each day and I only had one man working with me, a lad named James Collins of Highways Hostel fame.

It was summer. The weather was warm and the nights were light, so we decided we would work till dark and sleep on site, ready to start early the following morning. That meant we could be working instead of travelling. We had got to know the night watchman very well so he let us use the facilities in the offices.

We worked every night till eleven, just in time to catch the local chip shop before it shut, then went to the offices to eat. After we had eaten, we lay on one of the office floors and went to sleep. We had no blankets or pillows, just floorboards.

One night, at around two o'clock in the morning, I heard James moving around. What the hell was he doing? I sat up and asked him what he was up to.

'It's too draughty down there,' he said. Then I saw him lying on the top of the manager's desk using a bundle of papers for a pillow. We did that for several weeks.

In the following years, although we continued to work for lots of other clients, Cohen's were by far our biggest and we formed a good working relationship with their staff on site. Two of them were Bill Roberts and Bert Perry, both Scousers, both electricians and both good mates. One summer, Bert's wife decided that he needed to lose some weight so she put him on a strict diet, cutting down on everything, and packing him a much-reduced lunch to bring to work.

I can recall one day he was telling Bill how hungry he was. It was eleven in the morning and Bert couldn't wait till lunchtime but he didn't want to eat any of his lunch or there would be nothing left. Billy said, 'Have a couple of my sandwiches, my wife always packs too much.'

'Are you sure?' asked Bert.

'Yeah, get what you want,' said Billy, and Bert gratefully did, as he did again the following day and the next and the next, sometimes also taking a cake or a couple of biscuits. This went on for weeks and one day Billy said to me, 'Bert's been on a diet for six weeks and lost nothing. I've not been on a diet but I've lost eight pounds.'

Bert was a street-lighting boffin through and through. It was a bit like farming was to my dad; it was his life, and no one knew more about street lighting than Bert. Within the industry, a lamp post is always referred to as a lighting column. One day Bert asked me if we were going away that year.

'Yes' I said 'We are going to see friends in Germany.'

'Beautiful country,' he replied. I thought he was going to describe it to me and tell me where to visit when he said, 'I spent two years in Germany and never saw one rusty column.' To Bert, that made it a beautiful country. Well, what more do you need?

One job we did for Cohen's was to cable the central reservation of the M62 in the Irwell Valley, otherwise known as Death Valley. Both fast lanes were coned off for us to work in and there was a mobile cabin for us to use as a canteen. Because the two fast lanes were closed, traffic in the remaining two lanes moved very slowly and we used to watch the vehicles crawl past as we ate our lunch to see if we could spot any familiar faces.

One day, as we sat eating our lunch and gazing through the window, we suddenly realised that we were keeping up with the traffic. 'We're moving!' shouted one lad. The next minute, ten of us were crowding through the door all at once, with chips and pies flying in all directions. Then we stood and watched the canteen roll down the M62. Unknown to us one lad from another firm, not realising we were inside, had reversed up to the cabin with the tractor, hooked up and was moving it down site. There were hundreds of motorists having a good laugh at our expense!

One year Cohen's got the contract to install cable and columns on the A627M, the motorway that links Rochdale to Oldham. It was a good job, as the embankments where we were working were very sandy, meaning trenching was fast and easy. This meant I could make good money – better than when the ground was rocky and therefore progress was slow.

One day we dug a very long length of trench out and didn't manage to get the cable in, as the police don't like you to work after five o'clock when everyone is driving home from work and the motorway is busy. That meant the trench remained open all night. The following morning a lot of it had filled up with water, which had to be pumped out.

It never ceases to amaze me all the things that you find on the hard shoulder – things that you would never expect. That particular morning, as I was walking along the hard shoulder, I found a large fresh salmon. It was a beauty. Don't ask me how it got there as I have no idea. However, I then noticed three of Cohen's lads walking towards me a few hundred yards away, so I picked up the salmon and dropped it into the muddy water in the trench. I got down on my knees, put my arms in the water and pretended to be battling with it.

By this time the Cohen's lads had reached me. 'What are you doing?' asked Dave Barnes.

'Trying to catch salmon,' I replied, then just as the ridicule started to fly, I flipped it out of the muddy water, caught it, pretended to struggle with it then bashed its head on the ground. 'There. Got the bugger!' I said.

They all stood in amazement, with blank expressions, and then the inevitable happened. One of the lads, Frank Ledley, gave his version of how it got there. 'I saw a seagull flying over with it in its mouth then I saw it drop it right in the trench.'

Sorry, Frank, no you didn't! That was a lie, and anyway a two-ounce seagull can't carry a six-pound salmon.

Another job we did for Cohen's was on the A59 at Samlesbury on the dual carriageway heading towards the M6. On the day in question, there were only two of us on site – James Collins and me. It was a Bank Holiday Monday and not really a working day but I wanted to get the job finished so James and I went out. I was driving the trencher and James was working as a banksman further down the site. When it got towards one o'clock, I decided we should stop for lunch so I beckoned James to come up.

By now, the traffic had ground to a halt and, as it was a very hot day, all the motorists were sitting in their cars with the windows open. James was walking past all the families and, as he got closer, I could see he was carrying something in his hand, something that he had found in the grass. And as he got even closer, I didn't like the look of it.

You won't know this, but James has five daughters. When he got up to me I said, 'What are you doing with that?'

'I'm taking it home for the girls to play with,' he said.

It was a ten-inch vibrator! 'Do you know what it is?'

'Yes,' he replied 'It's a *Star Wars* gun.'

'No it isn't, James. And please don't take it home for your daughters.'

In the years that I worked for Cohen's, as well as being friendly with the lads on site I also got very friendly with the two bosses, George Northwood, Contracts Manager (who took my very first phone call) and David Linnington, the director. Things ticked along very nicely. In fact we sometimes went out socially and I was always invited to Cohen's Christmas parties and other gatherings.

But, as with the milk round and the landscape gardening, I always knew that being a subcontractor would only be a stepping-stone – not the end product. Again, I got the urge to crank my business up a gear, but how? Well, as I said before, opportunities do present themselves and one certainly did for me, from a most unexpected source.

One day I went to Cohen's depot in St Mary's Street, Preston, to be told that the three Cohen brothers from Manchester had sold the street-lighting department (in other words, the Preston branch I worked for) to a multi-national company, BKI. BKI were already big in the street-lighting sector and everyone suspected that the only reason they bought Cohen's was to close it down and eliminate a competitor. Everyone decided they would have to look for another job and that is how it turned out. BKI did keep the company going for a short time under the name of BKI Translight, but all the confidence had gone and the men were unsettled and gradually found new jobs. In theory that meant I was going to lose my best customer but, if I played my cards right, this could be my golden opportunity to take the business to a new level.

I decided to speak to George Northwood, as he was the man responsible for tendering and winning all the Cohen's contracts. He was well respected by the workforce and clients alike and had years of experience of building up contacts. My plan was that, with him in the office tendering and me running things on site, we would make a formidable team. Also, he would bring all of his Cohen's contacts with him, not forgetting that I had also built up a large number of clients in addition to Cohen's, so we had a good reputation already in place.

At that time I ran the business from home, home being Town House Farm, which was not ideal but adequate. I rang George to arrange a meeting and found that he had been thinking along the same lines, so a deal was done and we agreed terms. He accepted that I couldn't pay him a massive salary but, as he was likely to be made redundant anyway, he had nothing to lose. We agreed that I would pay him the salary that he had been on with Cohen's, which was £8,500 plus company car. I think the year was 1981 so it was a decent rate, and there was the understanding that if the company prospered so would he.

During the years that I worked for Cohen's, George and I got on fine. However, when he came to work for me, it became obvious from day one that this would not be an easy relationship. In fact it was anything but. For a start, he was very moody. You never knew from one day to the next what sort of mood he would be in. On the days when he was in a good mood everything was fine and nothing was too much trouble, but on the days when he was in a bad mood he was nasty and nothing was going to alter that. Meanwhile, his former boss, David Linnington, had started his own street-lighting company. Margaret and I couldn't initially understand why he didn't offer George a job – but it was beginning to dawn on us. Maybe he'd had enough of George's moods.

In fairness, George did bring some work in, some of which was quite profitable like the job we did for a Norwegian company, Norse Marconi, at Blackpool Airport. It was these profitable jobs that persuaded me to keep going with him and tolerate his moods. Our contact at Norse Marconi was an old friend of George's from his Cohen days, a German chap called Heinz Mayner, who was a real character and a good asset for our company. He was an ex-German prisoner of war who had married an English girl and stayed over here.

One day he rang to say that he had the chance to supply a large amount of runway lighting equipment to Stansted Airport and asked if we would put in a price to install it. Of course, the answer was yes. Arrangements were made to go to London, carry out a survey and tender a price. George said that it would take three days to survey the site and do the maths, so the airport manager, John Rigby, allocated us a vacant office and we booked in at a local hotel. George, in fairness, got his head down and with his calculator (a new thing in those days) spent three days working out the price. When he had finished, he put the tender in his briefcase and off we went to see John Rigby. The price that George had come up with was £27,000.

I discussed with George whether we should play around with the price, put it on to knock it off, in the hope that we might not have to. It was a common procedure but George was adamant that this was as much as we could hope for. It doesn't seem a lot today but it was thirty-five years ago. I hadn't worked on the price, as airport lighting was completely foreign to me so George had done it all. In fact, I just hung around for three days and didn't actually need to be there.

In the three days we spent at the airport, I got on well with John Rigby; I kept him well-fed and well-watered, if you know when I mean, so I knew he was a man that I could deal with. I also knew that he would – and could – be bartered with.

We went into his office and sat down. John said, 'Well? What's your price?'

Before George had chance to open his briefcase, I asked, 'How much can you afford? How much have you allocated?' They were questions that I shouldn't really have asked but, after having had a couple of nights out with him, I knew how far I could go.

'Tell me your price,' he demanded.

'£40,000,' I replied.

'Too much,' he said.

'By how far?' I asked.

'A couple of thousand,' he said. We shook hands at £38,000 and he never saw George's quotation.

In a way I felt sorry for George, as he had spent three days carefully working out his prices and he didn't even open his briefcase. Also, he didn't show any pleasure that I'd gained another £11,000 for the company. I think he resented the fact that I'd achieved more in ten seconds that he had achieved in three days. Maybe he felt belittled. He certainly didn't congratulate me. It was a quiet drive home and I wondered if perhaps another mood was coming. But on that occasion, I couldn't care less. Maybe my three days hanging about were well spent after all.

I gradually realised that when George came to work, his main priority was to get the day over with and get back home. He was obsessed with getting home early and never missed a chance to take someone out to lunch. He loved it. He also tried to water things down by talking in clichés. For instance, he never said that he was taking anyone out for lunch, he was taking them for a 'beer and a butty' or 'a pie and a pint'. He was never on his way anywhere, he was always 'betwixt and between', and he never said he was going home, rather he was 'heading south'. If he decided he didn't want to get involved with anything, he wouldn't – that was it, end of story.

One occasion that I remember vividly was a large job that we had done round the junction of the M6 and M63 (now the M60). When the work was completed, it was time for the measure to enable us to send in the invoice. I told George to go out and measure it up on site but he insisted that he could measure it equally well from the drawings. He laid the drawings out and measured everything, then priced up the materials, always finishing in time to 'head south' by three o'clock. On the day that he completed the measure, he came into my office and proudly showed me the invoice that was ready to be sent to the client. It was for £47,000. He put it on my desk and 'headed south'.

The following day, without telling George, I told Steve Leighton, the foreman on the job, to do a measure on site and then do 'his' invoice, which he handed to me the day afterwards. It was for £63,000. George had been prepared to sacrifice £16,000 rather than spend time on site and perhaps not get home as early as he liked. It was now clear to me beyond doubt that he had to go – but there were a few contracts that needed tidying up that only he could do. I decided that I would hold back and pick the time that would be most beneficial to me. However, one day he was in a particularly bad mood and I had to go to a meeting at eleven o'clock. The meeting lasted about three hours and I was on the way back to the office by about 2.30pm. I knew that by three o'clock he would be going home, and I had had enough of his unpleasantness for one day.

I parked up at the motorway service station and read the paper for half an hour to give him time to leave the office before I went back. It was whilst I was reading the paper that I thought, 'This is ridiculous. What am I doing this for? You can't run a business like this. He has to go and go now.' That night I told Margaret and she was in full agreement, as he was by then nothing but a liability.

I decided that I would meet him first thing the following morning and do the deed, no matter what the consequences. Nothing could have been worse than the last few months. Also, the workforce had started to notice the bad feeling between us and that was not good.

At around nine o'clock that night, the house phone rang and I answered it. The voice on the other end was George's. 'Hi, Fred,' he said in a very friendly voice that took me completely by surprise. 'George here. I'm ringing to tell you that I've got another job. No hard feelings. I just feel that it's time to move on. I will be in tomorrow to clear my desk and maybe you fancy a pie and a pint? This time it's on me.'

What a result! I almost punched the air. Thank God he was gone. I may have had a pie and a pint with him (I don't remember) but we parted on good terms, at least on the surface, so I hadn't burned my bridges if I needed any information from him.

I was now back to running the business how I wanted it run it without his constant criticism. Although I had lost my most qualified engineer, I had by now employed other electricians who could do the job. I felt liberated.

We were doing a lot of work for local councils – Lancashire County Council, West Lancashire County Council and Chorley Borough Council – but far and away our biggest client was Greater Manchester Council, who booked us to work on the Manchester motorway network. The lighting superintendent at County Hall was a man named Jack Thompson. I hadn't met Jack as I always dealt with his second in command, Harry Holcroft, a man in his sixties with whom I got on very well (and looked after).

One day Harry told me that there was a column (lamp post) painting contract to be put out for tender and he thought that I should price for it. I applied for the bill of quantities and duly submitted my price. A week or so later, I received word that my tender had been successful (how I used to love those phone calls) and asking me to arrange a meeting with Jack Thompson at County Hall to go through the details of carrying out the contract. At this point I had never met Jack Thompson but his reputation went before him; he was a hard taskmaster who loved to humiliate his subordinates, and you would cross him at your peril.

The night before the meeting Margaret, who at that time was a district nurse, suggested that as I didn't possess a briefcase I should take hers. It would look more professional than the plastic bag that I usually used. So I did. It was a very hot day when I went to County Hall and on arrival I was escorted to Mr Thompson's office on the seventh floor, where I was introduced to him and two of his young engineers, Peter Odlin and Ron Atkins, who would be supervising the contract.

The office ceiling was made of glass and the sun was shining through very strongly, which I hate. We spent the first twenty minutes or so making small talk, as you do, when I did my best to impress them with my professionalism. Then it was time to get down to business. Ron Atkins laid the drawings out with all the specifications and so on, and I put my briefcase on the desk to get out the prices that were inside. Then the worst thing possible happened – I couldn't open it! There was a hidden button that released it, but where was it? No matter what I did, I couldn't open it. All the while, the three of them looked on in silence. Then the inevitable happened and I started to sweat. It was due to the heat coming through the ceiling, mixed with the embarrassment I was feeling. I was sweating buckets but still getting no nearer to opening the briefcase and the more I panicked, the more I sweat.

Luckily for me, a girl came in with cups of tea. Her mother had a case just like it and, hey presto, the case opened! In later years I became good friends with Ron and Pete and that briefcase episode always came up after a few pints!

Throughout all my years of street lighting, the premier lighting company was David Webster of London, or DW as they were usually referred to. They were London based but had offices throughout Britain and you couldn't travel very far without seeing their vans or wagons with their distinctive livery. But as the years went by, I started to win contracts that they expected to win and the gap between our two companies narrowed, until by the time we sold out to McAlpines we were much closer in terms of turnover and profit.

One day, shortly after the takeover, Graham Northrop rang me to ask if I would accompany him to London to meet DW's chief executive with a view to one or two joint ventures. I agreed.

The following morning, I met Graham at five o'clock at the Barton Depot and we set off for London. When we arrived, we were shown to the chief executive's office and we introduced ourselves. Graham and the chief executive started to talk business but the chief executive was very dour and did not contribute much. I had never met him before so I didn't know if this was the norm for him.

Eventually he looked at me and said to Graham, 'I'm sorry if I'm not being very helpful but I just see that man as the enemy.'

I couldn't believe what I was hearing. The chief exec of DW saw me as the enemy! How good was that? He made my day. I don't think any work came out of the meeting but hey, what the hell, I had unknowingly been a worry to David Webster's.

Another contractor who had tendered for the GMC work was York Lighting from Yorkshire who, apparently, were very keen to win it and not happy that this new kid on the block won it. I was told by various GMC engineers that he was parking up on motorway bridges spying on us and getting on the phone to County Hall, pretending to be a member of the public if he saw us commit any (in his opinion) misdemeanour. The people he spoke to knew it was him phoning and let me know, so it actually did him more harm than it did me.

In contracting, sometimes the council will pay what is known as 'rained-off rates', meaning that if the work is halted because of inclement weather they will pay you a reduced rate while you are stopped. Because of the nature of the painting contract, rained-off rates did not apply. In other words 'it's raining, so hard luck' – and no pay. Of course, I didn't pass this on to the lads; I paid them just the same even though Fred Smith Street Lighting was not getting paid.

One day we were working on the fast lane of the M62 at Rocking Stone Moss, which is the long uphill length past Rochdale and the border between Manchester and Yorkshire. I had three hydraulic-platform wagons working with two men on each wagon, me being one of them. The rain was torrential and we sat in the cabs until the motorway police came and said that we would have to pull off and they would remove the traffic cones, as we were making road conditions very dangerous. It was about eleven o'clock, so we agreed that if it brightened up in the afternoon we could go back and salvage part of the day. We took the wagons off the motorway and went to Milnrow Motorway Maintenance Depot to kill an hour or two, read the paper etc., and see if the weather cleared up. As well as us, there were also a dozen or so council workers in the Milnrow Depot. By now most of my lads and the council lads knew each other and everyone was chatting away.

I was talking to one lad that I didn't know and it soon became apparent that he didn't know me either. I happened to mention that I didn't get paid while we were rained off, to which he replied in a very loud voice that everyone could hear, 'You don't get paid but you can bet that f*****g Fred Smith will be getting paid. You're all out here getting piss wet through while he's sitting in his nice warm office or driving his fancy f*****g Range Rover. While you lads are making him a fortune he's paying you f**k all. You should tell him to f**k off.'

Everyone in the room fell silent, realising that he didn't know that I was Fred Smith. Eventually one of the council men, Peter Morris, said, 'Joe, can I introduce you to Fred Smith?' This was followed by a few seconds of silence, which were then followed by an outburst of uncontrollable laughter!

The painting contract became an annual event and meant painting around 4,000 columns per year. I was to go on and win for the next two years, meaning I won three years in a row until some jobsworth in County Hall said that Fred Smith should not be allowed to keep winning painting contracts as we were not even a painting company. The following year we were not allowed to tender and the contract was subsequently won by a painting firm, which suited the politically correct councillors.

All went well until they were instructed to paint a long length of twelve-metre twin-arm columns. With twin-arm columns, both sides of the fast lanes had to be coned off at a tremendous cost to the council. When the contractors moved onto site, it soon became obvious that while they may have been experienced painters, they were not experienced motorway contractors. They put all their wagons on site and started to paint until they got to the second arm, which was over the other fast lane, and the shocking truth dawned on them – their hydraulic platforms weren't big enough to reach the farthest arm. So what happened then?

It was decided that, after all the columns had been painted, they would move over to the other side of the motorway. All the traffic management would have to be put on again to allow them to move into the other lane and paint the one arm that they had not been able to reach. But what made this whole operation unacceptably expensive was that each arm needed four coats, so it would involve weeks of traffic management. In the end, after much debating between the council and the contractor, it was decided that the end result did not warrant the cost so one arm never got painted on thousands of columns; thousands of twin-arm columns had one arm a different colour to the other arm. Yes, you get what you pay for, although on this occasion Greater Manchester Council didn't get what they'd paid for. That'll teach 'em.

As the man said, motorway contractors are not painters but, as I said, painters are not motorway contractors. Motorway contracting is a strange and specialised line of business.

When we painted the motorway lighting columns, the final coat was known as Battleship Grey. It was a very thick paint, almost like a liquid plastic, which was designed to protect the columns in the most hostile weather conditions.

One of the painting team was a chap who all the lads called Pipi La Pew. Don't ask me why, but that was what he was known as. He drove a little bottle-green minivan of a type that was very popular at the time. Practically all of them were bottle green. He used to drive it into the depot near Barton Bridge and park it up in the same place every day, right outside my office. He would then come into the office to clock in.

One morning, when I happened to be there, he did exactly that. Although his van was parked in full view of the office and I was looking straight at it, he came in the office, said good morning, clocked in, discussed that day's programme and left to get into the wagon and go to the site. He never mentioned the fact that the minivan, that was bottle green the day before, was now Battleship Grey. Also, he never spoke about it to any of the lads and so it became a standing joke that he must have assumed no one had noticed.

There is a massive development at Preston called Red Scar, which in days gone by belonged to a company called Courtaulds. They were textile giants and they had been there for over a hundred years.

At the turn of the twentieth century, all the old concrete columns had been converted from gas to electricity. Around 1980 Courtaulds moved out, and the old Central Lancashire Development took it over and converted it into a business park. We got the order to go and refurbish all the columns, some of which had not been serviced since they were converted from gas. I sent Bert and an assistant to go and do whatever was necessary to bring them up to scratch.

At the same time, I had a painting contract at Lytham and one afternoon I decided to have a ride out to Lytham to see how the lads were doing. As I was on the way, I saw coming towards me in the distance what looked like one of my wagons. It looked like the one that Bert was using and, sure enough, as it got closer I saw Bert behind the wheel. I couldn't get my head round what he was doing in that area when he should have been on the Red Scar Business Park, so the following morning I asked him to explain. It turned out that all the cutouts and fuses (in fact everything inside the columns on B3) were so old that not only did no one stock them, but they had gone out of production years ago. However, Bert had remembered that the lighting columns on Blackpool seafront were the same age and were identical.

So he had gone to Blackpool in his street-lighting wagon, turned on the flashing lights, donned his hi-vis jacket and stripped everything out, then gone to Red Scar and installed it in those columns. 'They're all lit,' he said in his strong Scouse accent. 'You can send your bill in.' He had literally stripped everything from the columns in broad daylight but, because he looked official, no one batted an eyelid.

That night, out of curiosity, I had a ride out to Blackpool – and the entire Golden Mile didn't have one street light lit.

By then Fred Smith Street Lighting was fast becoming Greater Manchester Council's favoured motorway maintenance contractors. I had started to employ a much larger workforce who all got on well with the GMC site lads, as I did with the engineers at County Hall. All was helped, of course, by my legendary corporate hospitality skills (the one thing that I was good at) and many a contract was won with the help of a few large cognacs and a taxi home. County Hall at Minshull Street was becoming almost an extension to my office.

One day I had reason to go to County Hall, which was situated next to the Crown Court. At the time there was a very high-profile court case going on; it was big news, the papers and TV were full of it and security was watertight. No vehicles were allowed in the area so I, along with everyone else, had to park away from the area and walk to my destination. Just as I was walking along Minshull Street towards County Hall, a police car screeched to a halt at the side of me.

There were four police officers inside, two in the front, two in the back. The one nearest to me on the back seat jumped out, obviously in a hurry, and the one in the front passenger side opened his window. I was convinced I was witnessing some incident, something I could tell everyone about when I got back.

As the one in the back leapt out, his colleague in the front said 'Did you get that?'

'Yeah, Sarge, I got it,' said the officer. 'Chips, fish and peas twice, and chips, pudding and peas twice.' He was going to the chippy.

I once invited Peter Odlin out to lunch. His boss objected to young engineers going out for lunch with contractors, but this didn't worry Peter too much. 'I know a place that's out of the way,' he said. 'And he'll never know.' So, Peter directed me to this out of the way place in the middle of nowhere. We walked in and who was the first person we saw? Yes, his boss, but (and again it's a big but) his boss was with a young lady who he definitely should not have been with. So very brief eye contact was made and the event wasn't ever mentioned again, by either party.

In the early eighties, GMC was by far our most valued client and we had formed an excellent working relationship with both the lads on site, managed by Harry Holcroft, and the bosses in County Hall, headed by Ron Atkins and Peter Odlin. We had other good clients too, such as Balfour Kilpatrick, N G Bailey, Lancashire County Council and West Lancashire Council. In addition, my lads were well thought of by clients, which is always good. Quite often, we quoted for a contract that we didn't win which was then awarded to one of our clients who, it must be remembered, were also our competitors. In many cases they would win one of these contracts then find that they were too busy to carry it out, so they rang me and subcontracted it to us, knowing that GMC would be happy with that arrangement. So every time I tendered for a contract I knew that if we didn't win it as the main contractor, I would get a second chance as a subcontractor. Happy days.

THE BULK LAMP CHANGE (BLC) AND GMC

There was, however, one prestigious contract on the Manchester motorway network that had always eluded me, both as a motorway contractor and a subcontractor, and that was a contract known as the Bulk Lamp Change (BLC). This involved changing all the lamps on the motorway columns and carrying out any repairs required, including cleaning the plastic bowls, which as you can imagine got very grimy. This was a contract that had been traditionally won by the big boys, the multinationals; in recent years it had been monopolised by a Yorkshire company named York Lighting, owned by a fellow called Martin Collins, that didn't subcontract as all the work was done by his own labour force.

I remember driving along the motorways and seeing his vehicles in a long line with the men working on the lights, thinking how impressive the whole operation looked and wondering how could I get all those wagons to have my name on the side. It must be remembered that working on live motorways, although a very dangerous way to make a living, is the best shop window in the world. Just about everybody sees you and potential clients are very impressed, as only the best are allowed to carry out motorway maintenance. These motorway contracts were elevating my company better than any advertising could ever do.

Anyway, back to the BLC. Martin Collins coveted this contract and had no intention of letting anyone take it from him. He had won it for about five years in a row and it was coming up for tender again. I don't think he even considered me a threat – how wrong can you be?

By then, I had been working closely with Harry Holcroft for quite a long time and Harry's days were split between Barton Motorway Maintenance Depot and County Hall. Harry knew that I was desperate to win the BLC and I asked if he could get me some inside information, which I assured him would benefit him as well as me. I had no conscience about doing this after the dirty trick that York Lighting had played on me with the painting contract. This seemed to appeal to Harry, so it was time for him to get to work (devious as it was).

One particular day, he timed his visit to County Hall so he'd arrive at lunchtime when the seventh floor (the street lighting floor) would be at its quietest. He knew where all the tender documents were kept, so he casually walked over, pulled York Lighting's Bill of Quantities (i.e. figures) out, took them back to his desk and copied out all the figures in his own handwriting, then returned them to their rightful place in good time before everyone returned from their lunch break.

He then rang me to meet him to look at *some work* on the M62. I agreed to meet him an hour later and we pulled up on the hard shoulder of the off-slip on the Manchester/Yorkshire border, where he handed me a blank writing pad, a pen and the set of figures for me to copy out. I handed him my appreciation envelope. The reason for this was so the figures, should they ever be found, wouldn't be in his handwriting. He told me that Martin Collins traditionally increased his prices by 5% per annum so if I went in at approximately those prices I should win the contract.

That night at home, I went through the rates and decided that I would not go in at those prices but would knock off approximately 5%. This I did, and when the day came for the tenders to be opened at midday I couldn't concentrate on anything else. Peter Odlin had promised to call me whether I'd been successful or not, so I knew I was going to get a call but what would I be told? Also, it must be remembered that other contractors were tendering as well so there was no guarantee. I understand that David Linnington also tendered. The call came at about 3.30pm, and it was Peter. 'Congratulations,' he said. 'You've won the BLC.'

What a relief! This would take my company to a new level. We were now the major motorway lighting company in the North West and we were in the top five in Britain. A large Jack Daniels was in order that night!

Not having done the BLC before, I needed a bit of guidance. Harry had told me that the best material for cleaning the bowls was muslin. I found a place called Adlington Knitting Factory, which I was told sold muslin. I rang them and the man on the phone was very helpful and invited me to go to the factory to meet him, which I duly did. He was very friendly, got someone to bring tea and biscuits and apologised that the managing director wasn't in to meet me. He suggested that, if I wanted, he would arrange a meeting later on in the week.

I must admit this royal treatment took me by surprise, especially when he invited me on a tour of the factory to show me how they operated. Then the truth gradually dawned on me: he assumed (don't ask me why) that I wanted tons of the stuff and he started to talk about discounts and delivery dates. I kept nodding my head, terrified that he would ask me what quantity I required – which thankfully he didn't. I made an excuse to rush off. Just as I was leaving, he got a large plastic bag which he filled with muslin and said, 'Here, take this sample and see what you think.' I walked away with the bag in my hand and a smile on my face – that bagful was all I needed and I never went back.

One man at GMC that I knew well was Mark Brody. After GMC's

abolition he went to work for Thameside Council. Many years later I saw him in a restaurant having lunch with some of his colleagues and, after a chat, he introduced me to his friends. He said, 'I would like you to meet Fred Smith. This is the man that took motorway lighting out of the public sector and into the private sector.' Up until that moment I hadn't realised that I had done that; in reality I hadn't, as it was Margaret Thatcher that did it. Still, it was good to hear. I still see Mark occasionally.

1987 was a memorable year for the company and the changes came from a very unlikely source – Margaret Thatcher, of all people. If winning the BLC elevated Fred Smith Street Lighting, then Margaret Thatcher was to elevate it even further. At that time Ken Livingstone was the leader of what was then the Greater London Council and he was a thorn in Margaret Thatcher's side. So, according to legend, she decided to get rid of him. She abolished four major councils and put them in the hands of private contractors in what was known as PFI, Private Finance Initiative. London was one; I don't remember the other two but Greater Manchester was the fourth.

This meant that all work previously carried out by the council had to be carried out by private contractors. Maintenance of the motorways was an enormous undertaking to companies that had no previous experience. All the companies that were tendering were keen to win, as this was a revolutionary move that could mean millions to private companies. The structure was that one large company would oversee everything and subcontract various aspects to specialised subcontractors. The street lighting and signs, including twenty-four hour accident call-outs, were the biggest single contract of them all.

There was no doubt that my company was in pole position, having been GMC's main subcontractor, so all the main contractors were keen to talk to me. However, that did not guarantee anything and a lot of other street lighting companies were keen to jump on the bandwagon. We all realised that this was the chance of a lifetime and something that had never happened before. No one knew this more than a firm from North Wales called Mews. It was owned by Ray Mews who, although I didn't know it at the time, was always going to be a thorn in my side. In the run up to the tendering date, things started to get tense and the demise of GMC and the privatisation was all that anyone talked about. You have to remember that literally hundreds of people were about to lose their jobs and they needed to know who they could apply to for re-employment. It was a very stressful time, but also a very exciting one for me.

But back to Ray Mews, who was definitely making his presence felt and was making it clear to everyone that he was going to be a serious contender. 'I'm going to be hard to beat,' he said, and over those weeks everyone kept telling me that he was going to be the successful tenderer. In fact, I got fed up of everybody telling me about Mews. It was Mews this, Mews that, Mews everything, until the day arrived when the tenders had to be submitted. So that was that. The tenders were in and nothing could be done except wait until they had been analysed.

We decided that now the tendering was over, Margaret, Carmen and I would have a few days in London while things were quiet. Carmen booked us in at The Goring, a wonderful hotel at the back of Buckingham Palace. This was my opportunity to forget about the contract and most of all to forget about Mews. I said to Margaret and Carmen, 'I don't want to hear the word Mews while I'm away, I just want to forget about him.' I'd heard of nothing else for weeks.

We arrived at about 4pm and had a pleasant evening and a lovely meal in the hotel, then an early night. The following morning I got up early as usual and decided to have a short walk before breakfast. That's when I decided that I must have done something really bad in a previous life and I was now being punished for it. Every street

I walked down had the street name at the end and every one of them ended in 'Mews': Kensington MEWS; Knightsbridge MEWS; Windsor MEWS. Of all the places in Britain we could have gone, we had to pick that area!

Anyway, it seemed certain that Greater Manchester Council was to be abolished on a certain day. As that day approached, I invited Ron Atkins, Pete Odlin and Jack Thompson to lunch at the Piccadilly Hotel, Manchester.

When I was getting ready to go to Manchester to meet them, the inevitable happened – I had put weight on and none of my clothes fitted. There was nothing else for it; I just had enough time to nip into Preston, get a new suit from Halliwells and then make my way to Manchester.

All went well until I got into the centre of Preston and there was a major holdup. Traffic was hardly moving. I did not need delays, I only just had enough time as it was – and to make matters worse, I was not sure where Halliwells was situated. I could see a multi-storey car park quite near to where I was but had no chance of getting there till the traffic started moving. I was beginning to panic and there were no mobile phones in those days to let them know I would be late.

I happened to look to my right and realised that I was sitting right outside Halliwells. I took a risk and rushed into Halliwells with the car outside, engine still running. The first suit that I tried on fit me, so I put the old suit in the bag, paid the man then got back in the car in my new suit just as the traffic was starting to move. I even got to Manchester and the Piccadilly Hotel on time.

It was a cordial lunch (perhaps rather too cordial) but hey – this was the end of GMC, which was something that had played a very large part in all our lives. It all went very well and, as it was reaching its conclusion, I went in search of a public phone to ring for taxis. I was told that there was a phone in the lobby, which was down a small stairway of about four stairs. I went down the stairs and there was the telephone booth in front of me. It had a glass door and I could see the phone inside, but I couldn't work out how to open the door. No matter what I did, the door wouldn't move. I tried everything and was just about to get my fingers under the glass when a member of staff came and asked me what I was doing.

'I'm trying to get in here,' I replied.

'Why are you trying to get in there?' he asked.

'To use the phone,' I said.

'What phone?' he asked.

'That phone,' I said, pointing to it.

'Oh, you mean *that* phone,' he said, pointing in the opposite direction. I turned round to see the phone behind me. The glass door I was trying to open was actually a mirror and I was trying to get into a central heating flue.

Incidentally, on the day the GMC abolition took place the television cameras were at County Hall to film the staff leaving work for the last time. Some had worked there for many years, as often their parents and grandparents had, and many were in tears. But two people who did not expect the cameras were Peter Odlin and Ron Atkins, who were about to go self-employed and start their own consultancy business. They came out of County Hall carrying a desk, which they put into a GMC van to take to their new offices – all while being filmed live on TV.

NUTTALLS

O n our return from London, I received a phone call from Peter Odlin to say that the successful contractor for the overall contract was Nuttalls. With that information, I rang their Wirral offices and arranged a meeting for the following day. Paul Rotherham, our company accountant, came with me although, in truth, that was only for cosmetic purposes to make it look more official.

The two men that we met were Stuart Knutt and Chris Edwards. The former had come from head office in London to work with Chris Edwards in setting up the contract and would then return to head office once the contract was up and running. Chris Edwards would be in charge of the whole operation, which was a two-year contract. The meeting went well and, although Stuart Knutt was giving nothing away, I was getting good vibes from Chris Edwards, who I had never met previously.

My strong negotiating point was that motorway contracting was very specialised and was unlike any other kind of contracting, particularly the street lighting and communications aspect, and the twenty-four hour accident call-out. You could not afford to make mistakes. Also, the contractor had to work closely with the motorway police, with whom we had built up a very close working relationship. This relationship was important and I stressed this point. I also stressed, rather patronisingly, that as no main contractor had ever carried out this kind of work before and it was completely new to them, the last thing they needed was a subcontractor who had never done this kind of work before either. They needed a subcontractor who could take the worry from them and just get on with it. This seemed to appeal to them and there was much nodding of the heads.

They asked me questions about other aspects of the contract and things that were nothing to do with my department. It was obvious they were picking my brains and I was only too pleased to help them all I could, as this only strengthened my case. I couldn't answer some of the questions they asked but that didn't mean I didn't; I said what I thought was right, and said it very assertively and confidently. They seemed impressed – it was going well.

I came out of the meeting feeling good. They needed me as much as I needed them – it seemed that way anyway. Although nothing had been finalised, other contractors didn't seem such a threat anymore. I drove home that afternoon in good spirits. I just needed to wait for 'the' phone call that would arrive in a couple of days at the most. But, as we all know, that's not the way it works and a week later, there was still no phone call. My life seemed to be on hold. No matter what I was doing or who I was with, my mind was half on the Nuttalls' phone call. My confidence started to wane. Had someone undercut me to such an extent that they couldn't refuse?

Well, on about the twelfth day, the call came through. Could I get to their offices again to discuss things? This time I went on my own, again to meet Stuart Knutt and Chris Edwards. The meeting was, in their words, to look at the prices that I had submitted. This is normal procedure when placing an order and I knew that winning the contract was now within my grasp, providing they didn't want to drive my prices too far into the ground. As with the first meeting, Stuart Knutt was expressionless and his body language non-existent (he would make a good poker player).

Also, as with the first meeting, Chris Edwards was much more outgoing and friendly. This pleased me because, if we were to be successful in winning the contract, Chris would be the man in charge and I felt that I could work with him.

After what seemed like hours of trawling through page after page of figures, mostly with them looking for a reduction in rates, we reached a situation that they seemed happy with. Stuart Knutt almost managed a smile and said, 'If you are happy with those figures, we would like to place the order with you.' I was! And they did!

It was a defining moment in my life and the life of the company. The journey home was one of the most pleasant I've ever made and the first people I told were my family. That evening another large JD was in order and, of course, a takeaway – life doesn't get better.

The following weeks were spent preparing for the big day when Nuttalls would take over from GMC and we would take over the lighting, signs, communication and twenty-four-hour police call-out. As subcontractors to Nuttalls, I needed more plant and vehicles as well as staff, and this was mainly sourced by buying the ex-GMC plant and recruiting ex-GMC staff. By then they were mostly good friends because we'd been working alongside them for several years.

The first TMCs were described as 'free issue contracts'. This meant that I had to price for all the plant and labour but that the Highways Agency supplied all the materials – cables, columns, signs, and everything electrical apart from sand for the cable bed. I did not supply any materials or equipment; when the tendering documents were sent out, at the top of every page was printed: 'THIS IS A FREE ISSUE CONTRACT, ALL MATERIALS WILL BE SUPPLIED BY THE HIGHWAYS AGENCY.'

MARKER POSTS

One day I was sent an order to install 2000 marker posts for which I had submitted a price of £5 each. When the work was about to start, I rang Nuttalls to ask where I was to pick them up. Only then was I told that I had to supply them. 'But this is a free issue contract,' I argued. 'All materials to be supplied by Highways Agency.'

'Yes,' said Chris. 'Everything except marker posts.' I dug out the tender documents and the marker post page was the only page in the entire document where it didn't say that they would be supplied. It was down to me to supply them and I had absolutely no idea where to get them from, or how much they would cost.

I frantically started to make enquiries and managed to track down just one company that could quote me. It was a company near Blackpool called Glasdon. They gave me a price of £18 for a complete unit, and I needed two thousand of them. That was £36,000 that I hadn't priced for – what a slip up. This meant instead of the job being a nice little earner, it would be a financial disaster. Something needed to be done.

I put on my thinking cap and came up with the idea of acquiring my own tooling, then finding a plastic extrusion company to make my own. This I did. The tooling cost me about £8,000 and the extrusion company charged me a further £8,000 for the marker posts, meaning that the overall cost was £16,000 not £36,000. This was a great saving but I was still £20,000 down.

However, good working relationships are priceless (no pun intended) and over the previous months, through the monthly progress meeting, I had become friendly with a fellow called Peter Harrison. Peter was the person running the contract for the consultant WAP. In other words, he had overall authority over the contract. He was number one, full stop.

I'll never know whether he heard of my predicament or not but he issued an instruction that all marker posts had to be set in concrete, so a revised price had to be submitted.

This was music to my ears as it gave me the chance to disproportionately load the price of the concrete and again cut my losses. I don't remember what price I submitted but Peter accepted it and the losses were reduced still further. But the bonus was that when all the marker posts were made and installed, I still owned the tooling to make more posts and sell them to other contractors. There is a marker post every hundred metres on each side of all the motorways throughout Britain, and Glasdon seemed to be the only supplier. Here was an opening to exploit another opportunity.

Today, Glasdon do not sell marker posts and although the marker-post industry is not massive, we now are the country's biggest supplier; this was another one of my excellent mistakes. I often wonder if Peter Harrison asked for them to be set in concrete to give me the opportunity to reduce my losses. I will never know this but I will always be grateful. No marker posts since then have ever been set in concrete. Also, without a doubt, this was the accidental conception of what today is Blakedale.

While I was writing this piece, many, many, years after the event described, I received an invitation from Peter and Glen to attend Peter's seventieth birthday party. How good was that? What a coincidence.

DAY TO DAY BUSINESS...

I t was in the first few weeks of TMC when we got an emergency call to attend an accident on the M62. One of our wagons had gone out to remove a lamp post that had been hit, but (would you believe it) the wagon broke down at the scene of the accident. I got a very irate call from one of the consultants to get another wagon out there fast, as the whole motorway was grinding to a halt. This was my worst nightmare as it was very early on in the contract and I was eager to make a good impression. It was not good and I set about trying to divert a wagon from another job.

Just at that moment, James Collins walked into the office at Barton and stood in front of me, obviously wanting to talk to me, but all I was interested in was trying to locate another wagon. I was making phone call after phone call but not having much luck. The consultant, Geoff, was also constantly on the phone for an update as he had the police on his back. By now the M62 was at a standstill and the tailback was getting longer but still James Collins continued to stand in front of me, waiting to speak. I just wished he would sod off as I couldn't concentrate, but no, he was going nowhere.

Then the worst possible thing happened: one of our wagons was able to go to the accident, so went to replace the broken-down one, which was in the fast lane. However, that one had a puncture as it was travelling along the hard shoulder, so now the motorway was blocked and so was the hard shoulder. The police were going ballistic. I was desperately trying to locate yet another wagon when I got a call from one of our lads at the accident scene to say they had managed to repair the broken-down wagon and remove the column/lamp post and the traffic was now moving. Thank God for that.

That has got to be the longest hour of my life and all the time James Collins was standing in front of me, waiting to speak to me. What the hell could he want? What was so important that he would stand there through all this panic? When I tell you what he wanted to speak to me about, you will not believe it; but, as I wrote in the introduction, this may be the most boring book you will ever read but it will be factual. If it's in this book it happened and what I am going to tell you is the honest truth.

I put the phone down, slumped back in my chair and said, 'Right, James, what can I do for you?'

'Fred,' he said. 'How long does it take you to slice a tomato?' Friends, I kid you not – that is what he wanted to know. That is what he had stood in front of me for over half an hour to ask me during a major crisis. What a prat!

Apparently he had been to one of those country fairs the previous weekend where salesmen peddle their wares. One of the salesman was selling revolutionary kitchen knives and he had been demonstrating by slicing tomatoes, a feat which had obviously impressed James . If I could have got my hands on a revolutionary kitchen knife at that moment, I would have sliced *his* tomatoes!

James had a passion for anything that was free. If it cost a shilling or less he would have no use for it, but if it was free or if he found it, then it was just what he was looking for. 'Just what I need,' he would say. 'I can use that.' I'm convinced that if he'd found a crutch he would have broken his leg to get some use out of it.

As well as Nuttalls moving in as the new contractors, the admin and supervision (which had previously been carried out at County Hall) was awarded to a firm of consultants by the name of Ward,

Ashcroft and Parkmen or WAP for short. However, the supervision of the lighting etc., basically all my work, was subcontracted to some more ex-GMC engineers, Ron Atkins and Peter Odlin, who had taken redundancy and formed their own consultancy, Atkins, Odlin and Partners. This was good news for me as we had worked well together for several years. We had also become good friends socially, although I must stress that even though we were good friends they had a very professional approach to their business and demanded a very high standard of work – friends or no friends!

One member of their staff who I had also worked with during the GMC years was Geoff Old. Geoff was a stickler for quality, a trait that doesn't always endear a supervisor to contractors, as some contractors are rough and ready and adopt a 'near enough is good enough' attitude, which Geoff would not tolerate. Even though we had worked together for quite a few years and got on well, he still always referred to us as 'the best of a bad bunch'. Although I certainly did not put my company in that category, we got the sharp edge of Geoff's tongue on occasion.

I remember one day, when we were several months into the contract, Geoff rang me to say that he had done an inspection of a number of our jobs and was not happy with the quality. He asked if I would go round with him to allow him to show me his concerns. We arranged to go the following afternoon.

By then our main depot was at Swansey Mill (where we still operate from), but the maintenance contract was run from the Barton Depot (near Barton Bridge) that we had inherited from GMC.

The following afternoon I met Geoff at his office, as arranged, and we set off to inspect the various sites. We left Geoff's number two, John Higgins, looking after things in Geoff's absence at his office. We were driving to different locations on various motorways for about two hours, the last site being near Sale Waterpark on the M63 (now the M60). After the inspection we got into his car to drive back. As we drove round the roundabout and got under the motorway bridge, there was one of my wagons parked up with four of my lads in it – and they were all fast asleep.

Geoff hit the roof. 'I don't pay your men to sleep on the job,' he said. 'I will have to make a report out about this. I'm not letting it go.' He gave me earache all the way back to Barton Depot, where he asked me to go into his office while he made out his report.

We walked into his office together – and there was John Higgins, fast asleep. 'Yes, there is a God,' I said to myself. In fairness to Geoff, he immediately got out his camera and took a photo of John to show to him when he woke up. I don't ever remember seeing the report about my lads. John is now in his nineties and not in good health; Geoff and I still take him out from time to time, Geoff more than me. Two days after I wrote the sentence above, Geoff rang me to say that John had died. He was a true gent, a devoted family man and a devout Christian.

Although live motorway work is very stressful, not to mention dangerous, everyone worked and got on well together. I had some good lads working for me. Obviously, there is always the occasional bad egg but, by and large, they were a good group of men doing a difficult job.

When I first met Chris Edwards, I got the impression that this was a man I could work with, and that was how it turned out. Chris was very professional, very knowledgeable and much respected by both his staff and the clients. He treated the subcontractors fairly and never tried to take them to the cleaners, as many main contractors do.

Quite often in the evening he and I were the only ones left at Barton, Chris catching up on his office work and me in my office catching up on mine. So maybe at about 7pm to 7.30pm, a couple of drinks in the Swinging Bridge would be in order. The Swinging

Bridge pub was newly built at that time. It was where the entrance to the Chill Factore is now, and was knocked down when they started to build the Trafford Centre, about the time that I sold the company. I sometimes think it was built just for my duration at Barton. Maybe, maybe not.

We once did a Quakers Yard job at Merthyr Tydfil in South Wales for a client called N G Bailey. They were a massive electrical company and their man in charge was a guy called John Gerhity, a guy that I got on with really well.

One night after work, he asked me if I fancied a drive out for a pint and maybe a takeaway so I agreed. At the end of the night we set off back for the hotel, looking for a chippy on the way but there was none to be seen. We spotted a couple walking along the footpath, so we stopped to ask if they could tell us where to find one. 'Sorry,' said the fellow. 'There's none round here.'

At that point his wife said, 'If you'll give us a lift home, I'll make you some chips.'

'Jump in,' we said. We took them home and the fellow opened some beer for us while his wife made some chips and egg. They also made some for themselves, and we sat down to supper with these complete strangers. How good was that?! Lovely Welsh people.

On occasion, a contract will arise that is not part of routine maintenance so this will go out to tender to three or four contractors, Fred Smith always being one of them and my old adversary, Ray Mews, being another. These were a chance for him to get his foot in the door for when the next maintenance contract came round and also a chance for him to keep a presence on the motorway. Apparently he was very precise in his tendering and would calculate to the nearest half penny, whereas I was a 'near enough' person and worked in round figures.

One contract came up that we both tendered for and somehow our overall pricing was similar, to such an extent that AOP, the consultants, asked us both to come in to see them separately to go through the figures. Although I don't remember this, Geoff told me years later that we had both priced trenching and cable laying at £5 per metre.

When asked individually how we arrived at £5, Ray Mews explained thus: 'Excavate trench £1.02; clean trench 12p; sand base 68p; lay cable £1.07; sand covers 68p; backfill trench £1.01; tidy site 42p – overall price for cable laying and excavation £5.'

At my meeting they asked me the same question: 'How did you arrive at £5 per metre for excavating and cable laying?'

My answer, 'You wouldn't pay me six and I wouldn't do it for four.'

I got the job.

At the start of a two-year contract, the end seems like a lifetime away but, as we all know, two years is soon over and the whole tendering process begins again. In fact, the re-tendering begins after eighteen months, so there is another stressful six months ahead. Although this was not the only work we did, it made up about fifty per cent of the company's turnover and constantly required between forty and fifty staff, so it was a significant commitment for the company.

Apparently Nuttalls, under the leadership of Chris Edwards, had made a good impression on the client, The Highways Agency, and the consultant WAP, so they were automatically included on the list of contractors invited to tender for TMC2.

It is also recognised in the contracting industry that the 'sitting tenant' is always difficult to remove, as they have more knowledge of the requirements and the pitfalls. In other words, they can easily differentiate between the jobs that are easy to make money on and the jobs that are difficult to make money on. This means they are able to price accordingly and put together a more professional tender; this obviously always impresses the client. In addition to this advantage, the majority of plant and vehicles required had already been purchased for TMC1, so a lot of the cost had been absorbed in the previous contract therefore it could be spread over a longer period – another advantage. Even so, nothing can be taken for granted and, by that point, other main contractors had been alerted to the fact that the PFI was there to stay and would be extended to other areas, so all the big boys were eager to get a foot in the door.

Another predicament I found myself in was that, while I was anxious for Nuttalls to be successful as we now had the perfect working relationship, I also had to be mindful that all the other main contractors were aware that Fred Smith was the major lighting subcontractor. They wanted to talk business with me, so it was a balancing act to convince them all that they were the main contractor that I wanted to work with, while at the same time pledging my allegiance to Nuttalls.

I knew that Ray Mews would be working furiously behind the scenes, as would other street lighting companies who were waking up to the fact that PFI was the future, so there was no place for complacency. Once again, we had a few stressful months.

About a month before the end of TMC1 and the start of TMC2, it was announced that Nuttalls had again been successful in securing the second term. I treated myself to another large JD and takeaway. Again, life doesn't get better. By that point though, through constant and an ever-increasing presence on the motorways, FSSL was the most recognised name in motorway maintenance. We were even more recognised than the main contractor or all the other subcontractors. I largely attributed this to the fact that Fred Smith is such a stupid name – it's almost like being called Joe Bloggs. But it is a name that everyone remembers because of its simplicity and also because, wherever you were on the north-west motorways, there would be a Fred Smith vehicle somewhere near. People used to laugh at the name but no one ever forgot it.

One year I went to London with Margaret and Carmen to see two or three shows. The first one we went to see was *Aspects of Love*; by the interval I had decided it was not for me. I decided that I would leave the theatre, go for a drink and meet them back at the hotel. Off I went, found a pub and was having a quiet drink at the bar when a fellow came up to place an order for his family and friends and we got talking. I asked him what he did for a living. He said that he was a long-distance lorry driver. He asked me where I came from; I said near Preston.

'Oh, I deliver to that area quite often.' He then asked me what I did for a living.

'Motorway lighting,' I replied.

'Motorway lighting,' he said. 'You must work for Fred Smith.'

I liked that but when I related the story to my kids, I just got scornful looks. Maybe they were right when they said, 'Don't let it go to your head.'

Although by then we were a major motorway lighting and telecommunications contractor, it didn't go unnoticed that I had absolutely no qualifications for the type of work that we were doing, and this was occasionally pointed out to me. 'How can you run a motorway lighting company when you are not even an electrician?' was a question I was often asked. To which I always replied, 'Do you ever see Alex Ferguson score goals?'

The answer is no, because that's not his job. His job is to build a successful team, a team to go out there and do him proud. And that is what I saw as my job. Even though the bosses at the Highways Agency knew that I had no qualifications, they were always happy for FSSL to win contracts, as the job would be right and they knew I employed fully qualified engineers so that everything was above board.

As with TMC1, the months flew by and soon everyone was talking about TMC3, which we were told would be a three-year contract, a year longer than the two previous contracts. This would be a good one to win and a bad one to lose. Again, as the time got nearer to the end of TMC2, everyone was focusing on what was going to happen. It was a very unsettling time and on this occasion there was a new kid on the block, a company called Prismo from Rowfant in Surrey.

Along with the other competing companies, they asked me to submit a tender, which I obviously did. I gave all the companies the same price except for Nuttalls (I gave them a preferential discount to help them win the contract). But this time it was not to be and they were not the successful contractor. Prismo had come from nowhere and obtained the tender.

What was going to happen now? Everyone wanted to know! As disappointed as I was that Nuttalls hadn't won, I needed to throw my cap in the ring with Prismo as this contract was too important for my company to lose. I made Chris Edwards aware of my intentions and he understood completely, wishing me good luck.

I have got to say that securing the contract with Prismo was much easier than I expected. We had discussions over the telephone and, in what seemed like quite a painless and short amount of time, we reached a verbal agreement. Did they need me as much as I needed them? It seemed that way. After ironing out a few anomalies over the phone, it was eventually agreed that I would go to Rowfant to sign the contract. I would fly to Gatwick Airport and Prismo would pick me up and take me to a hotel that they had booked me into.

I decided to have a couple of days down there so Margaret came with me. We were picked up at the airport by John Abraham, the person I had dealt with on the phone, who I had also met on a couple of occasions when he came up here to meet the consultants. He took us to the hotel and, as it was late afternoon, he dropped us off and agreed to pick me up the following morning at eleven o'clock. It was then that I would go to their offices to sign the contract and be introduced to some of John's colleagues who would be moving up North to run the contract.

At this point I digress slightly because, as I waited in the hotel lobby for John to arrive, I was sitting close to two men who were sitting at a table. One of the men looked like he was close to retiring age and the other one was in his early twenties. On the table in front of them was an assortment of cakes – the kind you get when you order afternoon tea. It soon became obvious that the older of the two was a cake salesman and the younger one an employee of the hotel. It also became obvious, through lack of rapport and body language, that the younger one just didn't want to be there. I could hear everything they said and I felt sorry for the older one as the younger one was showing no interest, but still the salesman was very polite and kept going.

Eventually he cut a piece from one of the cakes and gave it to the younger man to try. He watched him while he ate it, waiting for a reaction which never came. Eventually the old fellow said, 'They are very moreish, aren't they?'

'Yeah,' said the young lad, totally disinterested. Then I think he had decided enough was enough. He wasn't going to hang around any longer and told the older fellow, 'It's not me you need to see. I am the assistant restaurant manager. You need to see someone who is in charge of afternoon teas.'

At that point, if I was that old man, I would have felt like saying, 'WHAT? You have let me waste all this time talking to the wrong person, you arsehole.' But instead the salesman said, in a very quiet voice, 'Oh, I see. Well thank you for pointing that out to me,' as he started to put all his cakes back into his case and leave. Bless him. I hope that by now he is happily retired or selling his cakes at the pearly gates.

John duly arrived and drove me to the offices, introduced me to some colleagues and the deed was done. I had now won all the first three contracts, totalling seven years, and this one was for three years, so that meant three years of steady work and steady cash flow, which is the lifeblood of any business. Prismo turned out to be excellent clients and another good working relationship was soon built up.

Again, as with the first two contracts, Geoff was in charge of several aspects as well as the lighting. One was the maintenance of the six motorway maintenance depots. One of the first instructions issued to Prismo was to install a new septic tank at the Westhoughton Depot. On receiving the instruction, Prismo asked Geoff what size the tank should be so Geoff asked them how many people would be working at the depot using it. Twenty-five, they replied. Now anyone who knows Geoff knows that he has a tremendous sense of humour; at this point Prismo didn't, but they were soon to learn. To answer their question, or at least give them a clue, he went to a joke shop and purchased an imitation poo, then carefully concealed it in a consultant's official jiffy bag and posted it to them. 'Try and work it out from this,' he wrote on an official letterhead. You can only imagine what Prismo thought on receiving this information (such as it was) at the start of a brand-new contract.

Over the years I have had many nights out with Geoff, including two trips to New York to watch boxing at Madison Square Gardens. On the first trip we flew back on Concorde. Incidentally, it was the only plane to take off from New York that morning as it was snowing very hard and the runways were deep in snow, but they cleared one runway so that Concorde would not be held up. How good is that?! The flight took three hours and twenty minutes, and the food was exquisite, like at a top hotel.

By that point I was employing around eighty people, most of them good and reliable, but one of the electricians, a fellow named Dave Grant, was very left wing and spent a lot of time trying to cause unrest among the staff. It got to the point where I had to get rid of him. He spent more time trying to cause trouble than he did working. One day I called him into my office and laid my cards on the table, telling him that in the best interests of the company I was going to dismiss him. This did not go down well. All of a sudden this was a good company to work for and I was a good boss; nevertheless, I had made my mind up and he had to go.

The spin-off from this was that his best mate, Frank Cooney, still worked for me and, although I have no proof of this, I am convinced that Frank Cooney embarked on a policy of making deliberate mistakes (very expensive mistakes) with an attitude of, 'This is for sacking my mate Dave.' So that was it, Frank Cooney also needed to go. Yet another office confrontation and another sacking.

I was well aware that, as I had not followed the correct dismissal procedures, he could have put in a claim for wrongful dismissal. I weighed up what that would cost me against what he was costing me anyway and I decided that losing a wrongful dismissal claim was the cheaper of the two options, so he had to go.

Predictably, it wasn't long before the union officials were contacting me to arrange a meeting and I was advised to employ a solicitor who specialised in such matters. I did a bit of homework and contacted a firm of solicitors from Manchester, who were happy to represent me. They contacted me to say that the meeting had been arranged on a certain date to be held in the Oyster Suite at the Tickled Trout at 10.30am. They suggested we meet at 10am to set out our stall pre-meeting, so to speak.

I arrived at the Tickled Trout and asked the girl on reception to direct me to the Oyster Suite, which she did. I entered the Oyster Suite and was surprised to see not one but three solicitors there. My God, I thought, how much is this going to cost me? It got even worse when they told me they had arrived last night and stayed over. Why would anyone travelling from Manchester come the night before and why were there three of them? It seemed ridiculous but they were the experts and they knew best.

They offered me tea and biscuits, which I gratefully accepted, then we got down to business. After a few introductory questions we got on to the dismissal.

They started to fire questions at me that I couldn't make sense of. I wondered why they were asking those particular questions. Then one of them asked, 'How long have you been with the company?' The bomb dropped; they were not my solicitors – they were Frank Cooney's union representatives. As I realised who they were, they realised that I was not Frank Cooney. To say that their attitude changed is an understatement – they almost told me to get out, which I did.

I went into reception and there waiting for me was my solicitor and at the opposite side was Frank Cooney with a union representative from Wigan. At that point the other three who were in the Oyster Suite came to reception. They all sat down together and went into a conversation, as did I with my guy.

After about ten minutes, the union man from Wigan went to the centre of the room and beckoned me. I've got to say that I am not a fan of unions or shop stewards but this guy from Wigan was really sound, a real Wiganer. He and I sorted out the whole thing on our own without any involvement from either my solicitor or the three union men from London.

I don't remember how much I paid Frank Cooney but I remember driving back to the office feeling quite satisfied. Many months later, my son Richard was talking to Frank Cooney in a pub when he admitted he had been at fault. He told Richard he had a lot of respect for me and they shook hands. At a later date Frank did come back to work for me. It was a case of forgive and forget and he worked well.

One of the duties we had to carry out on TMC was the night

inspection, which required two men to scour the motorways looking for outages or other obvious problems. They would make out a report which had to be handed in to the consultants to allow them to issue an order for repairs. At the bottom of the report both inspectors had to initial it. The two lads who carried out the inspection were Steve Hardman and Ian Townhill; they took great pleasure in signing off every report with SH IT, at the bottom of the page.

One of our other duties was responding to the police call-outs. This was a twenty-four-hour commitment and every week two electricians were paid a decent amount of money to be on standby on a rota. I can't remember the exact amount they were paid but it was quite lucrative for them. The rule was quite simple: they must be in close proximity to the motorways to allow them to respond to an accident call-out within forty-five minutes and obviously they were allowed no alcohol. I couldn't believe it one day when one of the electrician's wives rang me to say that her husband liked to go out for a drink with his mates at night. She asked if it would be alright if she drove the van to the accident if he got a call-out after he'd been drinking.

I couldn't believe what I was hearing. The police call us out to attend an accident and the man turns up, after having had God knows how much to drink and no doubt smelling of beer – but, no problem, as he is not driving.

One of the bosses from the Highways Agency, who was more than happy to be taken out for a meal, was a Chinese guy called Tyze Lee. He was a very amiable chap who liked a good drink and a good meal and was a man after my own heart, so we got on very well. Usually when I took him out Geoff came as well, as he knew him better than I did. I will never know if Tyze Lee didn't know my name or whether he just couldn't pronounce it, but in his broken English he always pronounced Fred Smith as Fresh Meat. Close enough, I suppose.

One day at the Milnrow Depot, in the days before everybody had mobile phones, a Pakistani lady walked into the office and said that she had broken down. She asked if she could use the phone to ring her husband and the lad in charge was happy for her to do so. She rang him and proceeded to give her husband all the details (apparently in great detail) but as she was speaking in Urdu, the lad in the office couldn't follow what she was saying. After a lengthy discussion, she put the phone down and offered the lad some money, perhaps ten or twenty pence. The lad waved it aside and said that it didn't matter, for which she seemed very grateful. It was only weeks later when the telephone bill arrived that we saw the price of her call: I think it cost us £38! We realised that she hadn't broken down at all but had rung her family in Pakistan. Ten out of ten for initiative.

One day I interviewed a lad as a maintenance electrician. The interview went well; he seemed bright and I took him on. During the interview, I asked him about previous experience. It turned out he had street-lighting experience with another company, which he had left of his own accord. 'Why did you leave?' I asked.

'Well, to be honest,' he replied, 'the contracts manager who was my boss had been a milkman. What does a milkman know about street lighting? I'm an electrician and I'm not being told what to do by a milkman.'

One night there was what can only be described as a hurricane blowing in the Manchester area. It was worse than anyone could imagine and at Rocking Stone Moss and the Rakewood viaduct (two very exposed lengths of the M62 which approach the Yorkshire border), the twelve-metre twin-arm lighting columns in the centre reservations had to be seen to be believed; they were blowing from side to side like palm trees. Granada Television filmed them from a bridge and it was a terrifying sight – and all this was occurring while traffic was still using the motorway.

At about ten o'clock at night we got a call to muster all the men and vehicles that we could and get out there as soon as possible to remove the columns. The police positioned on the Manchester–Yorkshire border stopped all the traffic while we moved in to remove the columns. It was a very dangerous and arduous task and there wasn't time to take the columns down in the conventional way, which would have taken far too long and been even more dangerous.

It was agreed with the police that we would saw off the columns at six feet from the ground and lay them in the centre reservation, to be removed at a later date. So at ten o'clock at night in the pitch black, the lads got to work and in less than three hours had removed 127 columns. That was an amazing achievement which was all filmed by Granada. But while three hours is a very short time to remove 127 columns, it's not a very short time for the motorists who are sitting in their cars waiting. One of these motorists was a mate of mine, Les Simpson, and those were three hours that he never lets me forget, even today. And I always reply, 'Well never mind, Les, think of all the money I made. Money that I was making while I was in bed and you were sat on the M62.' That always makes him feel much better.

Today David Beckham is often referred to as 'Goldenballs', for whatever reason. Well, that was also a nickname given to me many years ago on TMC by Geoff and Peter Odlin. The reason behind this was that we were issued with a works order to rewire the computer suite at Milnrow Depot. I sent Bert Perry to do the job but (for whatever reason) he wired it up completely incorrectly. Peter Odlin went to inspect it and was not happy with what Bert had done. He told me we would have to strip it out and do the entire job again, this time doing it right, and all at our own expense.

We were just about to start the work when Peter rang me to say that the Highways Agency had been on the phone to ask if the work had been done. He had told them that it had but didn't tell them that it had been done incorrectly – there was no need, as we were going to strip it all out and do it again at our expense. At that point the guy at the Highways Agency said that there had been a change of plan and they had decided to do it completely differently. He instructed us to strip it out and rewire it to the new design, obviously at their expense. So I actually got paid for Bert doing it wrong, then got paid for ripping it out, and then paid for doing it again properly. After that, Peter, Ron and Geoff always referred to me as 'Goldenballs' – I could live with that.

As with TMCs 1 and 2, the three-year term flew by and we were soon back to the worrying period. We were up for tender again. Many more main contractors were anxious to get on the bandwagon and the sitting tenants were anxious to retain what they had got. Unlike in the early days when there was limited interest, there was now massive interest. In addition, more areas were being privatised. PFIs were big business and, as the profile of the contracts grew, so did the profile of the contractors. By then my street-lighting competitors, who had previously just been interested spectators, were anxious to oust me.

John Avery, the Prismo Chris Edwards equivalent, who I had worked alongside for the three years of TMC3, rang to ask me to attend a meeting with him and some of his colleagues, people that I knew well.

The meeting was to take place after working hours when everything was quiet and we wouldn't be interrupted; the object of the meeting was to plan a strategy to retain the contract. TMC3 had been very profitable for Prismo and they were desperate to hold on to it. Inevitably, since we were the biggest subcontracted department by a very large margin, our part of the contract was a massive influence on their final submission, so some fine tuning between FSSL and Prismo was called for.

We agreed that to get through all that we needed to would require two meetings per week for about a month. I was happy with that and there was no problem – until the phone call came that I was expecting and dreading. It was from my old friend and client, Chris Edwards. 'Could we arrange a clandestine meeting to plan a strategy to help Nuttalls to win back the contract?' he asked. HELP!!!

I was torn about what to do. By that time my relationship with Prismo and John Avery was on a par with Chris at Nuttalls. I couldn't have lived with myself if I went into meetings with Prismo where they took me into their confidence and we planned a pricing strategy together, then went to a similar meeting with Nuttalls to help them to take the contract from Prismo. As much as I wanted the contract – and indeed needed the contract – I just couldn't have done it, I wouldn't have slept at night.

As painful as it was, there was only one thing to do. I had to come clean with Chris and tell him that I couldn't give him a preferential price over Prismo, but I would give him a preferential price over the other companies that had asked me to quote. I could tell that he was disappointed but at the same time appreciated the predicament I was in. He asked me to submit the best price that I could and he would work with it. This I did.

Then the waiting game started all over again; the worry returned, fuelled by the inevitable rumours that always abounded (some accurate, others pure fiction) till the final announcement was made.

On this occasion the successful company was Nuttalls. Prismo were devastated, as they'd been very confident of being successful – but that's contracting for you.

After all the commiserations, I got on the phone to Chris at Nuttalls. 'Was my price good for them?' I asked. Were we to link up again? Sadly, the answer was no!

When I had told him that I couldn't give him a better price than the one I had given Prismo, he had phoned another contractor to ask him to submit a heavily discounted price on the gentleman's agreement that if Nuttalls were successful they would automatically award the lighting to Mews. We had lost the jewel in the crown. I was gutted, as were my family and all the workforce.

I rang Chris to see if he would talk but understandably he was tied by the gentleman's agreement that he had reached with Mews. I had to lay off about forty staff but they all kept their jobs as they simply transferred to Mews, as they had transferred to me from GMC, so at least there were no redundancies.

As with any other business, news gets around fast and rumours fly. It soon became common knowledge that Mews was not a popular employer and did not treat his men well. The employees that had left me to go and work for him were still mates with the lads that I had kept on, so I was kept up to date with all that was going on. I must admit to getting a degree of satisfaction when I heard derogatory reports about him and how he had upset the client.

I was once speaking to Chris on the phone and I asked how things were working out with Mews. He replied, 'We have a very professional working relationship.' I, rightly or wrongly, translated this as, 'We don't like him but we are stuck with him.' But Chris was too much of a gentleman to say that.

RECEIVERSHIP

One summer evening, we were working during the night on the M62 changing the lamps on the central reservation. Also working within our lane closure was a fellow named Tommy White, whose job was to install new signs. Tommy was an old friend of mine; we had worked on many of the same jobs up and down the country. He was also a friendly guy and easy to get along with.

While we were talking, Tommy was in his platform wagon (cherry picker) installing a sign and I was on the road, so he was shouting down to me. As we were talking he said, 'Have you heard about Budge?' A F Budge was a huge civil engineering company that both Tommy and I did contracts for.

'No, what about them?' I replied.

'They've gone bust,' said Tommy.

'Oh no, I've been working for them. They owe me some money.'

'Yeah, me too,' said Tommy. 'But there's nothing we can do. Apparently there's no money in the kitty, so there will be no payouts to creditors.'

This was the last thing that I wanted to hear, but Tommy seemed very relaxed about it. 'No point in worrying. Worrying won't solve anything,' he said.

I've got to say that Tommy's attitude was totally opposite to mine. I was panicking. As I drove home, all I could think about was how much they owed us. It was something I was determined to find out first thing the following morning.

At that time I was using a self-employed quantity surveyor called David Lester. This was another of the George Northwood/Martin Shepperd fraternity, i.e. a waste of time but he was handling the Budge account.

The following morning I went into his office. 'Have you heard about Budge?' I asked.

'Yes, I've just heard.'

'How much did they owe us?' I asked.

He got out their file. '£30,000,' he said.

I didn't know whether to feel worse or better, for although £30,000 is a large amount it could have been a lot worse. Also, it was a figure that I could absorb so I was prepared to grin and bear it. But, as I stated earlier, Metcalfe couldn't always be relied on and it turned out that his figure was the figure that we were due to receive shortly, and not the figure that we were owed in total. That was over £203,000! Things were serious. There was no way that I could absorb that kind of figure.

I was also about to be hit with another massive blow: losing our jewel in the crown, the Term Maintenance Contract. All of a sudden things were going from bad to worse. What was ironic was that the previous year we'd had the best year in the company's history and there we were, only six months later, in serious trouble.

I needed to do something so I reluctantly agreed to carry out a contract for a company that was renowned for not paying its sub-contractors. Another company that had a reputation for not paying its bills had a contract for a road widening scheme in the Midlands. Although most sub-contractors steered clear of Balfour Beatty, I had met the two young engineers who would be running the contract and they assured me that the company had had a change of policy, and that they would personally see that I got paid promptly. Unfortunately that was not to be; every time a payment was due, I got excuse after excuse as to why I would not be receiving a cheque any time soon. Of course, I went to see the engineers who had promised me prompt payment but all I got was, 'Well, we've passed your invoice for payment, now it's out of our hands.' In other words, the proverbial brick wall.

All this was getting too much, with the large amount of money owed by Budge and the constant source of cash flow from the term maintenance now gone. Also, I had paid out a large amount in redundancy when I lost the contract. After years of enjoying good profits and steady cash flow, I was now facing the harsh reality of receivership.

Receivership is the nightmare of any businessman, and it certainly was the case with me. From the very first day that I started in business at the age of twenty-two, there wasn't a day where it didn't cross my mind.

The year was 1993 and, due to pressure from the bank which also echoed my own judgement, I knew that receivership was inevitable. I reluctantly rang the bank to instruct them to go ahead and call in the receivers, which I had no doubt they would have done anyway. They informed me that they would go ahead but it would be a few days before they could proceed. That was no problem.

I had only just put the phone down when it rang again. It was Geoff, who I could tell was upset, and he was ringing to tell me that a mutual friend's seven-year-old son, David, had died. I was devastated. I went sick. The day that the bank brought in the receivers was the day of David's funeral, which Margaret and I attended. A child's funeral has got to be the worst thing ever, and when I went to bed that night I suddenly realised that the very thing, the one thing I had lived in fear of, had happened that day and that I had never given it a thought.

It was in February 1994 that Richard, Jonny and I attended a meeting at the receivers office in Manchester, bought the assets of the company back again and re-formed the company, albeit with a

1992. When I took Prismo for a birds eye view of the maintenance work which we were carrying out as their sub-contractors. Prismo were ideal clients.

1992. Letter from Prismo following the helicopter trip.

Prismo Limited
Rowfant, Crawley, West Sussex RH10 4NF, United Kingdom
Telephone: (0342) 714949
Telex: 95190
Fax: (0342) 715664

Prismo

Our Ref: EF/fr
26th February 1992

Fred Smith Service Lines Limited
Swansey Mill
Mill Lane
Whittle le Woods
Chorley
Lancashire
PR6 7LX

Dear Fred

Enclosed please find photos of the exciting trip by helicopter that you managed for us on the 28th January. It was disappointing that there was not room for you and John Avery to join us; but I don't think John needed an excuse not to come up! Despite the bad weather, Mike Yearwood and I were able to get a very close view of a substantial part of the network and in particular our recently finished Barton Bridge contract.

I was pleased that you were able to meet our new Chief Estimator, Ray Wescott at 'Swallowfields' last week. Apologies for not being able to make it, but I met Ray the following morning. It is very positive that we are already working together on the best way to secure the contract next time around. It is very important to us, as indeed it must be to your Company.

Once again thanks for organising the trip and we look forward to monitoring the continued good mutual trading relationship.

Yours sincerely
for PRISMO LIMITED

E FLOATE
OPERATIONS DIRECTOR

c.c. J C Avery

ef292x.1

Registered Office: 673 Galvin Road, Slough, Berks. SL1 4DL. Registration No: 871451, England.   Registered user of trademarks.

Cheshire
Constabulary

The Chief Superintendent
Operations Division
Police Motorway Unit
Toft Road
Knutsford WA16 0PA
Telephone (0565) 634100
Fax (0565) 651260

The Managing Director
FRED SMITH SERVICE LINES
Swansea Mill
Whitley Woods
Chorley
Lancashire

In reply please address for the attention of

RECEIVED
- 4 MAY 1993

Our reference	Extension	Your reference	Date
OPS/93/726/RT			30th April 1993

Dear Sir

I write with reference to an incident on the M56 Motorway in Cheshire on Sunday, 15th April 1993, when a horse box overturned on the carriageway allowing the two horses being carried to escape.

Staff from your company stopped at the scene. One of these, David JACKSON, had witness the incident. They assisted with looking after the horses and then, using their crane, put the horse box back onto its wheels.

We in the police service are extemely grateful to people who give professional help in situations such as this, and I ask you to pass on our thanks to Mr JACKSON and his colleagues.

Yours faithfully,

Chief Inspector
for Superintendent.

All correspondence (quoting our reference shown above) should be addressed to the Chief Superintendent

1993. Letter from Cheshire Motorway Police which is self explanatory.

2005. New York. Me, Gus, Peter Cooke, John Greenhalgh (front row), my brother-in-law Richard Ormisher and Keiran (back row).

Brindle Weightlifting champion, Fred Smith, with Michael Jennings

2009. Two champions! Me with Chorley boxer, Michael Jennings as he prepared to fight Miguel Cotto at Madison Square Gardens for the World Welterweight Title.

A CHAMPION weightlifter will be travelling to New York to support Michael Jennings in his fight against Miguel Angel Cotto – and expects to see another moment of history.

Title

Fred Smith, 66, has been lifting weights since 1960 and has won the British title twice and currently holds the British record.

He'll be in the crowd at Madison Square Garden on February 21 but it won't be the first time he's been at the Mecca of boxing.

The pensioner witnessed the famous Muhammad Ali versus Joe Frazier fight on March 8, 1971.

He recalled: "The atmosphere was out of this world, the place was packed with film stars and celebrities.

"There was only one seat left in the arena and that was because the organisers thought the President might turn up!"

Fred has got to know Jennings after his company Whittle-le-Woods based Kingsley Finance started sponsoring him.

Fred bids to lift world title

WHEN Fred Smith sold off his business in 1999 he was determined to dedicate more time to keeping fit, and three years later has the honours to prove it.

Fred, 63, of Sandy Lane, Brindle, recently lifted more than 22 stone in weight to become a British champion in a 'bench pressing' power-lifting championship in Birmingham, and this month he heads to Miami for the World Championships.

His success in the 60s-and-over section came shortly after Fred broke the British 'masters three' record for 60 to 70-year-olds, and Fred continues to pump iron.

Now it's intense training with his coach ex-British Olympic lifting record holder Alan Fairclough at the Adlington Barbell Club.

Fred is a regular visitor to the Oxford Street club, housed in an old air raid shelter, for four decades, having started lifting in

By Malcolm Wyatt

1960 at its previous converted stables base off nearby Park Road.

Fred, brought up in Adlington and a farmer in Heath Charnock before setting up his own motorway maintenance firm, has been based in Brindle for 30 years, but remains a regular Adlington visitor.

He said: "I've always worked out, but when I sold my business I joined the Shaw Hill gym too, and soon slimmed down from 23 stone to 16 and a half. I'm also a keen runner, and have completed four marathons in the last two years, having done London twice, and also Dublin and New York.

"But through my coach Alan Fairclough I was persuaded to go back to competitive weightlifting in an attempt to break records, and that proved to be the case."

Bench pressing is a part of the powerlifting discipline, involving 'dead lifts' while lying on a bench, with Fred breaking the British age group record in December at a NW Counties championships.

He added: "I broke the record in August, lifting 330lbs, but unfortunately that was not registered for drug testing through an administrative error. I went on to lift 319lbs at the regional championships, 5lbs more than the previous record.

"I then went to Birmingham for the British Championships, and won the masters three class there. I'm now set for Miami and the World Championships on April 20, and this September hope to lift in the European Championships in Russia. But a lot of credit for my success so far is down to my coach Alan."

US bid: Fred Smith, right, with Alan Fairclough

2006. Me with my coach Alan Fairclough, having just been selected to represent Great Britain in the world championships in Miami where I came fourth.

Fred pushing for fifth record

HE'S got the power! British weightlifting champion Fred Smith, 64, from Brindle, near Chorley, is flexing his muscles for the European Championships in the Czech Republic next month.

The Masters 3 British Weightlifting

Association weightlifter has already broken UK records four times.

Now he hopes to beat his personal best and bring home a medal from the tournament next month.

Pictures: IAN ROBINSON

2007. Training for the European Championships in the Czech Republic

1999. Me and Geoff on the return journey on Concorde. The food was out of this world (literally) and the journey took just 3 hours 20 minutes.

1999. Me and Geoff outside Madison Square Garden for the Evander Holyfield and Lennox Lewis fight. Madison Square Garden is the most famous boxing arena in the world. I understand that this is the third building to bear this name but it is the same ring used by Jack Dempsey, Rocky Marciano and Joe Lewis.

1999. Me reading the Wall Street Journal, pretending I understand it.

1999. Me and Geoff doing the touristy stuff, we both love New York.

Right:
Circa 1999. Me at 23 stone before I joined Shaw Hill.

Below:
2008. Jonathan and Carmen crossing the finishing line on the 2008 London Marathon, presumably ahead of me!

2008. Receiving my medal after completing the London Marathon.

work force of six as opposed to the eighty or so that I had previously employed.

Contracts were slow to come in at first and this gave us cause for concern but I was convinced that things would pick up and we would get up and running again. This is what gradually happened.

HERE WE GO AGAIN

Anyway, the years came and went and in no time at all it was contract renewal time again. I heard from some excellent sources, i.e. the consultants, that most of the main contractors were looking to FSSL to take on the lighting and comms contract again. This was music to my ears and I felt the old buzz coming back. My main competitor had completed the contract but not made many friends along the way; by all accounts, he was very contractual with no give and take. When the new contract was up for renewal, everyone was rooting for us to win it and the phone was red hot with people wanting to give me inside information, all of which I gratefully accepted.

Once again all the main contractors approached me for a price and, as with all previous contracts, the tension mounted. But, unlike the previous contracts, this time I couldn't lose it – I could only win it or not, as the case may be. However, the feedback I was getting gave me reason to be optimistic. As I stated earlier, more and more main contractors were showing great interest, all eager to have a bite of this very prestigious apple. It turned out the contract changed hands again, this time being won by the construction giant, Alfred McAlpine. We had submitted a price to them and it was not long before they were on the phone to open up pre-contract talks.

By now my son, Jonathan, had left his job as auditor for British Independent Hospitals and joined the company. When the talks with McAlpines opened, he attended all the meetings with me. I had been told in confidence that Macs wanted to place the order with us but were also in discussion with others, which is normal procedure; the winning of the contract had to be by tact and negotiation, not by divine right.

All meetings had to be taken seriously; we could not be overconfident. On the whole, the meetings went well and, as with other main contractors who had no previous experience of term maintenance, I was asked a lot of questions. I had it in my mind to help them and this gave me confidence. They wanted our experience, and that could only be good.

All the meetings carried on going well and I felt that things were moving our way, although there was one embarrassing moment. Just as I thought the negotiations were coming to a conclusion and we had it in the bag, they asked about our quality assurance procedure. We assured them that it was well in place and up to date. Then, one of Mac's men said to Jonny, 'Can you table it?'

'What the hell does that mean,' thought Jonny. But not wanting to be seen as ignorant he said, 'Yes, of course,' thinking that the conversation would move on and we could find out what tabling meant later. But the conversation didn't move on; everything went quiet as the three McAlpine men sat and waited. The five of us sat round the table with no one speaking, till eventually one of them said, 'Well, go on then, table it.'

It appears that 'table it' is simply jargon for 'put it on the table', jargon that neither Jonny nor I had ever heard. Jonny had to come clean and say, 'No, we couldn't.'

Anyway, that little embarrassing moment did us no harm and they awarded us the contract a few days later. It was time for another large JD and a takeaway.

I had the pleasant task of re-employing most of the forty men that I had previously laid off. Up till then my oldest son, Richard, had always worked on site, which is what bosses' sons should do, but he'd moved up to management. This move was hugely beneficial to the company as it allowed him to demonstrate his ability to strike some excellent deals, whether purchasing materials or quoting for contracts. I often compare the deals that Richard pulled off to the pathetic half-hearted deals that George Northwood handled.

I now had both Jonny and Richard alongside me running the business and what a difference it made, not only to me personally but also to the bottom line.

But one more personal acquisition was to take place. Geoff Old, who had previously overseen the contract as a consultant, now moved over to us as contracts manager to oversee the TMC on our behalf. This was a massive acquisition for us, as Geoff was well known and well respected in the industry. With Geoff, Jonny and Richard working alongside me, I was totally confident about the future of the company. We had also reinstated Steve Leighton, another very capable engineer, to assist Geoff. I am convinced that there wasn't a better motorway lighting team in the country. There definitely wasn't a more experienced one.

As with Nuttalls and Prismo, a good working relationship was established with McAlpines treating us fairly and appreciating that we, in turn, were doing a good job for them. One month they treated us not only fairly but rather lavishly. Jonny sent them an invoice for some work for the sum of £287,000 and they very kindly sent us a cheque back for the sum of £787,000, £500,000 more than we had applied for. But the good news, or the bad news, depending on your point of view, was that they didn't want it back, or at least they didn't want it back just yet. The reason for this was that the mistake would come to light and the person responsible would be in serious trouble, so it had to be kept quiet. This gave Jonny no concerns whatsoever; we now had half a million pounds of McAlpines' money to do whatever we wanted with until the day they asked for it back.

I'm not sure what Jonny actually did with it but he certainly made it work for us for, as the saying goes, money makes money. They (Macs) eventually asked us to give them discounts on future invoices until we had paid it all back, which is what we did. All money was returned in this way but it made a lot of money for us while we had it.

The months went by and the TMC was running well, as were the other contracts that were being run from the Chorley office, until one day we received a phone call from McAlpines that would change our lives. The call was from a guy called Graham Northrop, who was based at Macs head office at Birchwood, Warrington. The term maintenance contract came under his jurisdiction. It appeared that he had been keeping his eye on the amount of money that Macs had been paying us every month (which was substantial), as was the money coming in from other contracts. He liked what he saw, so he asked if he could come to see us. We arranged it for the following day.

Jonny, Richard and I were intrigued. Graham had said enough on the phone to make us suspect that there could be a takeover bid in the offing – and so it turned out. Although he did his best not to give anything away, he certainly had not come just for a cup of tea, or to talk about the weather. By the time he left, both parties had agreed that there was some common ground and arranged a second meeting, this time with their finance director, Neil McDougle, in attendance.

The meeting was arranged for the following week and again all went well. As with all meetings for takeovers, the buying party always play their cards close to their chest and try not to give anything away. The selling party spend their time at the meetings trying to read between the lines, see through them and glean truths from what they don't say as much as what they do say.

Again the meeting went well and a third meeting was arranged. This time it was to be with McAlpines' managing director, Derek

McCormick, in attendance. This was getting serious. The third meeting took place and mainly consisted of Derek and Neil asking us questions. We found both Derek and Neil very genuine and easy to get along with; Derek in particular was quite a character and a good laugh. Richard and Jonny had all the answers they required and were very confident. By then, Graham Northrop had dropped out of all the negotiations.

It was about the fifth meeting, after all the questions had been asked and answered, that we were in a position to talk money. I remember well when we all sat down at my desk, knowing that we were about to discuss the price of the takeover. Jonny and Richard both had writing pads in front of them and were keeping notes – at least, that's how it looked. What they didn't know, and neither did I, was that Richard was just writing notes about Jonny's reactions, because it's well known in our family that Jonny is money-orientated, to put it mildly. Richard's notes went something along these lines.

'Jonny's trying not to smile.' 'Jonny just won't look at me.' 'We are now talking serious money, and Jonny still won't look up at me.' That's how Richard's notes went for the entire meeting. I sometimes wonder if he still has them as they would bring a smile to my face

Eventually, after months of negotiations, the takeover was completed and I was very proud that McAlpines continued to trade as FRED SMITH and also trade from Swansey Mill. That meant no change as far as the workforce was concerned, which was good.

On the completion of the takeover there were a few obligations that I had agreed to fulfil, which were designed to assist McAlpines to ease their way into the running of FSSL. One of the things I had agreed to do was to attend monthly progress meetings at Birchwood, their northern head office, along with five or six of Macs men who were running FSSL. This was no problem to me as we had always held progress meetings at Chorley, so on the last Thursday of every month

I made the trip to Birchwood. It didn't take me long to realise that the progress meetings at Macs and the ones that I was used to at Chorley were on completely different planets.

The meetings at Macs would go on for five or six hours, whereas the ones that I was used to lasted about one hour. In reality, Macs' *useful* discussions lasted about half an hour with the rest being useless waffle. It did my head in.

Our previous meetings at Chorley were predominately about how much work had been carried out that month, the value of that work, the cost of carrying it out and the prospects for next month and beyond. Then we'd discuss the possible need for more plant and staff, etc. Simple. To me, that is what a progress meeting was for. But apparently that was not how big companies saw it. Oh no, that was far too simple.

After a few meetings, I decided that each of these guys had his own little empire within the company and each one was going to prove that his department was essential and important. This meant that each person went on at length discussing things like procedures, formats, systems, records, and health and safety. Basically they'd discuss a whole manner of things that meant nothing to me – and I suspect not much to them either, except to prolong the meeting and make the minutes look good.

I remember one meeting which lasted about six hours. It was just about to come to a conclusion when one of the men, I think it was Graham Northrop, produced a handful of forms. He handed them round, one form for each person to read and fill in. I read my copy and couldn't believe that they were forms requesting an analysis of our own performance at the meeting that we were still attending, and giving ourselves marks out of ten. Filling in the forms and the following discussion of them lasted another two hours. By the time the meeting was over, I was losing the will to live.

What was worse was that every meeting was the same. This was the norm. They were nothing like the simple and intelligent meetings that I'd held with Richard, Jonny, and Geoff at Chorley. It was plain to me that I contributed nothing to those meetings and it became apparent that Macs men had noticed that as well so I was formally excused from any further meetings. I was later told, by another member of staff who didn't attend these meetings, that it was noticed that my only contribution to the meetings was to make sure that no sandwiches got wasted. Well, it was a contribution of sorts.

So that was it then, the end of FSSL as I knew it. It was the end of an era and, although I didn't realise it at the time, it was also the start of another era in which my children would play an even bigger part.

A few years earlier, I had used a self-employed man from Great Eccleston named Martin Sheppard to do the company accounts. He had been recommended by Paul Rotheram, my accountant. He was alright and we got on reasonably well at the beginning, although it was to turn very sour later. But, as with most things that go bad, something good can come from it and that was certainly the case in this instance.

He had not been with us long when he informed me that he owned a finance company called MJS Finance. This sounded very good but, in fairness to him, he assured me that it was a very small company with only five customers. I admired his honesty. It appeared that he had found a niche in the market of taxing HGV wagons for other people, a niche that appealed to me.

One day, when he had been with us for about six months, he came into my office to talk to me about MJS and his optimism about the future. This was a meeting which ended in him asking me if I would be interested in: (a) buying into the company, and (b) lending the company £4,000. I had already decided that what he was doing was a good idea so I had no hesitation in agreeing to his request. I bought one hundred shares at £1 per share and wrote him a cheque for £4,000. At that time the debtor book (the amount of money lent out) was £163,000, which was not a large amount, but promising. Little did I realise at the time that this would eventually lead to the inception of Kingsley Asset Finance and a debtor book of £15,000,000.

At around the same time, I had decided to remove the marker post business, small as it was, out of FSSL and form a separate company. This was during a period when Martin Sheppard and I were getting on well and I was impressed with his enthusiasm. One of the things he had done, without me asking, was to get involved in preparing the marker posts to enable orders to go out on time.

I decided to offer him fifty per cent of the new company, in the belief that his enthusiasm and drive would carry it forward faster than I would, as at the time FSSL was keeping me fully occupied. He was very grateful for this; he saw it as an opportunity to build up a business that he never thought he would get.

We now found ourselves in a position where I owned part of his business (MJS) and he owned part of my new business, now called FRED SMITH Highway Supplies. For a time all went well and he still did the FSSL accounts. Both companies continued to expand and make profits, albeit on a moderate scale, but this was fine as it was how we wanted it to grow. But as time went by, I noticed that Martin was becoming less and less motivated. Whereas before he was bursting with enthusiasm and plans for the future, he was now becoming more and more withdrawn. If I asked him a question, I would get only the minimum information from him. Also, in the past he had always pushed for regular meetings and updates but he now shied away from them. If I suggested a meeting, he always had a reason why he couldn't make it and I started to feel uneasy. I realised that something was changing. I decided not to do anything but to keep an eye on things.

Then one day Martin came into my office and asked if I would mind staying behind after everyone had gone home as he wanted to talk to me uninterrupted. I agreed and after everyone had gone, he came to see me. He asked if I would be interested in selling my shares in the finance company back to him as he had plans for it that he would prefer to carry out alone.

To be honest, I didn't question too much what these plans were; providing we could come to a financial agreement, I was happy to be out. Without question, I just had a bad feeling about him.

The financial arrangements went very smoothly. I wanted the £4,000 loan paid back with interest and requested a further £4,000 for my one hundred shares. I had paid £100 for them but he agreed to this. Because of his recent behaviour, I also told him that I would probably start my own finance company with other partners. He seemed happy enough – not that he could have done anything about it.

Now I was out of MJS but we were still in partnership with the marker post company. However, it was a partnership that didn't last long. A couple of days later, I received a phone call from my solicitor, John Chadwick, to say that Martin Sheppard had been to his office to ask for a copy of the agreement. I wondered why he wanted one. I soon found out.

The following Saturday afternoon we were going to a wedding, so I went to the mill to pick up the mail. Most of the mail was pretty routine stuff but then, there it was – a letter from a solicitor representing Sheppard saying that I had violated the agreement and that he was dissolving the partnership. I can't even remember what the so-called violation was, it was so trivial. However by now, because he had been more or less running FRED SMITH Highway Supplies, he knew all the clients and contacts and he started his own company in competition with us. He just dropped the name FRED SMITH from the company title and called his company Highway Supplies, so to the customer very little had changed. He saw a chance to steal the company.

When I took him in as a partner, I genuinely thought that I was giving him a chance in life. He had told me earlier that his wife had walked out on him, leaving him with two children. He also told me that his own family didn't speak to him. Maybe I should have read something into that but I just wanted to give him a leg-up in life. I was now beginning to see why his wife and family didn't speak to him.

I found out later that he had got a relative to invest some money in the company and he had come in as a partner. I think the relative was an uncle, who apparently had spent most of his life working on boats. He was known as Tug Wilson. About two years later, I got a phone call from the uncle who told me that what Martin had done to me he had also done to him. He (the uncle) had lost all his money and the partnership had been dissolved, leaving Tug broke.

Anyhow, as far as I was concerned, as I stated earlier, out of everything bad something good can arise and that was to apply in this case.

By that time my daughter, Carmen, had left her equestrian career and was now running FSHS, as the only employee, having clawed back most of the customers that Sheppard had stolen. One day the phone call came that, yet again, would transform the company and our lives beyond recognition. It came by way of a complaint from a guy called Robert Radford who worked for Nuttalls at the motorway maintenance offices at the side of the M6 near the Tickled Trout.

The call was to say that the marker posts that we had supplied were not up to specification, as the reflective strips were not spaced apart to the correct distance. The complaint had apparently been made by a member of the public – and guess who that member of the public was? A Mr Sheppard. And guess who had actually assembled the reflective strips on the marker posts? The same Mr Sheppard. I sometimes wonder if, when he worked for me and he knew that he would be leaving, he deliberately spaced them wrongly so that as a member of the public he could lodge a complaint later.

In response to the phone call, Carmen and I went to meet Robert Radford, who I knew from when he worked at LCC. He told us of the nature of the complaint, which was later thrown out as too trivial to worry about. I mean, who the hell is going to pull up on the hard shoulder of a motorway and measure the distance between two reflective strips. However, at the initial meeting the complaint had to be taken seriously and I was anxious to let my client know that, no matter what the outcome, Nuttalls would suffer no financial loss and any cost or labour would be met by me.

This was when Robert Radford made a statement that got me excited and Carmen worried. He said, 'I appreciate what you say, Fred, but when you used to work on the hard shoulder you only needed three cones and an arrow. Now they insist that you use a crash cushion to protect the workforce and you can't get them for love or money. And when you do get them they cost an absolute fortune.'

Carmen sat there thinking, 'This could cost us a fortune,' but I was sitting there thinking, 'This could make us a fortune!'

At the end of the meeting, I asked Robert if he had any literature on crash cushions, which he had and gave to me. That night at home, I studied the leaflets and decided that crash cushions – or at least one crash cushion – was worth a try. I worked out that if the whole thing fell flat on its face and was a complete failure, I could still sell the wagon and scrap the cushion, so the worst-case scenario was that I would lose the cost of the cushion, about £20,000. This was a risk worth taking.

At that time, Ben was still at university. Richard had taken over a car wash at Padiham, which he still owns but now rents out. I remember when Richard was buying the car wash off a fellow called Ian McVeigh, Richard and I were in his office finalising the deal when he made a comment that almost made us laugh. He said, 'I worry that you will not be able to run this business as you've had no experience of running a car wash.'

We couldn't believe what we were hearing. We had just done twenty years maintaining all the motorways in the North, plus dealing with all the police accident call-outs and he didn't think that we would be able to run a car wash!

Jonny was running the finance company that we had started up following the split from Sheppard, and Carmen was fully occupied making marker posts and getting the orders out, so it was down to me to get this venture up and running.

I rang the company that supplied the cushions, which was a company called King, I think, and arranged a meeting with their sales manager, Dave Staiano, at Swansey Mill. Mr Staiano turned up at the appointed time and negotiations began. That was over ten years ago and the rest, as they say, is history. I remember saying to Dave, 'If this takes off, we could end up ordering seven or eight of these vehicles.' We now have around 250 and Dave is our business expansion manager. He often reminds me of that comment.

Having sold Fred Smith Street Lighting and being the age that I was, fifty-six, our company accountant advised me to sign all the shares in FRED SMITH Highway Supplies over to my four children. This I agreed to do. It wasn't so much that the shares were worth anything at that time (they weren't) but I saw the potential to build a successful company in what I regarded as a niche market. It was better that the children owned the company – although for some reason they dropped the name FRED SMITH and renamed it Blakedale.

At this point I must say how proud Margaret and I are at the professional and responsible way that the family have taken Blakedale forward to what is today, the country's leading self-drive company supplying protection vehicles for motorways workers, without any shouting or showing off. And Ben, who is carving out his own career and not involved in Blakedale on a day-to-day basis, takes a lot of good-humoured flack from his siblings regarding his twenty-five per cent share. He just laughs and says, 'Yeah, it's like winning the lottery without buying a ticket.'

My Later Life Sporting Careers – Muscles And Marathons

So with FSSL owned by McAlpines, Jonny running Kingsley Finance, and Richard and Carmen running Blakedale, I was more or less retired, which suited me.

While I was running FSSL and FSHS I may not have been the best businessman in the world but I was excellent at corporate entertaining. It was one thing I excelled at, but entertaining comes at a price and I don't mean just financial.

Because I had ceased to work on site those last few years, and my weight training had been curtailed, my body weight had ballooned. I remember calling at Anderton Service Station and getting weighed. The machine was one of those that gives you a print out, ie: what you are and what you should be.

I read it and it said my ideal weight was 11st 5lb, and that I needed to lose 11st 5lb. I smiled at the misprint but then I realised it read that my weight that day was 22st 10lbs. Oh my God, I was almost 23st at 5 foot 8 inches. I had to do something and that led to another life-changing moment.

At the time, Shaw Hill Golf and Country Club had recently opened a leisure section, which comprised of a gym, beauty salon and pool. Margaret was eager for me to go and look at it, but really my intention was to rejoin Adlington Barbell Club. Also, I had an excellent gym of my own. It had previously been a hayloft that I had converted when we first moved from Adlington. My training plans were in place and I was ready to go.

However, Margaret came home one day and said that she had been to view Shaw Hill and was impressed. Not only was she impressed but she said, 'I have met a man who says that he can help you and I would like you to go and meet him. His name is Gus O'Donnell and he is an ex-rugby player.'

The following day I went to meet him and he impressed me too, so I joined Shaw Hill Leisure. This was in June 1999 and, despite the age gap of about thirty years, Gus and I became good mates. We have had fifteen very eventful and interesting years, fifteen years of achievements and experiences that I never thought I'd have and memories that will last forever.

My early years of training with Gus were very rewarding physically. I soon started to lose weight and feel fitter. I lost seven stone, but a fringe benefit of losing all that weight was that I stopped sweating so much. Previously, at twenty-two stone, if I was out for a meal or at a party, I started to sweat very easily and then the embarrassment of sweating made me sweat even more. I got to the point that if I was in a restaurant or at a party, I would automatically look for the air con and get as near to it as I could. Now, suddenly, it was no longer an issue; it was simply not necessary as there was just no sweat.

One person that I haven't yet mentioned is Kieran O'Donnell. Kieran has played a major role in my time at Shaw Hill over the last sixteen years, both in training together at the end of the day, or with him bullying me to join his classes when I was training on my own, happy in my comfort zone.

I keep a diary and I am amazed when I look through my old ones how often I trained in the morning, then went back at the end of the day and worked out with Kieran on various muscle groups.

Many years ago, we decided to train for a month then have a bench-press contest against each other. We both got down to serious training and put posters up around the gym. Our posters read: 'Don't miss this big grudge match, Kieran (Cutie) O'Donnell (because all the girls fancied him) versus Fred (Fearsome) Smith.' We hoped that this would generate a bit of interest. Neither of us expected the level of interest that it did generate.

The contest was to take place on Friday afternoon. It was normally a very quiet period, but there must have been about fifty people there, some of whom I knew had definitely taken an afternoon off work. We both took our lifts, with Gus acting as referee, and we had to call it a draw when we both lifted 319lbs which was all the weight that was available at that time. It was a good contest and a fair result.

Some people said that I had scored a moral victory as I was almost forty years older than Kieran. Others said that Kieran had scored a moral victory as I was a dedicated and international power lifter, whereas Kieran only lifted on the bench press casually. So a draw was a fair result and we both agreed that afterwards in the members' bar.

Kieran is the only person I know who can run a marathon in less than three hours and lift 320lbs on the bench press. I would put good money on it that he is the only person in the country that could perform these two feats. I know that there are many who could do one or the other, but find me someone who can do both? You won't. He is now thinking of attempting to do one hundred miles in twenty-four hours and nobody would back against him.

I don't think I have ever met anyone as popular as Kieran and this is mainly because of the genuine interest that he shows in the members of Shaw Hill. If they have a training problem and go to him for advice, he helps them all he can but then follows it through and monitors their progress till the problem has gone away. This is very important, much better than just answering their questions then forgetting about them.

I often smile when I think of the difference I have seen in Kieran since he started working at Shaw Hill sixteen years ago. In those days he was what you might describe as a handy lad round Wigan on a Saturday night, but Marie and Carrick (his wife and his three-year-old son) have brought about a complete transformation.

In his younger days, his conversation on a Monday morning would always be along the lines of, 'There were a couple of nutters throwing their weight about on King Street, so I had to sort 'em out.' Or, 'Some guy tried to push me around in a bar, so I showed him who was boss.' These days I hear him talking to a young mother and he is saying things like, 'Is she on solids yet?' Or, 'Is he sleeping right through now?' Oh, yes, he is a devoted husband and father. He has done the Jack the Lad thing and has moved on. That's the way it should be: Jack the Lad to perfect dad.

It is not uncommon for someone who is training for a marathon to ask Kieran to train with them for support and he invariably agrees. The trouble is that they are training with a single goal in mind, whereas Kieran has to continue with his own training, plus all the classes that he takes, and somehow fit in their marathon training as well. Don't ask me how he does it but he does it.

One girl, Marie, who had previously weighed twenty-two stone, asked Kieran to help her lose weight. He did this very successfully and helped her to lose eleven stone, which was half her body weight. Then he entered her for the London Marathon, helping her with training. About a week before the marathon, she asked him what time he thought she would complete it in. He didn't answer but wrote it down on paper and put it in a sealed envelope, telling her not to open it until she had completed the marathon.

The day came and she successfully completed the marathon. When she got back to the hotel she took Kieran's prediction out of the envelope. He was out by only nine seconds.

My first London Marathon

I'D BEEN TRAINING at Shaw Hill for about four years and was sixty years old when one day Gus said to me, 'Next year, you're doing the London Marathon. I'll do it with you. You don't need to run it, you can walk the entire twenty-six miles but as fast as you can.'

'Yeah, alright,' I said because, as we all know, a year is a long way away. But again, as we all know, it comes round in a flash and in no time at all I was on the train with Gus on our way to London.

We travelled down on Friday and went to the Excel Centre to sign in on Saturday. By then, butterflies were beginning to kick in. The following day, Sunday, we got on the tube (which is free on this day) to travel to the start and I was getting really nervous. I kept asking myself why I was getting so nervous. Nobody knew me and I was not going to win; I just had to walk twenty-six miles which I had done in training several times. But it was the enormity of the occasion: all those thousands and thousands of people surging forward and the very loud music blaring over the tannoys. I later learned, by talking to several people, that nervousness is a common thing and most competitors suffer from it.

I will never forget the incredible feeling when the starting pistol is fired and everyone surges forward and you realise this is it, I am doing the London Marathon.

I remember on that first marathon starting to feel faint and sick at four miles. 'What's wrong with me?' I thought. I didn't mention it to Gus and, sure enough, the feeling went away, only for it to come back again, not once, but several times. It got to the stage where it didn't bother me as I knew it wouldn't last long, so it was no problem. Anyway, I kept my head down and kept going with Gus urging me on all the time.

At every mile there was a mileage sign to let you know where you were. You long for these signs to come into view so that you can knock another mile off. This marathon was one of the coldest and wettest of all time, and everyone was battling against the wind and rain. Gus carried no surplus weight so the cold affected him far more than it did me, therefore by mile twenty-four he was seizing up. For the first twenty-four miles he was, metaphorically, dragging me along but for the last two miles the roles reversed and I was dragging him along.

When we eventually got back to the hotel he ran a hot bath but was so cold he had to get into it fully clothed till he thawed out and could get undressed.

I can't begin to describe the feeling when you cross the finishing line and they put the medal round your neck. It's a feeling of elation, relief and everything else you can think of and the tremendous lift that you get from the roar of the crowd. How can these wonderful people stand there hour after hour and show such enthusiasm for people that they don't even know? At this point I must pay tribute to Gus, who stayed with me all the way even though he could have gone faster and finished in a much shorter time.

Our time was 6 hours 46 minutes 16 seconds and about 1500 people finished behind us, so that was alright. (We'll not mention the 38,000 or so that finished ahead of us.) But I had done the London Marathon – what a fantastic feeling.

A bonus of doing the London Marathon (I've now done four) is that I now love watching it on TV, which is something I never used to do. I love to spot all the landmarks and I know how the runners feel as they go past them.

Incidentally, at the 2004 marathon we had been out for about five hours and we were walking with three or four other people of a similar standard when we passed a group of children, probably aged five to eight. One little girl was obviously the ringleader and making the most noise. They were all cheering us on. By that time probably 37–38,000 had already passed that spot when the little ringleader shouted, 'You're all winners.' How lovely was that? It isn't only the landmarks that keep the runners going.

I imagine that the weekend of the London Marathon must be like Christmas to the hotel cleaning ladies, the reason being that when you cross the finishing line, apart from receiving your medal you are given a lucky bag. This is a large plastic bag full of presents from national companies. For instance, you will find things like a tin of salmon, a shampoo, a tube of toothpaste, probably about twenty to thirty free gifts donated by the manufacturers. The problem is you are already loaded up with luggage and these are very bulky bags, especially if you have to fly. As a consequence, most of their contents get left behind in the hotel rooms.

I also think it is a common feeling (understandably) when you are well into the marathon, in pain and the finishing line is miles away, you promise yourself, 'This is the last time I am ever doing this. Never again. Never ever again.' But it's not long, when the blisters have gone and the injuries are just a memory, before you start to think, 'Could I beat that time? Should I try another?' And so it was with me. I decided to discuss it with Gus but he had already decided and informed me that he had applied for entry to do the New York Marathon.

We did the London Marathon for Kidney Research and raised £4,500. We got a place in the New York Marathon to raise money for Galloway Society for the Blind, a Preston local charity.

My First New York Marathon

After a few weeks of rest it was back on the road again, as they say, with the New York Marathon in our sights. I needed to get a lot of walking under my belt but, as I said earlier, Gus was very fit and didn't carry any surplus weight, so he just turned up on the day and did it without any training. Alright for some!

On this occasion there were seven of us that went to New York: Gus; Kieran; Richard Ormisher; John Greenhalgh; Mike Briggs, and Peter Cooke (not Dudley Moore's mate).

Now no one needs to tell me that I don't look like your average marathon athlete. At age sixty-one and weighing seventeen stone, I attracted many a sarcastic comment, but it was all good-humoured fun and it gave me no concern at all. In fact, I rather enjoyed the banter – but the passport control officer at New York airport certainly didn't mince his words. He checked all my documents and, having done so, he said, 'Just a few more questions for security purposes.'

'Alright, fire away,' I replied, confidently.

The questioning went like this.

PCO:	Destination?
Me:	Manhattan
PCO:	Address at destination?
Me:	Modern Hotel West 55th
PCO:	Duration of your stay?
Me:	Four days
PCO:	Reason for your visit?
Me:	To do the New York Marathon.
PCO:	I'LL ASK YOU AGAIN. REASON FOR YOUR VISIT?
Me:	I've come to see my cousin.
PCO:	Thank you, visiting relatives.

He then banged my passport down in front of me and said, 'You'll not get through here any quicker by trying to be funny.'

'Very sorry,' I replied.

We arrived on the Friday and, as Sunday got nearer, again the butterflies started. On the day of the marathon we had to be up by five in the morning as the race started off from Staten Island, so hundreds of coaches were laid on to transport everyone over the bridge before people started to commute to work. Nobody got a good night's sleep as we all kept waking to check the time.

When the race eventually started, the first length was back over the bridge that we had crossed earlier in the coach. With my experience of working on motorways, I know what walking over a motorway bridge feels like. They aren't like other bridges as there are expansion joints every twenty or so yards, which means that the bridge is not rigid and moves about a lot. You don't feel it when you drive over it but you certainly do when you walk over and this was one walk that Gus did not enjoy, as he just wasn't expecting it.

I found New York harder than London and my time was seven hours and nine minutes.

As in all big cities, there is always someone accosting you to try to extract money. On the Monday, after the marathon, we were all walking in pairs on the footpath on Seventh Avenue. Gus and I were about fifty yards or so behind the others when in front of us we saw this scantily clad girl approach Richard Ormisher, my brother-in-law, and start talking to him very enthusiastically. 'I bet I know what she is selling,' said Gus. I nodded in agreement.

Now anyone else would have said, 'Not today, thanks,' and walked away but Richard is a very trusting soul and takes everything at face value (a sales person's dream). He was agreeing with everything the girl said. As we got closer, we began to pick up on the conversation and I heard Richard say, 'When can we go?'

'We can go now,' said the girl.

'Now?' said Richard.

'Right everyone follow me,' he said as he and the girl turned right down a side street, deep in conversation.

The other lads didn't follow but Gus and I thought, well, we fly home tomorrow and it would be good to enjoy the cabaret for an hour, so off we went. They were still deep in conversation till we got to a grotty building which looked like an old cinema, more or less just as we had expected. Another attractive girl was sitting at reception. 'Please sign your name here,' she said with a smile. Gus signed a fictitious name, as most men do at strip clubs. I signed my real name as everyone thinks it is fictitious anyway so there's no need to lie.

We followed Richard and the girl down a dingy corridor until we came to a door, which we went through. I wasn't quite sure what to expect but was surprised to find that the room was empty except for about twelve rows of seats facing an empty stage, which had a large screen in the centre. At this point the girl left us on our own. Gus and I decided that they were going to show us a film to get us in the mood. We didn't have a problem with that and, sure enough, after a few minutes the lights went out and the screen lit up. A large message appeared on the screen: 'WELCOME TO THE CHURCH OF CHRISTIAN SCIENCE.' I kid you not.

It was a religious gathering – and Gus and I had been waiting for the strippers to come on. We watched for about fifteen minutes then made an early exit although Richard, who had known all along what it was, not only watched it all the way through, but also spent $37 on a book about Christian Scientology. 'This all makes sense to me,' he said, 'I am going to read this book on the plane on the way home.'

That was over twelve years ago, and I recently asked him if he ever actually read the book. 'Did I bollocks,' he replied. The moment had passed.

MY SECOND WEIGHTLIFTING CAREER

IT WAS THE week after the 2004 London Marathon when I went to see my old weightlifting mate, Alan Fairclough, on a Sunday lunchtime at the Top Spinners pub in Adlington. I proudly took my marathon medal to show him. Although he was very complimentary and showed an interest, Alan was a weightlifter through and through; if a sport doesn't require a barbell then to Alan it's not a sport. Predictably the conversation soon got back to power lifting (there are two kinds of weightlifting, Olympic and Power).

Although I had not competed in well over twenty-five years, I had continued to train; under all the blubber, I was still in decent shape. Having lost about six stone, I was now in good condition. Alan said, 'Now that you're fit again, why don't you get back into competitions?'

He went on to explain that, unlike when I competed as a young man, they now had a category for older people so I could compete against weightlifters of my own age. This appealed to me and got me thinking.

'I'll tell you what,' said Alan. 'I've got a book at the Club (Adlington Barbell Club), with all the British records in, including your category. If you are interested, come down tomorrow night, Monday, and we'll look up your competitors and assess your chances.'

Again this appealed to me. That night I decided that I would go to ABC the following evening and discuss the possibility of competing again, this time against men in my own age group.

The following night I went and, sure enough, Alan was there with the book of British records. The British record on the bench press (the lift that I specialised in) was 314lbs, held by a lifter from London. Alan and I agreed that reaching that poundage was a possibility and we would go for it.

That Monday evening in April 2004, I began what I can only describe as my second weightlifting career, which provided me with almost ten years of enthusiasm and pleasure that I never dreamt I would ever have again. It gave ten years of the same for Alan, as his passion for his members was every bit as keen as theirs. He lived every lift that they performed, and he always liked his members to compete.

Some lads, as in any sport, like to train for pleasure. That's fair enough but Alan liked to see ABC members in competition. I don't think I am exaggerating when I say that ABC is the premier club in the North West and has been for almost sixty years. Despite being only a small club it has a big reputation, with many of its members holding British records and lifting at international level.

The following Wednesday night I was back at ABC, training on power lifting with the focus being the bench press. This meant that I was training at Shaw Hill under Gus's supervision in the morning for five days per week, and at ABC under Alan's supervision for three nights per week. This led to a conflict of interest, as Gus wanted me to concentrate on fitness and weight loss through cardio training, while Alan wanted me to bulk up and get strong through weights. It was a conflict of interest that would never go away. Neither of my coaches wanted me to train at the other place but, whilst Gus was reasonably light hearted about it and always referred to ABC as 'Your Adlington playschool', Alan didn't approve. I made a decision never to mention Shaw Hill or marathons to Alan.

My power lifting training went well and both Alan and I were happy and pleasantly surprised by my progress. This in itself ramps up the enthusiasm and on occasion after a good night's training, I would drive home on a high. It was reminiscent of when I was a young lad, and a feeling that I never thought I would experience again, certainly not at well over sixty. 'How good is this?' I used to think to myself. 'It's like being young again.'

MY FIRST BENCH PRESS COMPETITION

I HAD BEEN training for about three months on the weights when Alan informed me that the North West Counties Bench Press

Championships were to be held in December at the gym in Thorn Cross Prison at Warrington. The reason the contest was held at the prison was because they have all the best facilities – of course they do. So, as with the marathons, it was head down and focus; also, as with the marathons, the day was with us in blink of an eye.

On the day, we all met outside the Ridgeway, Adlington, at eight in the morning. I remember thinking it was like turning the clock back thirty years. It was just how we used to meet up all that time ago, although in those days it was everyone piling into my milk van. Anyway, we all got into various cars and we were on our way.

I remember early on in the day, long before I was due to lift, going for a cup of coffee. The prisoners served the coffee and refreshments and, as I approached them, I could hear the radio which the prisoners were listening to giving out the football results. When it was my turn to be served, I said, 'Does anyone know how Preston are going on?'

'Yes, we are winning 2–0,' said one of the prisoners.

'Are you a PNE fan?' I asked.

'Yes,' he replied. 'Have been all my life.'

'Do you live in Preston?' I asked.

'Yes, Lea, the better part of Preston.'

As I walked back with my coffee I thought, well – he comes from the better part of Preston and he's in prison, so what's the rough part like?

We had arrived at the venue at about 9.30, weighed in at 10.30 and then came the very long wait until it was my class. I was informed that there were no other lifters in my age group. Although that gave me a clear run to win and in that respect took the pressure off, I was a little bit disappointed as I was looking forward to a bit of a battle. However, the upside of this meant that I could now forget about beating opponents and concentrate on something that was even more important: qualifying for the British Championships. As a young lifter I had never qualified for the British, so if I did now it would be a first for me.

I remember standing in the dressing room waiting to be called to lift. I couldn't believe that at sixty-two I was again doing what I did forty years earlier. I was eventually called and, although not everything went according to plan, I lifted 308lbs and easily qualified for the British. As a bonus, although I was the only competitor in my class, I was also the official North West Counties Champion, so it was a very satisfactory day.

On the way home we called at the White Crow pub on Wigan Lane to relive the day. Calling at a pub on the way home was to become a tradition, as it was so good to analyse the day over a pint with the other lads.

Earlier in the day, when I was waiting to be called to lift, one of the other lifters, a lad from Wigan, walked into the dressing room having just finished lifting. He shook his head in anger and said through gritted teeth, 'Bastard, bastard.'

'What's the problem?' I asked.

'The ref failed my last lift,' he growled.

There are several infringements that a referee can fail a lift on, so I asked him, 'What did he fail it on?'

'I didn't budge it'

'Bastard,' I said, in mock agreement.

THE BRITISH CHAMPIONSHIPS

THE DATE OF the British Championships was Saturday 5th February 2005. I was up at 5.30am and met Alan and another lifter, Joe Bullock, at the Ridgeway pub. Joe was not lifting but was just coming to support me. The contest was being held at a sports hall in Birmingham. All the way there I felt very confident. I had broken the North West

Championship record at my last competition by 78lb, and I had a gut feeling that by tonight I would be British Champion. I couldn't have been more wrong, as the day proved to be a disaster.

They started the weigh in at 10.00am and there were about 130 lifters in total, from the flyweights to the super heavyweights. I stood outside the weighing-in room for about two hours waiting for my name to be called out but they never called it, and they eventually put up the closed sign. Alan, Joe and I stood there in amazement.

'Knock on the door and ask them what is going on,' said Alan.

This I did. A fellow answered the door and, when I asked him, he just said, 'We called for you but you didn't come so you are disqualified.'

I argued that I had been standing outside the door waiting to be called for over two hours and they had not called my name. After a heated argument, he agreed that I could go in and be weighed. But this was not good preparation.

I competed in one of the heavier classes so I was always one of the last to lift as they started with the lightest classes first. That means the tension is with you all day, which is again not good. It was about 4.30pm when Alan told me to start warming up, i.e. to start lifting lighter weights in preparation. This went alright, with Alan and Joe helping me; then, for my last warm-up lift, Joe was helping me to tighten my lifting belt when snap, the buckle broke. Now, a lifting belt to a lifter is like a golf club to a golfer, or a racquet to a tennis player. It is part of you and is what you are used to, so this was another mini-disaster and I was about to lift in a few minutes. Obviously your opponents are not going to lend you their belt, so Joe disappeared to try and borrow one from someone.

He came back in a few minutes with one that he had borrowed from one of the super heavyweights. It was far too big for me but it would have to do. The belt is supposed to feel very tight around your middle to give you support but this one was too big. However, it was better than nothing.

Then the man on the microphone called out for my class to go on stage to lift. This was it – the British Championships. I went out for my first lift, lifted it but got failed on an infringement. Disaster – it was like a football team conceding an early goal in the cup final. My second attempt came round and the same thing happened again: I lifted it but the referee ruled it out. Only one more attempt was allowed. It was my last chance. It would take 314lbs to win the title.

By this time the crowd were behind me as most of them were lifters or ex-lifters themselves and they knew what it was like to bomb out, especially at the national championships. Their vocal support was deafening. I was determined that I was not going to let them down, so I took a deep breath, pushed out my chest and strode manfully to the bar. Well, that was until I got halfway across the stage, when an old problem with my left knee came back and it gave way. I almost fell, I let out a loud groan and one of the loaders grabbed hold of me to steady me and helped me to the bar. It couldn't be happening. I attempted the 314lbs. which I had done many times before in the gym, but got my line completely wrong and the bar came crashing down.

So, with echoes of my first bodybuilding contest all those years ago, that was the end of my big day. Alan and Joe were devastated – even more so than me, in fact. It was a long and quiet drive home, except for members of my family ringing to ask how I had gone on.

But, as I always say, with every negative there comes a positive. I comforted myself with the fact that I had, at last, competed in the British Championships. Also, the British title had been won with 308lbs, the same weight that I had lifted at the NWC, so I must be there or thereabouts. Again, we had a pint at the White Crow and began to look forward to the next match.

NWC Championships

My next match was the NWC on Sunday 8th May 2005. This was at Rhinos Gym, Oldham. Again, I lifted 308lbs but took 319bs for my third and final attempt, which would have been a British record. I narrowly failed, although it was so close that they allowed me to have a fourth attempt (outside of the competition) but I just missed it again. However, I had qualified for the next British.

In between the British and the NWC Championships, Gus, my brother-in-law Richard and I did the London Marathon on Sunday May 7th in 6 hours 46 seconds. Don't ask me why, but it was the easiest marathon I ever did. I experienced no pain at all and at the end I felt as though I could have done it again. I expected to be sore the following day but I was not sore at all. I was delighted.

My Second British Championship

Saturday, February 4th 2006 was the day of my second British Championships at the same Birmingham venue as the previous year. Unlike that event when I drove there full of confidence, this time I was more apprehensive because I remembered how last year had gone.

As with the previous year, I picked up Alan and Joe at the Ridgeway Pub, Adlington, at 7.30am. We got to Birmingham in good time and I weighed in at 17 stone 3lbs. Because of the various contests I had entered over the last twelve months, I had got to know other lifters, especially from the North West; unlike last year, when the room was full of complete strangers, now there were many familiar faces. This in itself had a calming effect and the time waiting to lift went much faster.

I went out for my first lift at 308lbs at about 1.00pm. Again, as with the previous year, I lifted it but the referee failed it on an infringement.

Oh no, was this going to be another disaster? But no, when I took it again I lifted it perfectly. I knew then that I had won the title, as no other lifter was anywhere near my poundage. With the British title safely under my belt, I took 325lbs for my last lift for a new British record. Again I lifted it and one referee gave it a pass but the other two failed it, so I gained a British title but no British record.

But the icing on the cake was that, as British Champion, I was told that I would be invited to represent Great Britain in the world championships in Miami. Things were getting better and it was all happening thirty years after I had thought that my weightlifting career was over. A lifelong ambition had been achieved. It was a much better journey home, with plenty to discuss and analyse, and again the White Crow was a grateful beneficiary. This was the best part of the day, as all the pressure and tension were gone and I had gained a gold medal.

After the White Crow, we had a last one in the Ridgeway at Adlington. By now Alan was well away and my old idol was now idolising me (how good was that!). I was sure he would have forgotten about it in the morning.

THE WORLD CHAMPIONSHIPS

AFTER AN EASY week at the gym, it was head down to train for the World Championships in Miami. It was a three-day competition and I would be lifting on Thursday, April 20th.

Alan's enthusiasm for the sport and for his members has never diminished in sixty years. He was as keen then as he was as a young lifter, so from then until the championships he lived for the preparation and the training. To Alan it wasn't 'me' training, it was 'us' training. While he was also keen for the other lads, it was no secret that I was his number one priority, probably because I had been a member of

ABC for so many years and we were also good mates.

As with the marathons and the other weightlifting competitions, the day was soon with us. On Tuesday 18th April, Jonny took us to Manchester Airport, from where we flew to Amsterdam. It's interesting that, while we were waiting for the connecting flight, we started to see other weightlifters obviously doing the same as us. Weightlifters are easy to spot.

We went on to Miami, where we stayed at the Hyatt Regency Hotel. It was also the venue for the championships, and was a massive hotel. Every country's lifters and officials were staying there. Alan has lifted in many internationals himself so he is no stranger to big comps, but when we arrived he couldn't believe all the international flags that were flying. 'My God,' he said. 'I have never seen anything so impressive. This is a real world championship.'

I hadn't the heart to tell him that all the hundreds of Hyatt Regency Hotels throughout the world have these flags flying and that they weren't just for us. He mentioned them many times but I didn't want to spoil it for him.

Wednesday the 19th was not a pleasant day. It was a kind of nothing day, when we were just hanging about talking to other lifters and killing time. You couldn't even enjoy a drink and a good meal, as you had the weigh-in to think about. It was, as one lad put it, like waiting to be hanged. Even when you went go to bed you didn't sleep well. Anyway, I was not complaining. I was about to fulfil a lifetime's ambition.

Thursday the 20th was the big day, the day I became a fully-fledged international. It was 5.00pm when I lifted and by then I was pretty stressed out, but once you start to warm up you forget all that.

The Americans always put on a show. When you walk out to lift, the loaders and the officials treat you like you're a superhero. They cheer you on and make you feel special. Again, as with most of my other comps, I failed the first lift but got the last two. My final lift was 319lbs and got me fourth place. Fourth in the world – how good is that!

All the stress was lifted the moment I finished and all that was left was the pleasure and the analysis.

I hate the warming-up room where you go before you lift. I hate everything about it – the short tempers as lifters fight for warm-up bars, the fact that the light weights that you warm up with suddenly feel very heavy, and that you fret about what the heavy ones are going to feel like. I just hated it but after I had lifted – and if I lifted well – I just loved that room and could sit there and reflect and enjoy.

The countries in my class were USA (two lifters), New Zealand, Finland, France, Great Britain, Sweden and Denmark.

A pleasant spin-off was that in the warm-up room an American guy started to give me a lift. He was very friendly and helpful, then stood backstage to watch me and offer advice. It was only after the competition was over that I found out that his name was Dave Doan, the world light-heavyweight champion. For the next few days we got on very well and became good friends.

On Saturday the 22nd, we watched the lifting during the day then in the evening we attended the closing banquet. After a few drinks at the bar, we went into the dining room. The food was a serve yourself buffet and I have never seen a buffet like it. It was obvious that they had catered as best they could for all the countries, but (just my luck) I found myself queuing up behind the entire Japanese team. They were all in their national costume, and most of them make their living as Sumo wrestlers. I will leave you to imagine what it was like queuing up behind ten Sumo wrestlers at a buffet – but I decided not to complain.

Sunday was a free day so at last we could leave the hotel and do a bit of the tourist stuff. But back home, another sporting event was taking place for the Smith family: Richard, Jonathan and Carmen were all running the London Marathon – Richard in 4.16, Carmen in 4.26, and Jonathan in 4.58. They all thoroughly enjoyed it and want to do it again to beat their times. So, it was a memorable sporting weekend for my sporting family.

Uncle Richard went with them but didn't run. However, he was also quite determined that he would run it one day.

Like many other lifters, indeed anyone that takes part in sport, I've had my share of injuries. A few weeks before the world championships I went to see my mate Tony Smith, who is an acupuncturist, to give me treatment on my right shoulder. Tony lives in Hoghton, the next village to Brindle where I live. He has been in a wheelchair for many years but is always a very cheerful chap and has a great sense of humour. He is a big fan of the television programme "Phoenix Nights" and funnily enough I know Dave Spikey from the show quite well, he lives locally and for a long time we were members of the same gym. Dave is a great lad, very easy going and approachable. When I told him about Tony, he was only too happy to give me an original signed script for him. Tony was over the moon.

Over the next few weeks I went to see Tony twice a week and I know that the treatment helped a lot. A few days after I returned home from Miami, I went to the Sirloin, the local hostelry that Tony used to frequent. As I walked in, Tony looked at me expectantly and said, 'Well, how did it go?'

'I came fourth,' I proudly replied.

'Well that's not too bad,' he said sympathetically.

I couldn't believe what I was hearing because up till that moment I'd thought it was very good. 'Tony,' I said, taken aback, 'that's fourth in the world, not Hoghton and district.'

He suddenly realised what he'd said and put his head in his hands. 'I'm sorry Fred,' he said, through stifled laughter. 'That's not how I meant it to come out. Let me get you a drink. I'll get you a large one.'

To this day there isn't a time when we are having a drink that that conversation doesn't come up.

THE EUROPEAN CHAMPIONSHIPS IN FRYDEK-MISTEK

BECAUSE OF WINNING the British and taking fourth place in the world, I was invited to lift in the European Championships in the Czech Republic, in a backwoods place called Frydek-Mistek. Because power lifting is not a mainstream sport, the competitions are sometimes held in remote places. I love this, as you get to visit places that you would never go to on holiday and you get to see the real country. It was also noticeable that we never saw a takeaway, nor did we ever see a fat person, but almost everyone smoked. There were many cigarette kiosks on street corners, the kind that we had in Britain in the fifties and sixties. There must be a link here.

Friday, September 22nd 2006 was the day I lifted and also was a day to forget, because the British team manager couldn't make it to the competition. Alan was asked to take over as manager, which he did, and he did a good job. In reality, though, I paid for Alan on all these trips and paid for him to look after me as my coach, not as coach to the team. As a result of the distractions of being manager, I saw very little of him – and what a difference it made.

For the second time in my second career, I bombed out. Although I lifted all three attempts, I was failed on infringements. The most frustrating was the third attempt. I lifted it easily but beat the two-second pause before I pressed it out. What's more frustrating is that this would have got me a bronze medal, so it felt like a long journey home from the Czech Republic.

The night after the contest, Alan and I walked into town and popped into a bar. Frydek-Mistek was one of those remote places that didn't get many tourists, so as a result hardly anyone spoke English. Once in the bar we got a drink and sat down.

After a few minutes the proprietor came over to us. It was obvious that he wanted to know where we were from and, no matter how much we said England, he seemed convinced that we were Germans. We continued to shake our heads but we were getting absolutely nowhere. Then I had an idea and said loud and clear, 'Margaret Thatcher.'

His face lit up and the penny dropped. He nodded his head enthusiastically and said, 'Alex Ferguson.' I nodded in agreement. Then he said, 'Bobby Charlton.' By now we were all nodding and smiling as he carried on saying, 'Dennis Law. George Best.'

The locals round the bar smiled and joined in. After a few minutes, we shook hands and he returned to his duties, only to return shortly afterwards with a plate of local delicacies for which he would take no money. These are happy memories that helped cushion the blow of bombing on my lifts. Let's just remember the good things.

THE NEXT COMPETITIONS...

My next competition was the British at Birmingham, on February 17th 2007 where, despite an injury sustained during warm up, I managed to hold on to the title, although with a much-reduced poundage. But even so I qualified for the internationals, so again there was a happy landlord at the White Crow.

The World Championships were with us again, this time in Berlin. It was the only competition that Alan didn't come to, as his wife was very ill with cancer. Competition days are known for being very fraught and, no matter how much you tell yourself that it's only sport and not important, it just doesn't work. Until it's all over you are uptight, and you just have to live with it.

I don't know why, but I have always seemed to miss my first lift. This was what I did again and, as you were only allowed three attempts, if you missed your first one the pressure was really on. Fortunately lifts two and three both went well and I ended up in fifth place. I have therefore had a fourth and fifth in two world championships.

I was invited to lift in the next European Championships, which were to take place again in the Czech Republic in a place called Zlin.

THE EUROPEAN CHAMPIONSHIPS IN ZLIN

ONCE MORE THE day came round in a flash and on Wednesday the 21st November 2007 Alan, Joe and I flew from Manchester to Zurich. Next we took a plane to Vienna, and finally took a four-hour coach trip to Zlin and the venue. Because of the time of the flights, the other British team members had made the journey earlier in the day; so the organisers had arranged for the three of us to travel with the French team. It was noticeable that in the four hours that we were travelling we never once drove on a motorway. It was all narrow country lanes and through small towns and villages. Also, in all the journey not one French person spoke to us. Maybe they just didn't like the British.

Thursday the 22nd was another anxious day as all competition days are. I made the weight with no problem, and the contest started at 4.00pm. On this occasion I got my first and second lift passed alright, but the referees failed my third lift of 314lbs. None of us knew why. However, my second lift of 303lbs got me second place and a silver medal. At last I was on the podium at an international. Again, the evening was all about reliving the day, along with other British team members.

British Championships in Solihull

On Sunday, March 9th 2008 the British Championships were held at Solihull. I didn't lift because of my shoulder injury but went with Alan to spectate. A lifter called Ken Churchmore, who also established a new British record with 162.5kg, won my class, so by the time I set off for home I'd lost both my British title and British record. Still, tomorrow is another day.

Back home at about this time (2008) I thought of buying a static caravan in the Lakes. I mentioned this to Gus and he agreed that I should go for it. One day we took a trip to the Lakes and looked at a couple of caravan sites. We ended up at Fallbarrow Park where I saw one I liked and bought it.

Peter, the sales manager, informed us that another caravan park, White Cross Bay, was owned by the same company and the caravan owners from Fallbarrow Park could also use the facilities at White Cross Bay, which included bar and restaurant, pool and gym. Then he looked directly at me and said, 'But with respect, sir, I don't think we will ever see you in a gym.'

Gus fell about laughing. After fifty years of training, I still look like I've never been in a gym – how bad is that! Also, why is it that when someone starts off a sentence with the words 'with respect' you know that you are going to get anything but.

2008 London Marathon

My next sporting event was the London Marathon, held on Sunday, April 13th 2008. Seven of us travelled – Carmen, Bruce, Uncle Richard, my Richard, Julie, Jonny and me. We met at The Paddock (Jonny's house) on Friday the 11th and travelled to Preston South by minibus. We arrived in London about 8.30, had a drink and a Chinese, and then decided on an early night.

On Saturday the 12th, we met at breakfast then took various trains and tubes to the Excel Centre to register. I've got to hand it to Richard – he knows his way around London. We had confidence in him. I just went with the flow.

We duly registered and had an hour or two in the hall, which was crowded with marathon runners, their families and friends. It was a fantastic atmosphere.

After registering, which you can do amazingly quickly, we went back into London for a meal. Unfortunately Uncle Richard had gone down with a stomach bug and the marathon was looking more and more doubtful for him by the minute. That night, Jonny, Carmen, Bruce and I met Bill and Brenda, Bruce's parents, for a meal at the Union Jack Club. While we were there, at about 9pm, Jonny's mobile rang. It was Uncle Richard who wanted Jonny to go and find a chemist shop and get him something for his bad guts, but Jonny was having none of it.

'Where will I find a chemist open at nine o'clock on a Saturday night?' he asked.

'There will be one somewhere,' said Uncle Richard. 'I need something. I can't get off the toilet.'

'Look,' said Jonny. 'Ring for room service and order a bottle of red wine.'

'Why? Is red wine good for diarrhoea?' asked Richard.

'No,' said Jonny. 'But you can shove the cork up your arse.'

It was Sunday the 13th, and once again I'd got myself into yet another pressured situation. Again the butterflies kicked in but I comforted myself that apparently a certain amount of pressure is good for you.

By then Uncle Richard was on his way home. It was the first marathon I had done without Gus, so I got my head down and kept going. All the way round the bottoms of my feet were extremely painful but I kept telling myself that everyone was suffering and I was not the only one. I told myself to not be a wimp and to keep going. Incidentally, this was the marathon that six Masai Warriors ran and I believe that one of them didn't finish – so at least I beat him!!

Again the crowd were wonderful and you really got the feeling that they wanted you to do well. The feeling of relief when you crossed the finishing line was indescribable – coupled with pride that I'd done another London Marathon.

The problem then was getting back to the hotel, for (as I've said before) once you cross the finishing line, your body (well, mine anyhow) packs up as its job is done.

Just as I was pondering the problem, a young Chinese girl on a rickshaw came peddling by. I flagged her down. 'Are you looking for business?' I asked – on reflection probably it was not the wisest thing to say to a girl in the middle of London. Anyway, she knew what I meant and stopped, so I got in.

The girl was very small and my seventeen stone was a bit difficult for her to transport. Things became even more difficult when we came to a steep hill with traffic lights, which changed to red as we approached them. As the lights changed back to green the girl attempted to get going again, but her five stone of bodyweight wasn't going to drag my seventeen stone uphill.

She turned to me and said, 'Do you think you could jump out while I get going then catch me up and jump back in again?'

WHAT!! Was she joking? In short, no I couldn't. As a compromise, I got out of the rickshaw, somehow hobbled to the back and half pushed and half leaned. It got her moving and I managed to drag myself round and climb in again.

When we got back to the hotel she said, 'That will be £25 please.'

'You are going to be a very rich girl,' I said.

'Yes, but you were very heavy,' she replied.

'Fair enough,' I said.

THE 2009 EUROPEAN CHAMPIONSHIPS, AND OTHERS

MY NEXT BIG sporting event was the 2009 British Bench Press Championships at Birmingham, on Sunday, March the 1st. I lifted well and got a 314lb but was beaten into second place by the previous year's champion. Nevertheless it was a good day for me and Alan, which meant a good night for the White Crow.

The next competition was the NWC at Clegg's gym, Ashton Under Lyne on October 11th 2009. I got an easy 314lbs and narrowly missed 330lbs – but I won easily.

On October 21st, Alan and I flew to Brussels for the European Championships. When we arrived at the airport we were met by a World Power Lifting official, who was there with the bus, but we had to wait a further one-and-a-half hours for some Swedish and Norwegian lifters before we could leave for the hotel. When I say hotel, it was actually a building in the middle of an industrial estate. It had bedrooms and not much else. It didn't even have a dining room, just a sandwich vending machine. To make matters worse, there was a taxi on its way to pick us up and take us to the venue as I had been nominated as the British representative at the technical meeting, the meeting where all the last-minute problems were ironed out for all the competing countries.

When all the fees were handed over after the meeting, we had to wait for the official taxi to take us back to the 'hotel'. When we got back, I managed to get a bacon sandwich at a transport cafe, which was a great preparation for an international championship the next day.

On Thursday the 22nd we had 'breakfast' at the hotel then the official bus took us to the venue. There were about thirty lifters staying at the same place as us.

As at any competition, Alan goes over every little detail again and again. He left nothing to chance, even to the point of finding me a quiet area to wait in so that I wouldn't be distracted by others. We knew that the wait between the weigh-in and lifting was the time to get mentally fired up.

This was not to be one of my better days. I only got my first lift of 297lbs, failing twice with 319lbs. As always, the rest of the day and evening were spent mulling over the events of the day with a drink and a meal.

I was very philosophical about my performances even though they were not as good as I'd hoped, because I was doing something beyond my wildest dreams. Everything else was a bonus. By then I knew most of the British lifters and quite a few from other countries, which was great.

On Friday the 23rd I was supporting the British lads and watching the lifting, and then in the evening I was doing what I do best – eating and drinking. On Saturday, the 24th Britain had no one lifting, so we took an hour-long train ride from Le Louvre to Brussels, then had a day of sightseeing.

On Sunday the 25th we were up at 4.00am, took a taxi to the airport at 4.50am for our flight and got back home to an early night after another great experience. I am so lucky.

Michael Jennings and Madison Square Garden

In February 2009, there was another major sporting event in our family when Blakedale and Uncle Richard sponsored a Chorley boxer, Michael Jennings, in a world title fight against Miguel Cotto at Madison Square Garden. It was big news locally that a Chorley lad was competing against one of the world's greatest fighters for the world title – and we were proud to be part of it.

The fight was to take place on Saturday February 21st, and the family and I flew out on the Thursday and stayed at the same hotel as Michael. The following day we attended the weigh-in. Michael made the weight with no problem.

On Saturday, the day of the fight, I was sitting in the lobby of the hotel when Michael turned up to get ready to go to Madison Square Garden. He was soon surrounded by photographers and autograph hunters, whom he happily accommodated. I was sitting watching him, full of admiration, when he spotted me, came over and sat with me. I couldn't believe it. Here was a man about to fight for the world title in a few hours and he was sitting talking to me. He even apologised for not spotting me earlier. I had flashbacks to when I used to idolise boxers like Emile Griffiths, Howard Winstone and Sugar Ray Leonard, and there I was sitting with a boxer doing exactly the same thing. Just chatting away! How good is that?

The crowd in Madison Square Garden that night was about 15,000 strong and the fight was televised in more than twenty countries. Of the 15,000 crowd, about 14,900 were Puerto Ricans cheering on Cotto. Before the fight we were warned by several people not to antagonise any Puerto Ricans as they would knife you as soon as look at you. As we were going in to our seats, they surrounded us, all making plenty of noise. Don't ask me how it happened but we actually ended up being friendly and got on well. Richard, as usual, got his camera out.

Although Michael fought well and was a match for Cotto, in the fifth round Cotto landed a haymaker and Michael was counted out. But it was a good fight. It was also good to see the Blakedale Company Logo in the ring at Madison Square Garden. After the fight we had a drink and it was definitely a trip to remember.

2010 SPORTING EVENTS

2010 SAW THREE sporting events for me – one as a spectator and two as a competitor.

On Friday, 24th September, I flew with nine others from Shaw Hill to Berlin, where five of them were running the Berlin Marathon. I thoroughly enjoyed it and it was lovely going to Berlin without the pressure of having to run. Very enjoyable.

Sunday, October 3rd, 2010, was the date of the NWC Bench Press Championships at Ashton Under Lyne. There were four lifters from ABC – Rick Booth, Pete Radcliffe, Aaron Loham and me. Of course, Alan was team coach. All four of us won our classes so it was a good day all round.

On Wednesday, October 20th, 2010, I picked Alan up at Adlington and we went on to Manchester Airport, then took a flight to Amsterdam, going on to Luxembourg for the European Championships which were held in France.

On Thursday, October 21st, 2010, I made a reasonable 281lbs; while not good, it was not too bad. I was lifting with a shoulder injury, so I was not too unhappy.

The next two days we spent at the venue supporting the other British lifters. The accommodation was ten miles from the venue but transport was laid on. The lifters from various countries occupied about a dozen different hotels. Our hotel was almost as basic as the

Belgium hotel; watching *The Simpsons* speaking in French is definitely not the same.

On Sunday, October 24th, 2010, we were picked up by the coach at 3.00am. It was just Alan, me, and a lone Norwegian lifter called Hans Jorgan Jorganson, who I knew quite well. I wondered why they had sent such a big bus for three of us. I was soon to find out. After travelling for about five miles, the bus stopped at another hotel, then the worst thing possible happened: the entire Swedish team got on and they were all drunk. By then it was about 4.00am and they had been drinking all night. Many of them were still carrying bottles of spirits that they were drinking from the bottle and the noise was deafening. It was not good and I sensed trouble. Of course, you have to remember that these guys aren't your average man in the street and are some of the strongest men in the world.

Well, trouble did break out but before anything serious happened, the driver stopped the coach – we had arrived at the airport. Alan and I were sitting at the back but we still managed to be the first off. It had been another memorable trip.

THE 2011 BRITISH BENCH PRESS CHAMPIONSHIPS

ON SUNDAY, 30TH January, I was up at 3.30am, picked Alan up at Adlington, went on to Bolton to pick up Aaron Loham, then we all went on to the venue at Horncastle, Lincolnshire. Again I was lifting while recovering from an injury, but even so managed to lift 303lbs to win the title again. I was delighted, as was Alan. But the icing on the cake was that, for the first time, the judges awarded medals for the best-executed lifts. That meant the lift with the best style. Out of more than 150 lifts, my 303lbs was judged to be the best, so I received not one but two medals. It was a pleasant trip back from Lincolnshire.

Denmark World Championships and the London Marathon

On Wednesday, April 13th, 2011, Alan and I went to Manchester Airport and flew to Copenhagen. We had a two-hour wait for the team bus and a two-hour journey to the venue. The British team manager had told me that, as in all the other internationals, I would be lifting on the first day, i.e. Thursday. I had also got permission to fly home on the Friday, as opposed to staying with the team until Sunday. The reason for this was that I was doing the London Marathon on Sunday and I had to travel to London on the Saturday.

The venue was a Scandinavian holiday camp which was closed to the public, so there were just the officials and the lifters there. We checked in and were escorted to our chalet where another British lifter, Tom Collins, had already arrived. The news that he greeted us with shook Alan and I to the core: I was not lifting on Thursday, my class had been put back to Saturday, the day that I was due to travel to London. This was a monumental cock-up and Alan and I knew who had made it (no names mentioned). Alan was fuming. On Friday we had to fly back home, having had a very expensive wasted trip. It also robbed me of the bragging rights of lifting in the world championships and doing the London Marathon in the space of four days. I could have got some mileage out of that. My easily inflated ego could have milked that one dry. Alan is not as forgiving as I am and was fuming for weeks.

On Saturday, April 16th, 2011, Carmen and Bruce picked me up at 8.45am and we travelled to Preston Station where we met Richard, Jack and Jonny. Gus and Liam Morrow got on at Wigan and off we all went to London, where we stayed at the Grafton Hotel on Tottenham Court Road.

In the afternoon we all went to the Excel Centre to register and it was there that I bought a white T-shirt which had the words 'FRED – Am I last?' printed on it. It was something I was going to regret the following day. Uncle Richard joined us later as he had stayed behind to watch his beloved PNE.

On Sunday I was up early, had a good breakfast and I didn't feel as nervous as I usually do before a marathon. It was good, or so I thought. As usual by ten o'clock we were all on our way. Once the runners had started to thin out, the crowds spotted my T-shirt and they all tried to comfort me by shouting sympathetically, 'No Fred you're not last.' At first this was quite amusing but after about three hours of thousands of people shouting it, all thinking that they were the only ones to say it, we felt worn down to such an extent that Gus and Liam could stand it no longer and ran off and left me.

To make matters worse it was a boiling hot day and I was drinking water all the way; what I didn't drink I poured over myself to keep me cool. My finishing position was 34,470 out of 38,000, so it wasn't bad at all. In the evening, we treated ourselves to a Chinese meal and a moderate drink, ready to return the following day.

2011 COMMONWEALTH CHAMPIONSHIPS

THE NEXT BIG event was the Commonwealth Championships held at the Sports Hall at Bournemouth University on 18th December 2011. As I wrote earlier, I had been having injury trouble with my shoulder, so a couple of weeks prior to the contest I decided to have some physio on it. I made an appointment at a physio that Margaret recommended and duly turned up for treatment. He did a bit of exploratory work and I told him about the contest. He told me that, because the contest was so close, there would not be enough time for prolonged treatment. He said, 'If you don't mind throwing a bit of money at it, you would be better having a pain-killing injection.' He recommended a doctor at Gisburn Park Hospital.

I duly rang the doctor to check that: a) it was legal and not a steroid and, b) to ask the price. It was £300, so I booked an appointment for Wednesday the 7th December.

The day came and I turned up with my mate Les, with the intention of having a meal on the way back. The doctor discussed the injection to make sure that I knew what to expect and the more he talked, the more confident I felt. He certainly knew what he was talking about. On the way home Les and I called at the Eagle at Barrow.

For the next week I didn't train, as instructed by the doctor. The aching and the pain were exactly as the doctor had predicted, so I accepted them without a worry. The following Wednesday, the 14th, I went to Adlington to try some light lifts. I was bitterly disappointed as the pain was worse than ever and even the lightest weight was excruciating to lift. But I had to be positive, as I knew I could do well in this contest. I convinced myself that, as there was still four days before I had to lift, perhaps I had tried my shoulder out too soon. I decided the next four days would make all the difference and that I must put all negative thoughts out of my head. Wednesday the 14th didn't happen. My shoulder would be fine, no worries.

Sunday the 18th came round and Alan and I travelled to Bournemouth by train. Two other lifters from Adlington (Joe and Dr Rick) had travelled down the previous day. Both of them lifted well and won their classes. Adlington lifters definitely take some beating.

I weighed in at about 1.00pm and made the weight with no problem. Then it was the usual hanging around until it was time for me to lift. The time always dragged and relaxation was impossible, no matter how much you pretended to laugh and joke with the others.

I started to warm up and the pain in my shoulder was still there, so I kept the weight light. I had just worked up to 220lbs when someone came into the room and said that none of my three opponents from overseas had turned up. That was music to my ears as my shoulder pain was a worry. All that I would need to do now was make a lift and I would be Commonwealth Champion.

Alan decided that I should take the 220lbs that I had just done in warm-up and that would guarantee me the title. Then for the second and third lifts I would go heavy once the title was in the bag. This was ideal and an easy ride – or so I thought.

I went out for the opening lift and – disaster – my arm gave way. The pain was worse than ever and the bar came crashing down. The loaders grabbed it and prevented what could have been a bad accident. Where would we go from there?

I was clutching my shoulder and ready to pack in but that was not Alan's style. He got me to change my grip to distribute the weight over a different area. This I did. Then, to the surprise of the crowd (and me), I went out for another attempt. That time it was even worse. My injury was now worse than it had ever been and I had to retire from the competition and probably competitive lifting altogether. I have never lifted heavy since.

What the hell did that doctor inject me with? It certainly wasn't a painkiller. I'd had so much confidence in him and thought of confronting him for an explanation but decided it would get me nowhere, so I just walked away. It was probably the end of my career, but I still continue to train.

When I got home my son, Jonathan, summed it up in one scathing comment, 'So you had no one to beat and you still couldn't win?' No sympathy there then.

I was at my caravan in Bowness when I got a call from John Fairclough, Alan's son, to say that Alan had suffered a massive stroke and was not expected to recover. He died three days later. I came back from Bowness and went to see him when he was semi-conscious. I spoke to him and he put his arm around my neck and tears ran down his face. Before I left, I put some photographs on his locker of him lifting as a young man. I wanted everyone to know how amazing this frail old man had been. I think he would have liked that.

Since Alan's death, ABC has not been the same. That is not a criticism of anyone, it is just inevitable after sixty years, but still the club carries on and has got some good lifters.

2004 London Marathon

I'VE ALWAYS HAD a bit of trouble with my left knee, so when I started training for the marathon, I went to see a physio at Euxton Hospital. She was a young lady called Susan, and was an excellent physio. She treated my knee, did a good job and advised me to try to do most of my training on the flat, suggesting that the seafront was a good place. Because of this, I started to make regular trips to Lytham, where I parked the car and started to walk towards Blackpool, extending my walk on each visit, sometimes accompanied by Gus.

One Sunday we had arranged to go early and have a long walk but on Saturday night, Gus, who lived on his own at that time, rang to say that he couldn't make it as he needed to do some housework. It was no problem to me as I was happy to go on my own. I parked up on the front at Lytham and strode out towards Blackpool. When I got to Squires Gate the footpath ran out and there was a narrow ginnel that took you to the seafront. As I was making the short journey along the ginnel, which had a small stone wall to the left (beyond which was the beach), I happened to look down on to the beach and there smiling at me was the most beautiful girl of about twenty or twenty-one and she was stark naked.

I couldn't believe it but it was about to get better. 'Would you like to join me?' she asked. Well the last thing that I ever wanted to do was to offend anyone, so I leapt over the wall and that's when I saw him. When I say him, I mean the photographer. It was a photo shoot. Still not deterred, I ignored the photographer and introduced myself to this vision of beauty. She then invited me to join the photo shoot and I happily agreed, stipulating that I would be keeping my clothes on.

I've got to say that photo shoot was the most entertaining, interesting and pleasurable twenty minutes that I had spent in a long time. I was sad when it was over but a small crowd was beginning to gather and, as she explained, what she was doing was in fact illegal (which to me made it even better). We shook hands (just hands) and parted company.

I immediately rang Gus and said, 'Did you pick the wrong day to skip training!!'

2014 LONDON MARATHON

ON SATURDAY, APRIL the 4th, 2014, I went to the paddock where I met Jonny, Charlie and Suzanne. Jonny had seen Mo Farah interviewed on TV about the marathon and was telling Charlie about it. Charlie asked, 'Is Mo Farah doing the London Marathon?'

'Yes,' replied Jonny.

'Oh no,' said Charlie. 'Granddad's got no chance now.'

'Don't write me off yet Charlie,' I said. 'I beat a Masai warrior last time out.'

We went to Delph Way to pick up Richard and Jack, then on to Preston station where we met up with others from Shaw Hill and got the train to London. Gus and Sharon got on at Wigan, as did crowds of Wigan supporters who were on their way to Wembley (Wigan were playing Arsenal in the FA Cup semi-final). When I saw the hordes of supporters, all chanting and carrying the obligatory cans of beer, my heart sank. Oh no, I thought, this could be trouble and can I stand this noise for two hundred miles.

As it turned out, I couldn't have been more wrong. Everyone was friendly and the lads offered their seats to ladies and older people. I got talking to one or two of them and, when they realised what we were doing, a few of them even gave us a donation for the charity. I will never prejudge anyone again. It was another early night but we didn't get a good sleep.

On Sunday 5th, it was marathon day and I was up at 5.30am. I didn't feel great and couldn't face breakfast. Of course, you need food to help you round the twenty-six miles but I wasn't worried. I would be fine.

After breakfast, we got on the tube to Greenwich for the start of the marathon. I can only describe the atmosphere as 'the marathon day atmosphere'. There is no other way to describe it; it's almost electric with the whole mix of runners. It's unique. There were the elite runners, who would be leading and who hoped to win or at least be placed. There were the serious runners who hoped to achieve a good time. There were the fancy-dress runners, of course, and the average runners, who were probably doing it for the first time. There were emotional runners who were doing it for loved ones, either passed away or very sick, and there were some running for loved ones that were missing. Then there was my group, the walkers; although the television focuses on runners, there are actually thousands that walk it. I'm not the only one. So there is a section for everyone at any level.

On the day of the marathon, the pubs open at 9.30am, which means that the crowds can watch the runners while they enjoy a drink. The trouble is that by the time I went past those pubs (at about three o'clock in the afternoon) the crowds were all pissed and what was enthusiastic support at 10.00am had turned to sarcastic abuse, although of the good-humoured variety.

I remember one occasion (I'm not sure which marathon it was) when I was going past a pub with a crowd outside all telling me to go faster. A runner dressed as a banana overtook me, to the delight of the crowd, and they gave him a massive cheer as he pulled away. I thought it was great as they would leave me alone but one of the drunks shouted, 'Look out, Fred, there's a pork pie coming up on your outside.' And his mate who was equally drunk shouted, 'And if you hadn't eaten so many of them yourself, you would be going a bit quicker, you fat bastard.' About 200 drunken people fell about laughing.

That marathon, the 2014 event, was the one that I didn't finish even though I had put the miles in during training. My old left knee problem came back and I was struggling at mile four. By mile eight I was in great pain and was losing contact with the others. Gus kept telling me to keep going and not to give up, but I knew I was in serious trouble when we came across a group of kids and one of them said, 'They went that way.' That's when you know you have got a problem.

I kept going until we got to Tower Bridge and that was it, I wasn't going any further that day. Gus wanted to carry on and finish. I didn't have a problem with that but I was going nowhere – at least not on foot.

There was a big hotel near Tower Bridge so I hobbled in and asked a lovely girl on reception if she knew where I could get a taxi. She explained to me that it was the day of the London Marathon (was it really?) and that taxis weren't running in the city centre, but she would get a member of staff to take me to where taxis were running from. What a lovely gesture – I was so grateful. She sent this young lad to go with me till we found a good place. He was pleasant and we had a good chat before he eventually flagged a taxi down and I got in.

If the girl at reception was pleasant, and the young lad was pleasant, the taxi driver was equally as pleasant and very friendly. When I explained I was going back to the hotel because of my injury, he wanted to take me to near the end of the marathon where I could get out and join the other runners. He wanted me to collect my medal then get back in again so he could take me back to the hotel. It was a good idea but no, I couldn't do it. Nevertheless, I appreciated his concern.

When I got to my room, I realised that my mobile was missing. It had dropped out of my pocket in the taxi, but I knew that the taxi driver would find it and bring it back. I had every confidence in him and I was right, because that's exactly what happened. Just as I was sitting down with my first pint of lager I saw his taxi pull up outside the hotel. There was never any doubt that he would bring it back.

The funny thing was that by the time he got back to the hotel, he was on first name terms with all my family as they had been ringing to see how I was doing and he had been answering my phone. The first thing he said when he saw me was, 'Can you ring Margaret?' I found that funny.

The 2014 marathon was my last sporting challenge as by that point I was seventy-one. I am very grateful to have been given what I consider to be two sporting careers, one as a young man and the second after I had turned sixty. I must thank both Gus and Alan for their help and support. Regrettably, and for different reasons, I have no contact with either of them now. It's sad, but that's life.

FRIENDS THROUGH TRAINING

ONE PLEASANT SPIN-OFF from being involved in sport is all the people that you meet from all over the world. Because of my international power lifting, the two power lifters that I became most friendly with were Julian Massey and Steve De Miesse. Julian was a real character, very helpful and very generous. He was also very popular and, if we were abroad on an international, everybody knew him. The Americans in particular loved him. If you met an American lifter, the first thing they would say was, 'Is Julian coming?' Also, he was well known for his ability to sleep anywhere, and I mean anywhere, and at any time.

I remember at the world championships in Miami, I went back to the changing room after I finished my lifting. There was Julian, sitting on a chair, fast asleep. I knew that he was about to be called to lift so I shook his shoulder to wake him up. It was the world championships, for goodness' sake. Julian said he wasn't asleep but that he was closing his eyes to meditate and psyche himself up. 'Julian you were *snoring*!'.

Julian also believes in travelling light and takes no luggage with him. At bedtime he takes off what he has been wearing, washes it, puts it on the radiator to dry overnight and wears it again the following day. He told me that after one trip abroad, when he landed at Heathrow he had to go straight to a business meeting, so he had to find a clothes shop where he bought a shirt and tie then went to his meeting. Cool!

Steve was a massive guy and, apart from his power lifting, he was a judo instructor. I think he's a black belt; he also did the doors in nightclubs in Oxford. Like Julian, he was a very helpful guy, even to the extent of coming with me to collect a Kingsley bad debt in Banbury. When we got to the premises the fellow wasn't in and we couldn't find the goods that belonged to us. But Steve wasn't going away without having a good look so the staff called the police. I must add that Steve was a paramedic at that time and the police who turned up were the ones with whom he often attended violent situations, so it didn't look good that on this occasion he was the one causing the trouble. We had to get out quickly – but not before Steve accidentally caused a bit of damage. At least we got some satisfaction, but that was all we got. We didn't find our property and the guy never paid us. He was a crook, but that comes with the territory when you have a finance company. It's a risky business.

When I think back over my life, I marvel at the number of people who played a big part in my life for many years and then, for many reasons, went out of my life. I suppose if we all stop and think about it, it's a situation that applies to most people.

Apart from the power lifting lads, I've made many, many, friends through training and sport – friends for life. For instance, all the friends from Shaw Hill and, of course, everyone at Adlington Barbell Club, whom I've met over the last fifty years. It's great to bump into lads, now mostly granddads, and relive the good times. I owe training such a lot.

I am almost seventy-four now and I certainly don't see the end of my training life. I don't just mean going to the gym and going through the motions, I am talking about meaningful workouts and clothes wet through with sweat. Training like that is a wonderful feeling and one that I hope to enjoy for many years to come.

Incidentally, I recently saw someone wearing a T-shirt bearing the slogan, 'The Older I Get The Better I Was.' I thought it was a brilliant slogan and never more appropriate than for weightlifters and bodybuilders.

When I was in my teens and early twenties, I began to make a name for myself and people began to recognise me as a bodybuilder and power lifter. I would often get into conversation with older people who, according to them, had been weightlifters or bodybuilders in their youth. They loved to tell me about what they used to do and what they could lift in their day.

I used to go along with it, nodding my head in agreement and faking admiration, when what I really wanted to say was, 'What a load of bollocks.' What they were claiming they used to do would have made them world champions and far better than I could ever hope to be. In fact, every older person I ever discussed training with was completely out of my league.

Even some of the lads that I'd trained with for years (not the top lifters but some of the lesser lights) would exaggerate their achievements when I met them in later life. I used to look at them and think, 'You could do what? Do you think I'm stupid? I was there, I trained with you. No, you couldn't.'

Yes, the older I get, the better I was.

Stocking Fillers

Verruca

When I was a kid, aged around seven or eight, I discovered a kind of growth on the bottom of my right foot. I showed it to my mum but she couldn't say what it was. The years went by but the growth didn't go away. However, as it was giving me no trouble it was more or less ignored.

Many, many years later, after I got married, Margaret spotted it and said that it was a verruca.

'It can't be,' I said. 'I've had it for years.'

'I don't care how long you've had it, that's a verruca.'

We disagreed but again nothing was done until about eighteen years later, by which time Jonathan was born and was learning to drive. He had cause to go to a chiropodist in Preston so I went with him as the qualified driver. Margaret suggested while we were there that I let the chiropodist look at my foot and settle once and for all whether I had a verruca or not. I waited until he had finished with Jonny then asked him to look at my foot.

He put on a mask (which I thought was rather unnecessary) and then examined my foot.

'Can you tell me whether that is a verruca or not?' I asked.

He stood up, took his mask off and said, 'Yes, it is, but fortunately we have caught it just in time!'

Phew, that was close, another 40 years and, who knows?!

MAKE MINE A DOUBLE!

IN THE YEAR 2002, I went on holiday to America. It was with one of those escorted tours through a company called Titan Tours and (if they are still around) I can wholly recommend them.

We arrived at O'Hare Airport, Chicago, and were picked up by coach and taken to the hotel. When I went up to my room, I was informed by the cleaner that the room wasn't yet prepared but if I left my luggage and came back in an hour the room would be ready. This was no problem; I went for a walk down Michigan Avenue, a well-known area that was lined with bars and restaurants.

I decided to have just one drink at an outdoor bar. 'A double vodka and diet coke, please, with ice and lemon,' I said to the girl bartender. I promised myself I would only have one but, as we all know, after hours of travelling and an empty stomach just one double makes you rather happy. 'Oh sod it, I'll have another. Same again please,' I said to this young girl, who very obligingly poured me another. This one went down even better, as two doubles really do the trick.

Then my big decision was whether to have a third. Why not? I was on holiday, and that's what holidays were for. 'Same again, love,' I said. She gave me a big smile. The Americans really do love the Brits and she handed me my third double. By then, all common sense had gone out of the window.

The third drink was the best yet. As I was draining the dregs through the remaining ice cubes, it was decision time. Should I go for a fourth double or would that be too much, as by now I was well away and in happy land? I reasoned with myself that I was only a few hundred yards from my hotel and could go back, have a sleep and a shower and would be fine.

So, taking a deep breath so as not to slur my words (I know that Americans will not serve someone if they think they are drunk), I said, 'Same again please.' I waited to see if she would serve me or not, but there was no problem. 'Coming up,' she replied as she poured me another drink and gave it to me.

That time I watched her pour it and noticed she hadn't put any vodka in. As she gave it to me I said, 'You haven't put any vodka in this one.'

What she said next nearly floored me. 'I haven't put any vodka in any of them. I didn't hear you ask for vodka.'

I'd just been drinking Diet Coke – and the bill she gave me proved it.

HOUSE VIEWING

BEN WAS A pupil at Stonyhurst College. It was a well-known boarding school but, if you lived within a certain radius of the school, you could sleep at home. Ben had decided that there was no way that he was going to give up his beautiful, spotless and spacious bed for a dormitory bed, so he lived at home.

This meant that someone had to take him to school and bring him back every day; being a boarding school, that included Saturdays. By the end of each week we had clocked up 500 miles on school trips alone. Add to that out-of-school activities and the mileage became ridiculous. A decision was made to put THF up for sale so we could look for something much nearer to the school.

We duly rang an estate agent and had the property valued. I think the valuation was around £500,000, which was a lot of money over twenty years ago.

We had the usual viewers round, some genuine, some time wasters. Then, one day, Margaret received a phone call from the agents. Could a couple come to view it right away? Now anyone that knows Margaret knows that her day is planned down to the last detail and that no interruption is welcome, but as she was keen to get things moving she agreed. Sure enough, about an hour later a knock came on the front door. Margaret answered and was bitterly disappointed that the two viewers were not much more than teenagers. She thought they were more time wasters but started to show them round, while all the time she was thinking what else she could be doing.

Eventually she had had enough. She believe those two kids couldn't possibly afford the house, so she asked Carmen to show them round so that she could get on with her work. Carmen duly took over. When she had finished, she watched them get into their brand new Aston Martin and drive off. It was Ryan Giggs and an actress.

ADLINGTON CARNIVAL

ONE REGRET THAT I have is that, up till now, I have never been a great reader. I feel that I have missed out on so much, unlike my older brother Roy, who regards reading as his greatest pleasure. Also, although I spend a lot of time in front of the television I spend very little time actually watching it and more time just flicking over from channel to channel. However, one innocent pleasure I enjoy in the evening is to get into the car and drive aimlessly just listening to my beloved country music.

One summer evening a few years ago, I got into the car and set off with nowhere particular in mind and found myself heading towards Adlington and Rivington. As I approached Adlington, I realised that it had been Adlington's carnival day, which was a big event for such a small village. The roads in Higher Adlington were very quiet, as on carnival day all the villagers congregate on the bottom recreation ground to keep the festivities going.

I decided to head back home and turned down Railway Road towards the A6. As I got about a hundred yards onto Railway Road, a young lad stood on the side of the road and started to flag me down. I am always aware when young lads wave to me that it may be someone who works for me, or who has worked for me in the past and recognises me but I don't recognise him. That means I don't like to just drive past so, with that in mind, I pulled up. The lad opened the passenger door. He was not someone I knew but it was immediately obvious that he had been enjoying the carnival all day. In other words, he was pissed.

'Are you going to the bottom of Railway Road?' he asked.

'Yes,' I replied.

'Any chance of a lift?'

'Yeah, no problem, jump in,' I said, thinking that we were only talking about a couple of minutes.

But he didn't jump in; instead he shouted across the road, 'Here, Dad, I got us a lift.' His dad, every bit as drunk, came across the road and slumped into the back seat.

I was about to set off when the lad shouted in the direction from which I had just come, 'Here Mam, I have got us a lift,' and his mother appeared, just as worse for wear as the other two. 'Come on, get in here, Mam,' he said proudly.

His mam managed to get to the car and was attempting to get in, when I saw through the mirror that she was having trouble getting through the door. I realised she was carrying something. It was big and black.

What on earth is that, I thought? Is it shopping? Is it a suitcase? No, it was a big black Labrador that she sat with on her knee. The conversation going down Railway Road went like this:

WAYNE: I told you I'd get you a ride in style, Mam.

MAM: You did, Wayne, you're a good lad.

WAYNE: Do you love me, Mam?

MAM: You know I love you, Wayne.

DAD: We both love you, Wayne. You're a credit to us.

WAYNE: Well, you're the best Mam and dad in the world.

DAD: Well, you are the best son in the world, Wayne.

And so it went on until we got to the bottom of Railway Road. Oh my God, that was all I needed: three drunks and a massive dog. However, by the time we arrived, I was their best friend ever and it was hugs and kisses all round. Then it was time to get out of the car and into the beer tent. They were one happy family, at least up to that point.

TAE

ANOTHER MAN WHO worked for us, although only at weekends, was a fellow called Owen Fishwick. He was a very genuine chap and a good worker who spoke with a very broad Chorley accent. In common with a lot of people from Chorley would pronounce tea as 'tae' (rhymes with Tay) as in 'Would you like a cup of tae?' His wife, Nellie, was always trying to get him to speak properly and pronounce it tea. One week they went into a cafe in Chorley. Nellie sat down and told Owen to get the drinks. She reminded him to ask for two cups of tea, so Owen went to the counter and ordered two cups of tea and two tae cakes.

COINCIDENCE

IN 2014 ABOUT a dozen of us went to a Sportsman's dinner at the Midland Hotel, Manchester. The speaker was Harry Redknapp and the excellent comedian was Gary Marshall. There were about 800 people in the hall.

After the speeches, we were all sitting at the table drinking when I decided to go to the toilet. On the way I had to walk past the bar and, as I did, I spotted something on the floor. I bent down and picked it up and realised that it was a wad of twenty-pound notes. I went to the bar and asked the girl if anyone had reported losing anything, to which she replied no. I said if they do, tell them to ring this number and I gave her my mobile number.

I went to the toilet and then back to the table, to find Jonny frantically searching his pockets. As I sat down, he looked at me and said, 'I've lost the kitty.' What are the chances – 800 people in the hall, my son loses a load of cash and I find it.

After the Midland, the lads decided that they would go to a casino but that wasn't for me, so Richard flagged me a taxi. Just as I was getting into the taxi he said, 'Dad, just come here, there's someone I would like you to meet.' So I turned around and Richard said, 'Kevin, I would like you to meet my dad.' It was Kevin Keegan.

That is so typical of Richard; he talks to these people as though he has known them all his life. He paid the taxi driver and said, 'Dad, remember I have paid him.' That was because I'm famous when I have had a few drinks for paying the taxi driver in Manchester, then falling asleep on the way home and paying again when I get home and wake up. Before we set off I'll argue the toss over a fiver and then end up paying twice.

THANKS TO FRED!

ONE OF MARGARET'S closest friends is Pauline from Bamber Bridge. She is a lovely person, extremely kind. She's also a very religious lady; in fact, I have christened her St Pauline of the Brigg.

Pauline and husband, Tony, had three daughters. One of them, I forget which, was about to get married. Pauline had a cousin who was a Catholic priest; his name was Edwin but he was always referred to as Father Ed. At the time of the wedding he was working abroad on missionary work but had agreed to fly back to England to officiate at the wedding, for which the family were very grateful.

A week or so before the wedding, Tony rang me to ask if he could borrow a transit van to move some furniture to the newly-weds' house. I agreed. He came to pick up the van, did the job and returned the van the following day.

The following week the couple got married and Margaret and I attended as guests. The church service went well and then we went on to the reception. The meal was soon over and it was time for the bridegroom to give his speech, which he read from an A4 sheet. He started his speech by thanking people for their help and the first person he thanked was me for the loan of the van, which was fair enough. But then he went on to lavish an extraordinary amount of gratitude on me, far more than my small good turn warranted. He continued reading things like, 'If it hadn't been for Fred,' or 'We can't thank Fred enough.' Fred this and Fred that.

I couldn't believe all the thanks I was getting, till his bride asked if she could look at the speech. He handed it to her. She gave him a derogatory look and said, 'That doesn't say FRED, it says FR. Ed.'

JAGUAR

AROUND 2008, MARGARET and I were attending a wedding in Windermere and had booked to stay at a hotel over night. At the time I was not very familiar with the Lake District and I overshot the road that I should have turned down. 'Blast, I should have turned down there,' I said.

'Don't worry,' said Margaret. 'There's a garage here, you can turn round on their forecourt.' The 'garage' was in fact a Jaguar dealership. 'Oh, look at that Jaguar sports car, can we have a look at it?' said

Margaret.

Overshooting that road cost me £45,000. I have often said it would have been cheaper to have taken a different route and pay for the wedding, but Margaret kept the car for about seven years and loved it. On the day we sold it, it still looked the same as it had the day I overshot that damn road.

DODGY CHARACTER

ONE OF MARGARET'S greatest pleasures is a few days at Ragdale Health Hydro with Carmen, although years ago she used to go to a different one called Inglewood Health Hydro at Hungerford. One year I took Margaret and her mother there; I wasn't staying so I dropped them off and set off on the long journey home.

I decided that I would take a different route for a change, and that it would be nice to have a night in Stratford Upon Avon to break up the journey. I booked into a hotel, had a drink and then went for a gentle stroll round town. After about an hour I was leaning on a rail near some crossroads when I got a tap on my shoulder. I looked round and there stood two police officers who began asking me all sorts of questions about where I lived, where I was staying and what I was doing there. Question after question came at me, till eventually they seemed satisfied with my answers. I was curious why they wanted to know so much. According to them, everywhere I had been I had been studying a bank and they thought I was planning a job. Did I look like a bank robber? I didn't even know that I had been looking at any banks!

EASY MISTAKE TO MAKE

IN THE EARLY seventies, Dad bought a beautiful Daimler Sovereign.

It was a regal car and a real head turner, only one down from a Rolls Royce and a car loved by royalty.

At that time my mother was an active member of the Chorley branch of the Lady Farmers, the female division of the Farmers Union. Every week my dad would take her to the meeting, drop her off, and go back about 10.30pm to pick her up, as my mother never drove.

One week when he dropped her off it was pouring down and blowing a gale. When she came out about 10.30pm the Daimler was parked outside so, with her head down, my mother made a dash for it and got into the car – only to find that she was sitting next to a complete stranger. It wasn't our car. 'Oh, I am so sorry,' said my mother. 'I thought you were my husband.'

At that very moment, my dad pulled up. 'Oh here he is,' said my mother and got out of the Daimler Sovereign and got in with my dad into the Bedford milk van.

BEWARE OF SHELLFISH SELLERS

IN THE 1980s and 1990s, The Sirloin was my local. At about ten o'clock most nights, a fellow with one arm used to come in the pub with a tray of shellfish round his neck. He would go round the pub trying to sell his goods to the customers, which was a common practice in those days but seems to have died out now. On one particular night nobody was interested in buying any of his wares, so he made no sales.

I was about to leave and was going to ring for a taxi, when I asked him which way he was going. 'Towards Preston,' he said.

'Oh I live in the opposite direction,' I said. 'But if you give me a lift home I'll buy everything you've got.'

'You're on,' he replied and we walked out of the pub and got into his van. That's when I realised I should have stipulated I meant everything that he had got *on his tray*. He took my statement to mean everything he had got in his van as well.

I knew I was in trouble when he pulled into my farmyard and did a 180-degree turn, reversing up to the back door of the house. I don't mind telling you that you can get a lot of shellfish for £71, I could have got a taxi for £3. But I am a man of my word. I said I would buy everything he had, and so I did. Also I was a little bit pissed, but he must have gone home that night clapping his hand.

Margaret was in bed so was oblivious to what was going on. The next morning I got up and had completely forgotten about it, till I was making a cup of tea and went to the fridge to get some milk. Oh my God, it was like stepping into a Grimsby trawler. It goes without saying that Margaret did not see the funny side of it and I lived off shellfish for a week.

THE TROUBLE WITH TENANTS

IT WAS AROUND 1984 that Jonny, ever the entrepreneur, bought a lovely cottage near Cuerden Park to rent out. The property was called Lane End Cottage and he initially had two tenants who were no trouble. Both were short term, however. He then he got a third, named McCabe, who ticked all the boxes and convinced Jonny that he would be a good tenant. It didn't take long to realise that he was the tenant from hell. He was nothing but a troublemaker.

To give you an idea of what he was like, there was a primary school close by and every November they held a bonfire supervised by parents and teachers. This had gone on for years without the slightest problem, but this was not good enough for McCabe; he called the fire service to come and put out the fire, which he said was dangerous and was frightening his children. Despite the school's protests, the bonfire was put out.

Predictably it wasn't long before he started finding fault with the cottage and demanded that we had work carried out, even though when he had viewed the house only weeks earlier, he had found nothing wrong at all. He then stopped paying his rent and started having work carried out, instructing the contractor to send the bill to Jonny. This eventually – and inevitably – led to solicitor's letters going back and forth. Also the money involved (including contractors' bills and unpaid rent) had now accumulated to around £12,000, so things were getting serious. By then his wife had taken the two children and left him because of his drinking.

One Sunday afternoon, I decided to pay him a visit to see if we could settle things amicably. I spoke to Jonny, who had no problem with my actions, but Margaret just shook her head and said that I was wasting my time as he was not a person interested in settling anything amicably. She was later proved right.

Undeterred, I jumped into the car and went to the cottage. No one was in so I came back home and made a second visit later, but still no one was in. At about 7.30pm I decided to make one last visit. I got into the car and went back to the cottage. This time there was a light on in the upstairs bedroom, so now I had a chance to meet him.

I forget what month of the year this was but at 7.30pm it was dark. I knocked on the front door; through a window in the lounge I saw him coming down the stairs. 'This is more like it,' I thought. 'Let's hope he'll talk.'

Just as this was going through my mind, I saw what I thought was a flash in the sky. There was another, then another. I wondered if they were shooting stars or maybe a helicopter. I also wondered why McCabe had still not opened the door. I looked again through the lounge window and saw him again, this time going back upstairs. Then I spotted something in his hand: it was a camera, and the flashes

I had seen were not shooting stars or a helicopter. The bastard had taken photographs of me so that he could prove I had been harassing him.

Well, if it's proof you want, photograph this, I thought. I gave the door an almighty kick and it burst open. I had seen McCabe go upstairs so I followed him and tried to open the bedroom door, but he had wedged it shut. I shouted to him several times but he didn't answer. I calmed down and suggested that we talked things over in a gentlemanly way but still there was not a word from inside the bedroom, so I left. As I was leaving, it did cross my mind to do another bit of damage to something, just for the hell of it, but then I thought better of it.

It wasn't long after that, that the inevitable phone call came from Leyland police station asking me to attend regarding a complaint they had received from a Mr McCabe. I went to see my solicitor in Preston and met a lady called Jane Ashworth, who suggested that she came with me.

On the day, I met Jane outside the police station and she told me that unless she instructed me differently I should reply 'No comment' to every question. This is what I did, but I have got to say I felt stupid and found it difficult not to laugh. After the questioning Jane left, but I had to stay behind to have a mug shot and fingerprints taken.

The policeman told me to follow him and we went into a cell where he got out a camera and took some photographs, before taking my fingerprints. It was about this time that I noticed the truncheon that he was carrying. It was not like any other that I had seen and I asked him about it. Apparently it was a new model and was telescopic so you could make it longer as you were using it, as opposed to the old ones that were rigid. He handed it to me as he was taking my fingerprints so that I could see it better. Suddenly, he snatched it from me. I don't know for sure but I got the impression that he realised being locked in a cell with a prisoner and handing him your truncheon was perhaps not a good idea.

A few weeks later, I got the letter instructing me to go to court. I phoned Jane who said she would come with me. On the due date I went to Preston to pick up Jane, then went on to court in Leyland. Jane told me to plead not guilty. I had never been in a courtroom before, so I had no idea what to expect.

When I entered the room, apart from the magistrate and two other people on the bench, there were only three or four people in the viewing area. One was a odd looking individual who I recognised as I had seen him at McCabe's. He was obviously a friend or relative. It also transpired that McCabe had not turned up. I assumed that the weirdo was there to listen and report back to his mate, McCabe. As it turned out there was nothing to report; the court couldn't find the papers for the case, so it was adjourned to a later date.

Shortly afterwards I received another letter summoning me back to court. Again, I went to Preston to pick up my solicitor, then on to Leyland. For some reason, Jane had changed her mind and told me that I should plead guilty. I didn't have a problem either way as it was hardly the crime of the century. Again the courtroom was almost empty, again McCabe hadn't turned up and again the weirdo was there on his spying mission.

When it came time for me to stand in the dock, I assumed that by pleading guilty they would just impose a fine on me so I could be back home for lunch. I couldn't have been more wrong. They asked me for my story, then they discussed it at length. Then they called my solicitor for her version and again talked among themselves. Wondering what the hell was going on, I remember thinking I'd pleaded guilty so there could only be one outcome. I was wrong again, as they found me not guilty. How does that work? I pleaded guilty and got found not guilty. I didn't think it could happen but they then also went on to award me £15 expenses. I couldn't believe it. Maybe I should have kicked the bedroom door down as well, as they might have awarded me £50. I'll never know why they reached that conclusion but I do know that McCabe spent his life taking people to court, so perhaps they were teaching him a lesson. Who knows?

On the way home I had to go past Lane End Cottage and, as I did, who should be standing at the door in deep discussion but McCabe and his weirdo mate. I assumed they were discussing the events of the morning so, being a friendly sort of a bloke, I wound the window down, blew the horn and gave them a big smile and a thumbs up. Would you believe it, I got no response. How strange.

The final chapter in this story was that one day I was in a long queue at a filling station at Clayton Brook, waiting to pay for my petrol. Just as I got to the front of the queue, I happened to turn round and at the very back of the queue was the policeman who dealt with me at Leyland police station. When he spotted me, he shouted in a voice loud enough that everyone in the room could hear him, 'Did you get off?'

'Er, yes,' I said. 'Thanks for asking.'

AM I NEAR...?

ONE SUMMER NIGHT I was working late on the trenching machine on Thornham Roundabout. It is the roundabout that spans the M62 and is actually on the A627M – a short motorway that links Rochdale and Oldham – just west, or maybe it's east of Manchester.

It was a lovely summer night. At about nine o'clock, and I spotted a very old Morris Minor van pull up on the hard shoulder on the opposite side of the M62 to the one that I was working on. It was travelling in the Leeds' direction. The driver's door opened and a little Chinese fellow got out. He looked about seventy-five years old or more and was wearing a big trilby type hat. He was waving at me with a big smile on his face. He continued to wave frantically, all the time shouting something to me that I had absolutely no chance of hearing. Then, oh no, I couldn't believe it – he looked both ways and started to make his way across the three lanes to get to the central reservation. I was frantically trying to get him to go back, but to no avail. I decided that maybe I was making matters worse so I stopped waving.

He made it to the central reservation, then started to negotiate the other three lanes. Don't ask me how he did it but he did. He got across to the hard shoulder, but because I was working on the embankment, he then had to scale the batter (the embankment) to get to me. He made the entire hazardous trip with a massive friendly smile on his face.

I really wasn't ready for what he said when he got close enough to me. He leaned on the side of the machine in order to get his breath back then said, still smiling, 'Am I anywhere near Edinburgh?' In a word, no! At nine o'clock at night, in a beat-up old Morris Minor.

I helped him all I could and off he went, still smiling. I showed him a safer way to get back to his van and watched him drive off to God knows where.

WHO IS LES SIMPSON?

LES AND I have been mates for many years. We first got to know each other in an unusual way. We were both regulars in The Sirloin pub in Hoghton. We had known each other around 12 months when one night a mutual friend, Eric Derbyshire, joined us at the bar and began a conversation that was not making sense to neither Les nor me. He started referring to what discounts Les offered me and did I get good service from Les? None of this made any sense to either of us and it was only when Eric assumed that we did business together that the penny dropped, Les being an electrical wholesaler and me being an electrical contractor. We just looked at each other and realised we had been doing business together for years without knowing who the other one was. We would talk to each other on the phone in the afternoon and meet up in The Sirloin at night, neither of us realising that Les's company and my company were doing business together. After that night I always had to pay my bills on time to avoid any embarrassment in the pub!

Les loves to hear a good story and he loves the one about me accidentally having to turn around at the Jaguar dealership forecourt, a mistake that cost me £45,000 (pages 228-229). I am convinced that when we are in the area he deliberately goes out of his way to drive past that dealership just to cheer me up.

I must say that because of Les and his friendship with sporting celebrities, I have met many of my sporting heroes who I never thought I would, for instance Duncan McKenzie and Kevin Gallagher (football), John H Stracey and Michael Jones (boxing), Brian Close (cricket) and Andy Gregory (rugby). Also, I have started to enjoy days out at Lancashire County Cricket Club, something I never thought I would.

I won't mention the night he spent three hours sat on a freezing cold motorway while we closed the roads to remove 127 dangerous lighting columns. The icing on the cake was that he had recently sold his company so didn't even have the comfort of knowing that he was going to supply all the new equipment. Sorry about that Les, you should've hung on a couple of months.

But I *will* mention the day he very kindly took me to Lytham to pick up my car, taking a short cut through the Preston docks road. He came out at the other end £80 poorer – those damn speed cameras! He has told me that if I need a lift anywhere in future, he will give me the money for a taxi, it'll be cheaper.

Fred Smith, The Reluctant Poet

The Lancashire Poem

The year was about 1980 and Carmen was a pupil at Westholme School for Girls, when one day she came home and told me that all her class had been informed that they had to write a poem. The poems had to have a Lancashire theme. They could be about anything at all, provided it was Lancashire.

This worried Carmen, as she just couldn't write poetry, so she asked me for some help. I suggested writing about the cotton mills of days gone by and the very bad conditions that people were expected to work in. We agreed that this would be a good subject then Carmen immediately washed her hands of the project and left me to get on with it.

I wrote what I thought was a reasonable poem and Carmen duly took it to school as her own work. I didn't realise it but this poetry writing was actually a competition with a professional poet, Joan Pomfrett, who came to school to judge the poems. Carmen was judged to be the winner and the poem was published in the *Blackburn Telegraph* and goes as follows.

The Cotton Mills

Through cobbled streets at break of day
In clogs and shawls they made their way
Through gas lit streets and morning chills
To go to work in the cotton mills.
Booming, banging all day clanging
Dusty rooms and noisy looms
Dyers and tacklers, spinners and weavers
Women and children working like beavers.
Machines that were manned by mother and daughter
Driven by steam, provided water
The water wheel, the mountain streams
A never-ending source it seems
To keep the cotton mills in fuel
For Spinning Jenny and Crompton's Mule.

After that, whenever there was an event in our very large family – a birthday, wedding, anniversary, or any kind of family gathering – I was always asked to write a poem for the occasion.

PUBLISHED POEMS

MY WRITING WENT on for many years and there were a lot of poems accumulating. One day I received a phone call from my niece, Jane Maudsley. Jane is a professional opera singer and a very successful businesswoman. She is also a trustee of a small but very worthwhile charity called *Sophie's Silver Lining*.

Jane had rung me to suggest that we round up all my poems that were now scattered throughout the family and have them published. Jane's reason for doing this is printed below and is self-explanatory.

How has this book come about?

We are all so busy, as individuals and families, rushing around on a day-to-day basis, we rarely take time to reflect and appreciate our lives; the things that have made us laugh, giggle and actually those that mean the most.

I spent quite a lot of time planning and reflecting upon my company, Little Voices, and my life as a whole at the end of last year.

I am a trustee of a charity called Sophie's Silver Lining Fund. They sponsored me through my Masters degree and I am now in the privileged position of being able to 'give back' in my work as a Trustee. Dame Judi Dench is the Patron and it is a very small yet worthwhile charity to be involved with, especially as it aligns so well with everything that we do at a national level with Little Voices.

Sophie's parents set up the charity by using the funds from publishing a book of Sophie's writings, poems and prose after her tragic death at age nineteen. Luckily Sophie had all her work written down in books for her family to find and take solace from after her accident.

In my reflection on my life last year, I started to think about my huge family and the special moments that we have shared. We come together at funerals, weddings, christenings and birthday celebrations and most events have been marked by a poem by Uncle Fred. However it made me think, and I became quite sad; when he is no longer with us, how will we, as his extended family, have access to his humorous words and his own unique portrayal of family occasions. He marked Grandma's funeral so eloquently with his words and we will all remember that phenomenal day as we celebrated together the life of our remarkable grandmother.

I decided that I wanted a record of his poetry and a book that I could read to Olivia about the different family events of our past. If I wanted this, I thought that it would be also nice for Uncle Fred's grandchildren and generations beyond to have the same, so that his children could recite his poems, remember and reflect.

So I telephoned Uncle Fred unexpectedly, explaining my thoughts and how special I felt that it was that we had a book of his words! I think that he was flattered but I really just hoped that he would agree and we could once and for all document his talent!

I did not imagine that this book would top the Amazon number-one best-seller list. That was never the vision nor the intention, but I do hope that I have achieved my purpose and documented some special, family moments that we, as a family, now have in print. I hope that it is as welcome an addition to your family bookcase, as it is to mine.

Jane.

Jane also suggested that we hold a launch party, which we did. We held it at Brindle Village Hall and we raised £1,060 for her charity.

WORDSWORTH POEM ON TRAFFIC CONES

LAST SUMMER I was travelling through Grasmere and was approaching Wordsworth's Dove Cottage when I began to imagine what it must have been like in the days of Wordsworth and his poetry. When I eventually arrived at Dove Cottage it couldn't have been less like the poem *'Daffodils'*, with miles of road works going on outside, temporary traffic lights and miles of traffic cones. I decided that the poem needed to be brought into the twenty-first century.

I wandered lonely through a cloud
Of dust and fumes and grime
When suddenly my thoughts went back
To a tranquil bygone time

241

And as I sought a place to rest
To ease my aching bones
I viewed the sights of amber lights
And a mile of traffic cones

I watched as lark and dove took flight
And head for yonder hills
To ease the burden on their ears
From six pneumatic drills

In hi-vis clothes and waterproofs
Men braved the summer showers
I wondered would we see again
That sea of dancing flowers

Through sweat of brow a job well done
Their hearts with pleasure fills
But now a field of concrete
Which once was daffodils.

Tribute to a Legend

This is a short poem I wrote for Margaret on Valentine's Day 2011. To put it simply it sums up Margaret perfectly. That's all I need to say, other than that it is a fitting end to this book.

Forty-six years with not a wrong word
no moan or complaint has ever been heard.

Nothing but joy you leave in your wake
ready to give but seldom to take.

Life's simple pleasures are all you request
and tending to others is what you do best.

And all that you do, you do to perfection
and you do it with love, with care and affection.

And what of the children you brought to our life?
No gift could be greater from any man's wife.

Their esteem and respect places no one above you
and there isn't a day they don't say that they love you.

So just keep on loving the children and me
we're here for you now and always will be.

LOGIC

Throughout my life I have never been what you might call, a machine man. Some people are natural machine drivers and others are not. I fall into the latter category. Looking back, it's amazing that it was machines that channelled my life and my business in a completely different direction to that in which they were seemingly heading.

First, in 1966 there was the little Merrytiller rotavator, for which I paid £63, which took me away from milk deliveries and towards landscape gardening. Five years later, it was the Davis trenching machine which cost £1200; that took me away from gardening into cable laying and street lighting. Then, many years later, the first crash cushion, costing £50,000, which was to be the start of what Blakedale is today. I sometimes cannot believe that something I wasn't interested in played a bigger part in my life and my family's life than anything else. It also happened just by following my instincts. Logic played no part. In fact, logic would have prevented it.